THE RETURNING

JASON STARR | ANDREA MUTTI

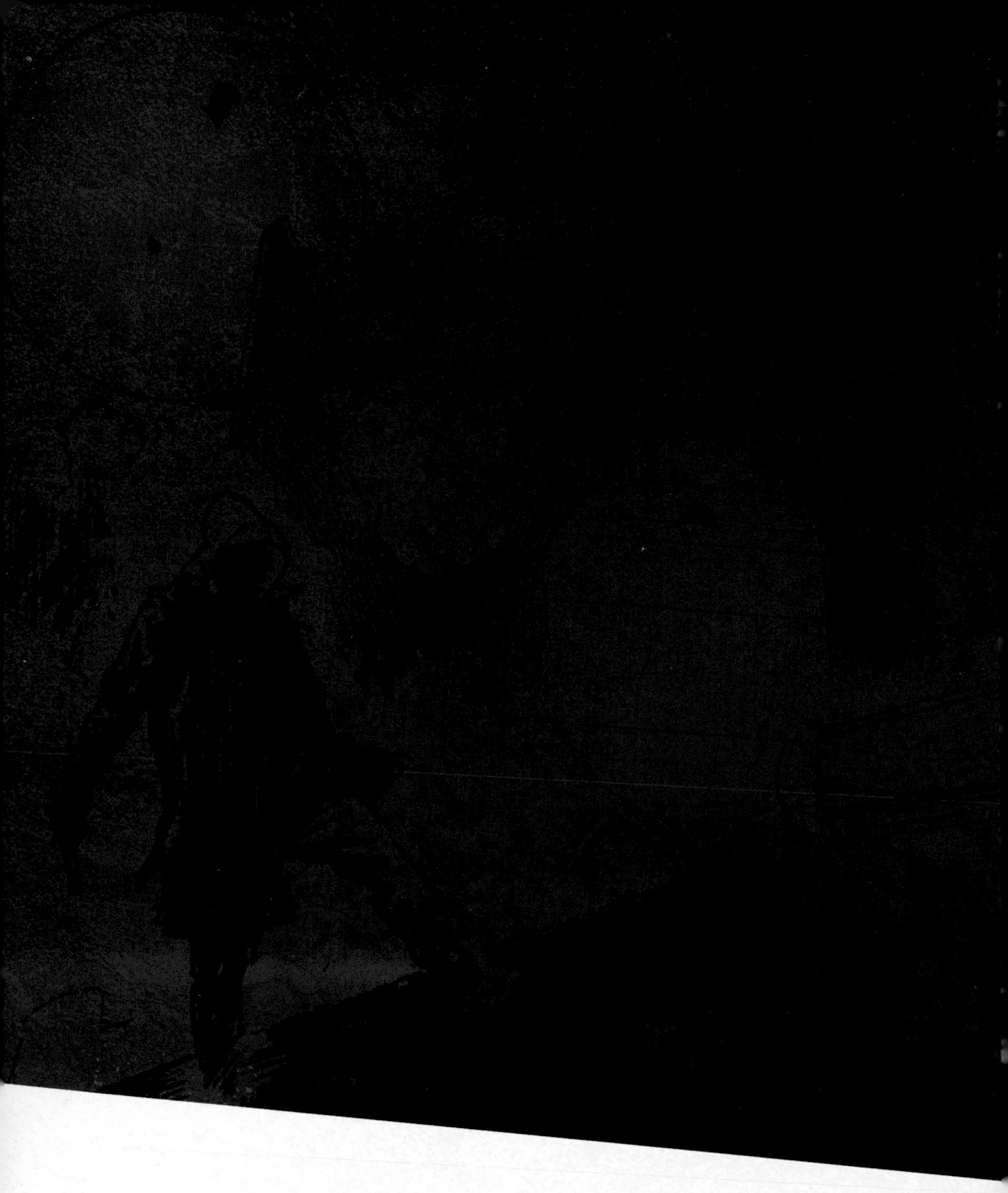

BOOM! STUDIOS

ROSS RICHIE CEO & Founder • MARK SMYLIE Founder of Archaia • MATT GAGNON Editor-in-Chief • FILIP SABLIK President of Publishing & Marketing
LANCE KREITER VP of Licensing & Merchandising • PHIL BARBARO VP of Finance • BRYCE CARLSON Managing Editor • MEL CAYLO Marketing Manager • STEPHEN CHRISTY President of Development
IRENE BRADISH Operations Manager • CHRISTINE DINH Brand Communications Manager • DAFNA PLEBAN Editor • SHANNON WATTERS Editor • ERIC HARBURN Editor • SCOTT NEWMAN Production Design Manager
IAN BRILL Editor • CHRIS ROSA Assistant Editor • ALEX GALER Assistant Editor • WHITNEY LEOPARD Assistant Editor • JASMINE AMIRI Assistant Editor • CAMERON CHITTOCK Assistant Editor • REBECCA TAYLOR Editor
KELSEY DIETERICH Production Designer • JILLIAN CRAB Production Designer • DEVIN FUNCHES E-Commerce & Inventory Coordinator • ANDY LIEGL Event Coordinator • BRIANNA HART Administrative Coordinator
AARON FERRARA Operations Assistant • JOSE MEZA Sales Assistant • MICHELLE ANKLEY Sales Assistant • ELIZABETH LOUGHRIDGE Accounting Assistant • STEPHANIE HOCUTT PR Assistant

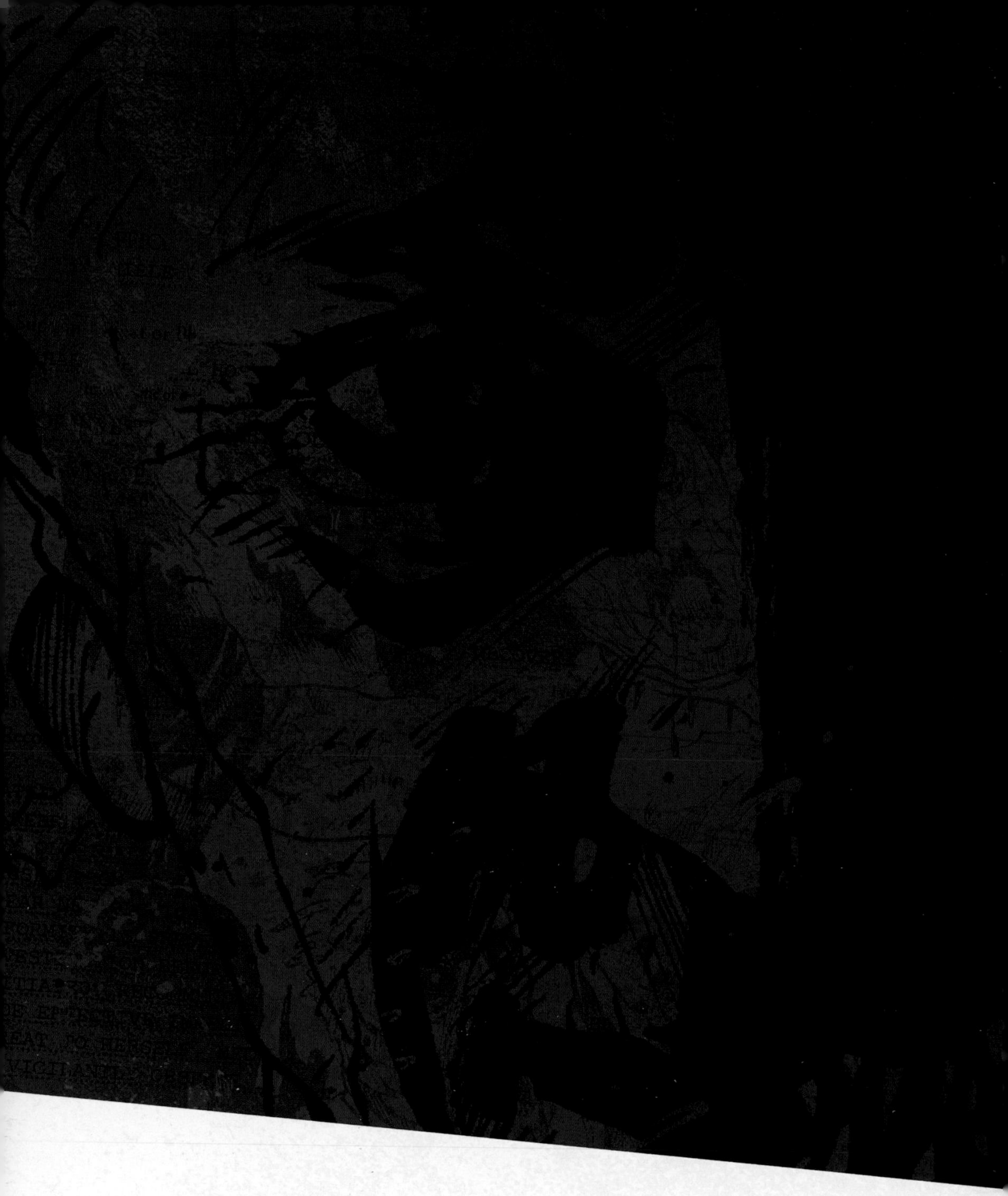

WRITTEN BY
JASON STARR

ART BY
ANDREA MUTTI

COLORS BY
VLADIMIR POPOV

LETTERS BY
ED DUKESHIRE

COVER BY
FRAZER IRVING

DESIGN BY
KARA LEOPARD

ASSISTANT EDITOR
CHRIS ROSA

EDITOR
DAFNA PLEBAN

THE RETURNING CREATED BY
JASON STARR AND ANDREA MUTTI

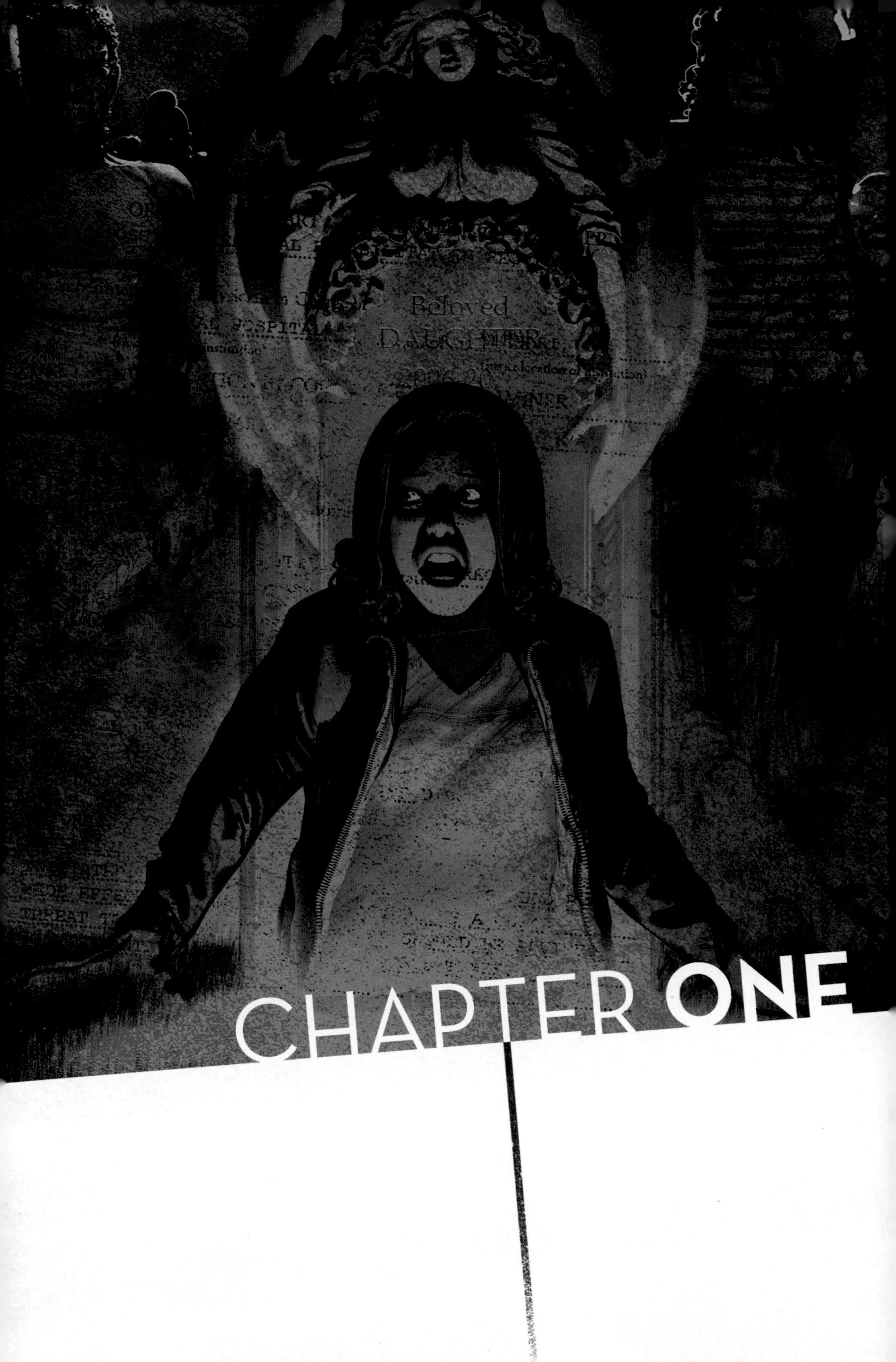
Beloved
DAUGHTER

CHAPTER ONE

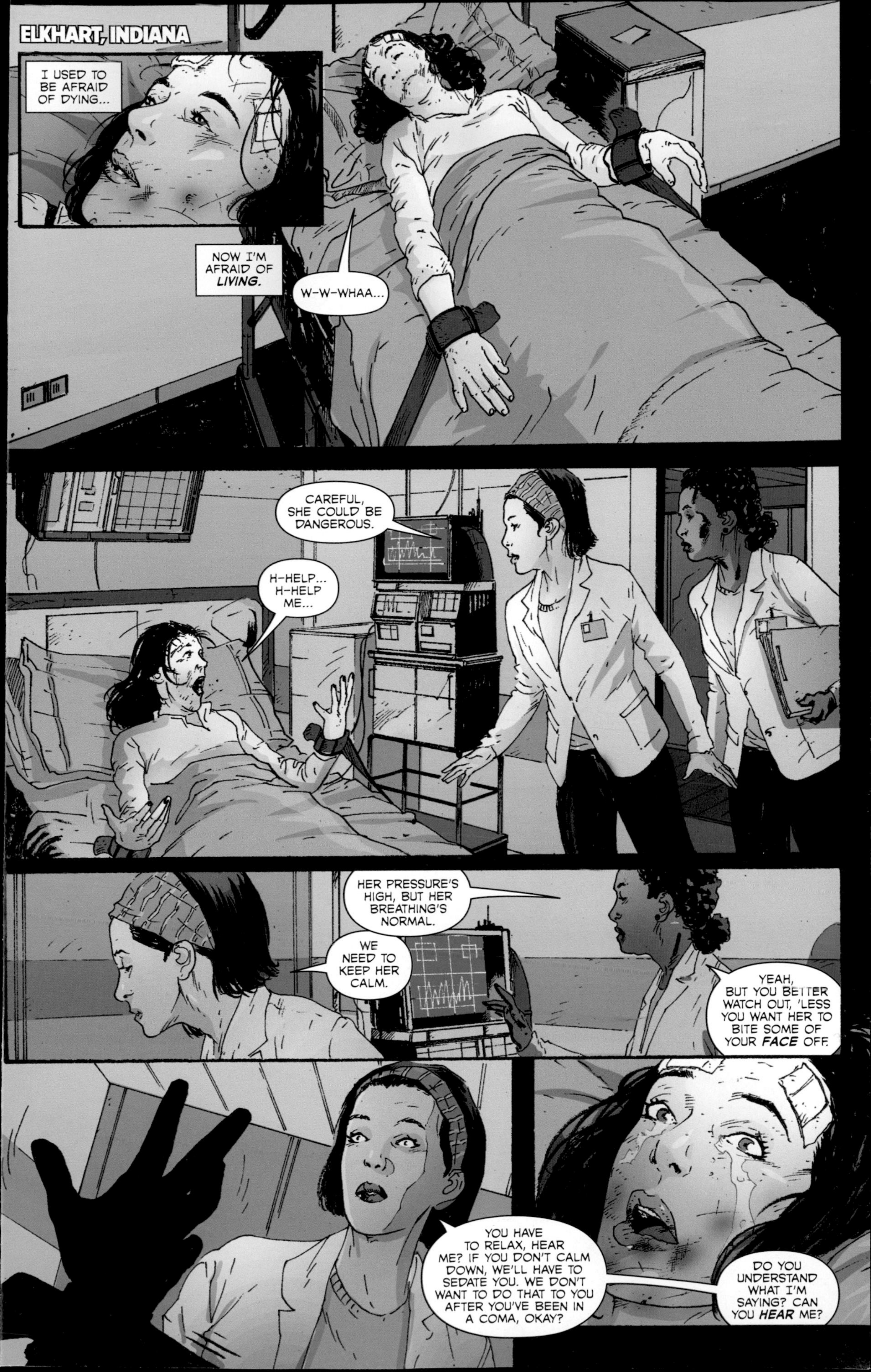
ELKHART, INDIANA
I USED TO BE AFRAID OF DYING...
NOW I'M AFRAID OF *LIVING.*
W-W-WHAA...
CAREFUL, SHE COULD BE DANGEROUS.
H-HELP... H-HELP ME...
HER PRESSURE'S HIGH, BUT HER BREATHING'S NORMAL.
WE NEED TO KEEP HER CALM.
YEAH, BUT YOU BETTER WATCH OUT, 'LESS YOU WANT HER TO BITE SOME OF YOUR *FACE* OFF.
YOU HAVE TO RELAX, HEAR ME? IF YOU DON'T CALM DOWN, WE'LL HAVE TO SEDATE YOU. WE DON'T WANT TO DO THAT TO YOU AFTER YOU'VE BEEN IN A COMA, OKAY?
DO YOU UNDERSTAND WHAT I'M SAYING? CAN YOU *HEAR* ME?

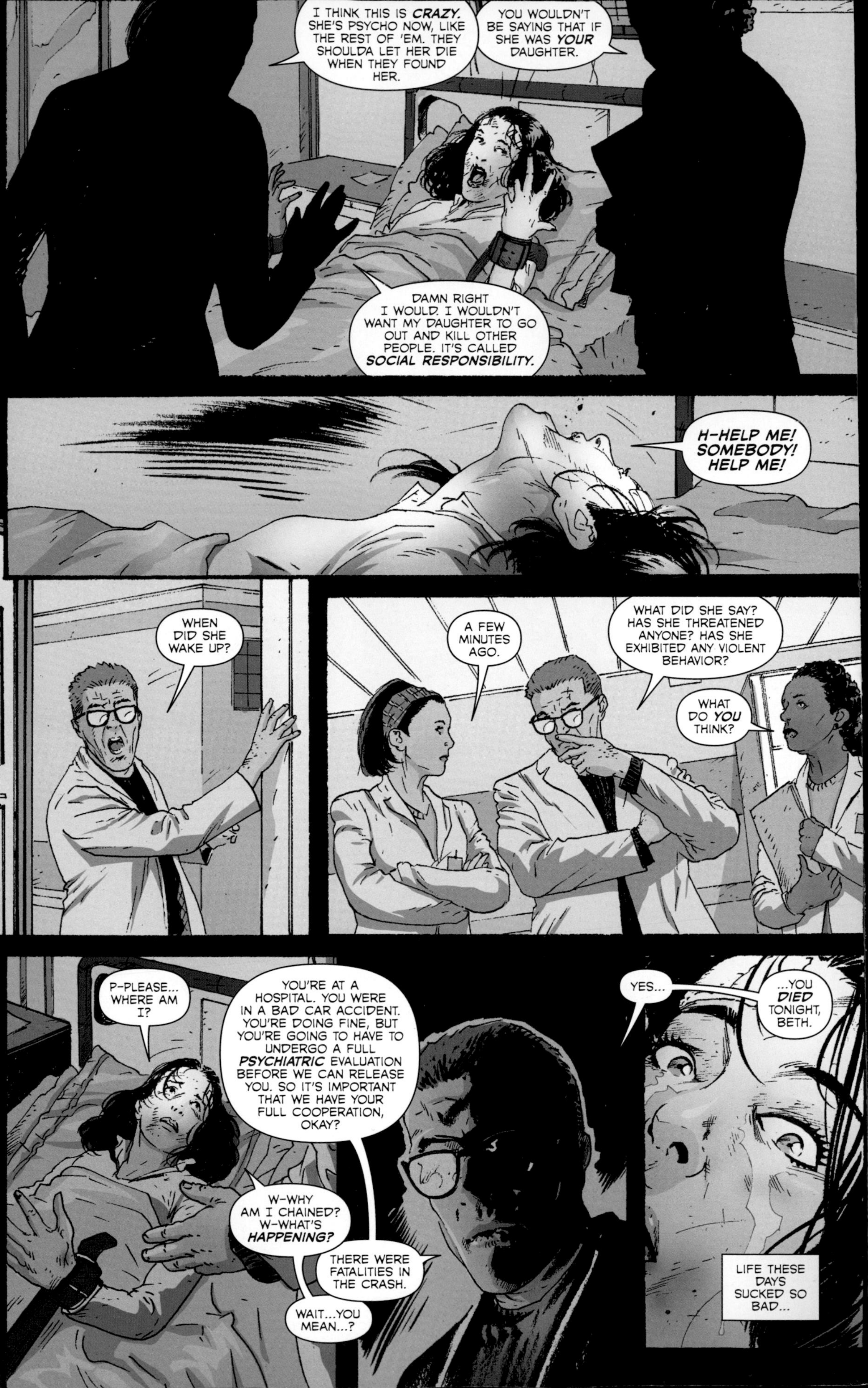
I THINK THIS IS CRAZY. SHE'S PSYCHO NOW, LIKE THE REST OF 'EM. THEY SHOULDA LET HER DIE WHEN THEY FOUND HER.
YOU WOULDN'T BE SAYING THAT IF SHE WAS YOUR DAUGHTER.
DAMN RIGHT I WOULD. I WOULDN'T WANT MY DAUGHTER TO GO OUT AND KILL OTHER PEOPLE. IT'S CALLED SOCIAL RESPONSIBILITY.
H-HELP ME! SOMEBODY! HELP ME!
WHEN DID SHE WAKE UP?
A FEW MINUTES AGO.
WHAT DID SHE SAY? HAS SHE THREATENED ANYONE? HAS SHE EXHIBITED ANY VIOLENT BEHAVIOR?
WHAT DO YOU THINK?
P-PLEASE... WHERE AM I?
YOU'RE AT A HOSPITAL. YOU WERE IN A BAD CAR ACCIDENT. YOU'RE DOING FINE, BUT YOU'RE GOING TO HAVE TO UNDERGO A FULL PSYCHIATRIC EVALUATION BEFORE WE CAN RELEASE YOU. SO IT'S IMPORTANT THAT WE HAVE YOUR FULL COOPERATION, OKAY?
W-WHY AM I CHAINED? W-WHAT'S HAPPENING?
THERE WERE FATALITIES IN THE CRASH.
WAIT...YOU MEAN...?
YES...
...YOU DIED TONIGHT, BETH.
LIFE THESE DAYS SUCKED SO BAD...

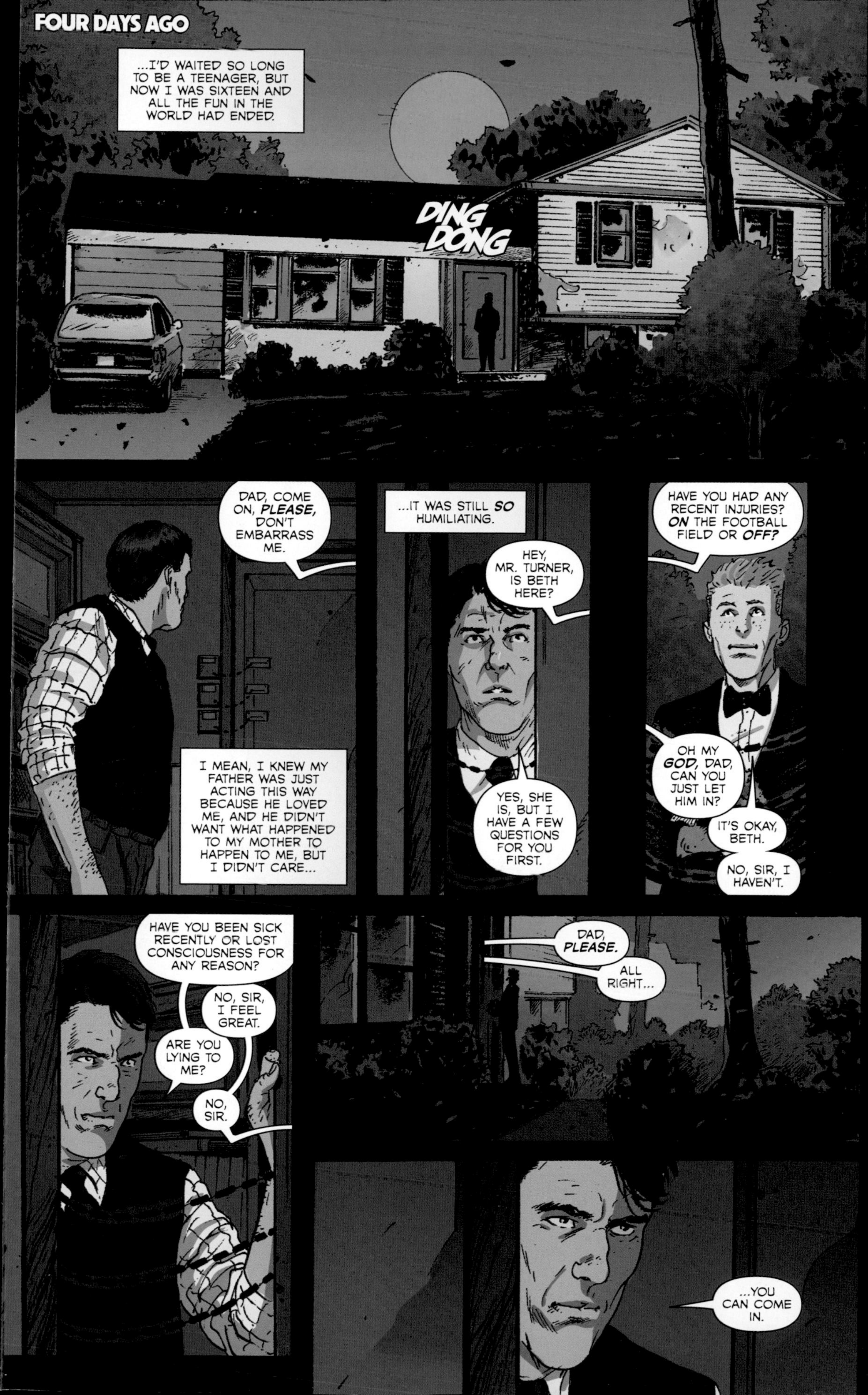
FOUR DAYS AGO
...I'D WAITED SO LONG TO BE A TEENAGER, BUT NOW I WAS SIXTEEN AND ALL THE FUN IN THE WORLD HAD ENDED.
DING DONG
DAD, COME ON, PLEASE, DON'T EMBARRASS ME.
I MEAN, I KNEW MY FATHER WAS JUST ACTING THIS WAY BECAUSE HE LOVED ME, AND HE DIDN'T WANT WHAT HAPPENED TO MY MOTHER TO HAPPEN TO ME, BUT I DIDN'T CARE...
...IT WAS STILL SO HUMILIATING.
HEY, MR. TURNER, IS BETH HERE?
YES, SHE IS, BUT I HAVE A FEW QUESTIONS FOR YOU FIRST.
HAVE YOU HAD ANY RECENT INJURIES? ON THE FOOTBALL FIELD OR OFF?
OH MY GOD, DAD, CAN YOU JUST LET HIM IN?
IT'S OKAY, BETH.
NO, SIR, I HAVEN'T.
HAVE YOU BEEN SICK RECENTLY OR LOST CONSCIOUSNESS FOR ANY REASON?
NO, SIR, I FEEL GREAT.
ARE YOU LYING TO ME?
NO, SIR.
DAD, PLEASE.
ALL RIGHT...
...YOU CAN COME IN.

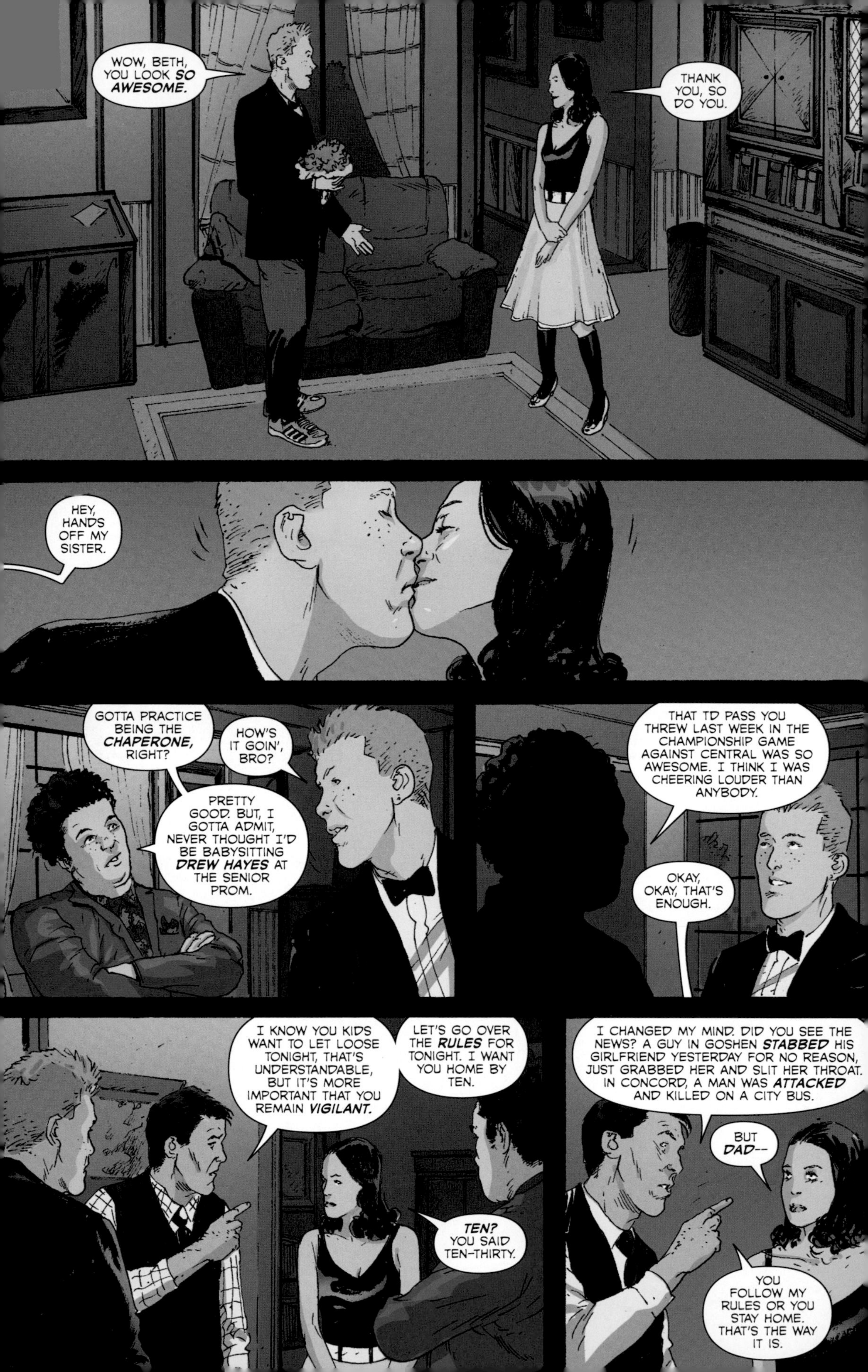
WOW, BETH, YOU LOOK SO AWESOME.
THANK YOU, SO DO YOU.
HEY, HANDS OFF MY SISTER.
GOTTA PRACTICE BEING THE CHAPERONE, RIGHT?
HOW'S IT GOIN', BRO?
PRETTY GOOD. BUT, I GOTTA ADMIT, NEVER THOUGHT I'D BE BABYSITTING DREW HAYES AT THE SENIOR PROM.
THAT TD PASS YOU THREW LAST WEEK IN THE CHAMPIONSHIP GAME AGAINST CENTRAL WAS SO AWESOME. I THINK I WAS CHEERING LOUDER THAN ANYBODY.
OKAY, OKAY, THAT'S ENOUGH.
I KNOW YOU KIDS WANT TO LET LOOSE TONIGHT, THAT'S UNDERSTANDABLE, BUT IT'S MORE IMPORTANT THAT YOU REMAIN VIGILANT.
LET'S GO OVER THE RULES FOR TONIGHT. I WANT YOU HOME BY TEN.
TEN? YOU SAID TEN-THIRTY.
I CHANGED MY MIND. DID YOU SEE THE NEWS? A GUY IN GOSHEN STABBED HIS GIRLFRIEND YESTERDAY FOR NO REASON, JUST GRABBED HER AND SLIT HER THROAT. IN CONCORD, A MAN WAS ATTACKED AND KILLED ON A CITY BUS.
BUT DAD--
YOU FOLLOW MY RULES OR YOU STAY HOME. THAT'S THE WAY IT IS.

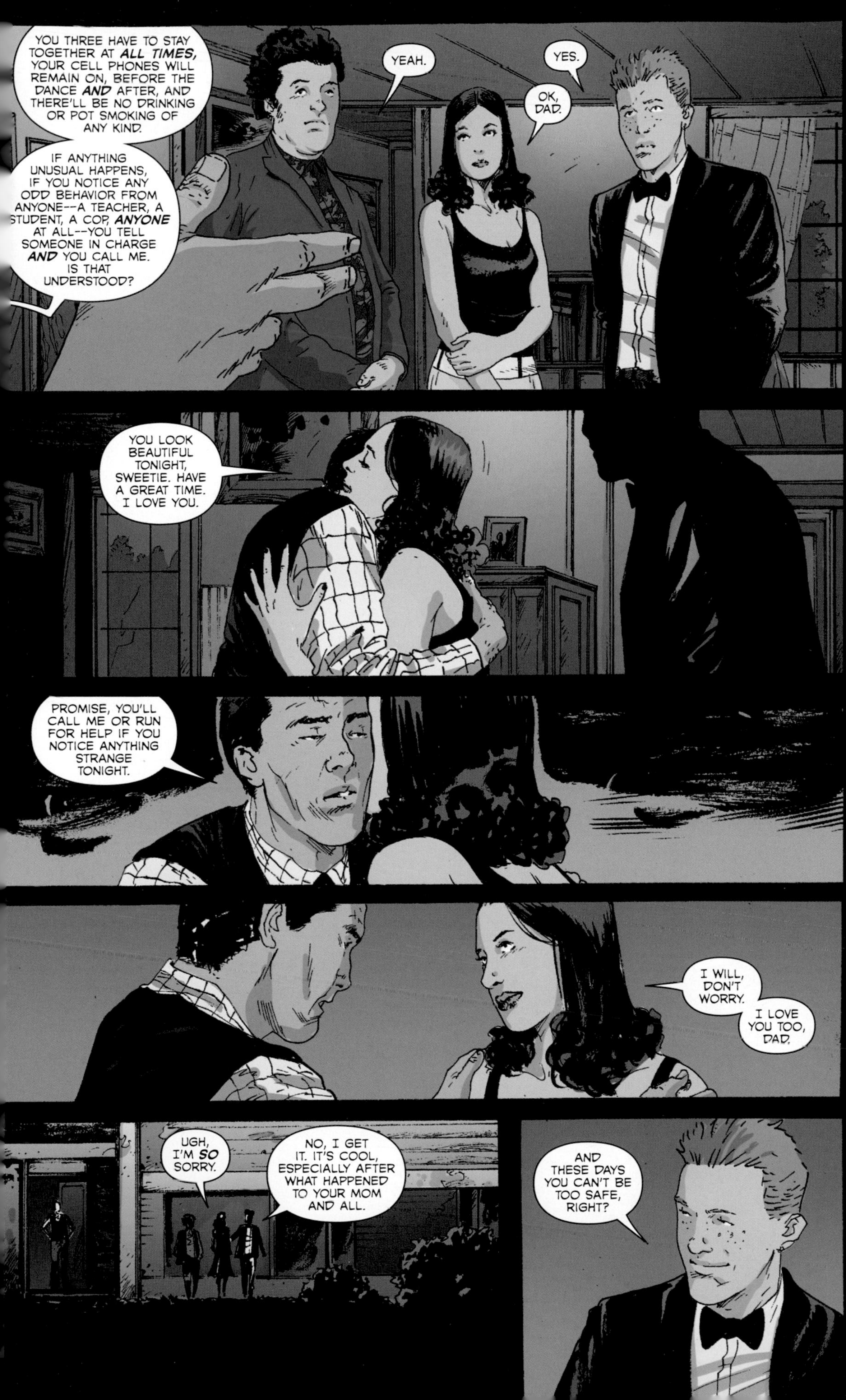
YOU THREE HAVE TO STAY TOGETHER AT ALL TIMES, YOUR CELL PHONES WILL REMAIN ON, BEFORE THE DANCE AND AFTER, AND THERE'LL BE NO DRINKING OR POT SMOKING OF ANY KIND.
IF ANYTHING UNUSUAL HAPPENS, IF YOU NOTICE ANY ODD BEHAVIOR FROM ANYONE--A TEACHER, A STUDENT, A COP, ANYONE AT ALL--YOU TELL SOMEONE IN CHARGE AND YOU CALL ME. IS THAT UNDERSTOOD?
YEAH.
YES.
OK, DAD.
YOU LOOK BEAUTIFUL TONIGHT, SWEETIE. HAVE A GREAT TIME. I LOVE YOU.
PROMISE, YOU'LL CALL ME OR RUN FOR HELP IF YOU NOTICE ANYTHING STRANGE TONIGHT.
I WILL, DON'T WORRY.
I LOVE YOU TOO, DAD.
UGH, I'M SO SORRY.
NO, I GET IT. IT'S COOL, ESPECIALLY AFTER WHAT HAPPENED TO YOUR MOM AND ALL.
AND THESE DAYS YOU CAN'T BE TOO SAFE, RIGHT?

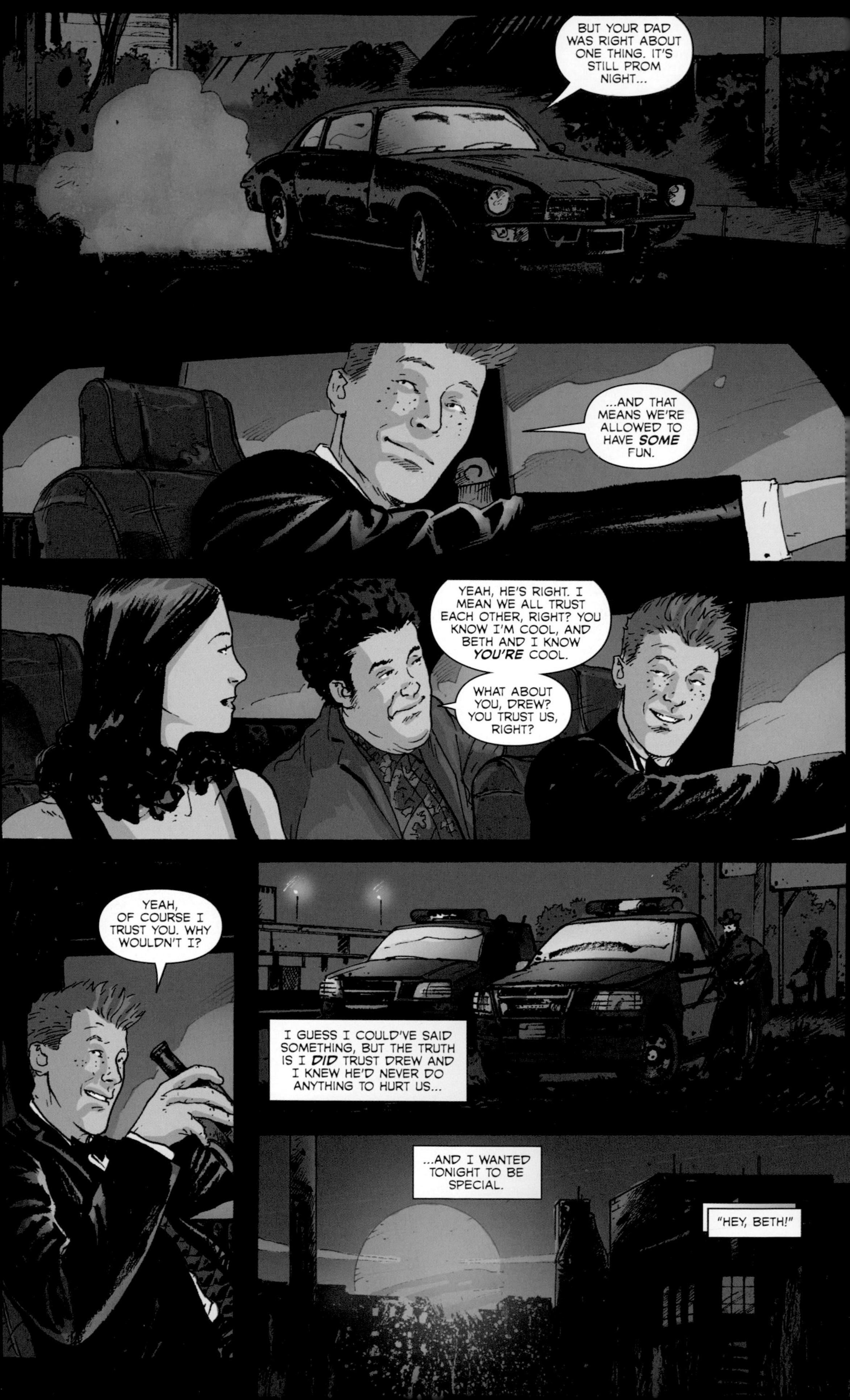
BUT YOUR DAD WAS RIGHT ABOUT ONE THING. IT'S STILL PROM NIGHT...
...AND THAT MEANS WE'RE ALLOWED TO HAVE SOME FUN.
YEAH, HE'S RIGHT. I MEAN WE ALL TRUST EACH OTHER, RIGHT? YOU KNOW I'M COOL, AND BETH AND I KNOW YOU'RE COOL.
WHAT ABOUT YOU, DREW? YOU TRUST US, RIGHT?
YEAH, OF COURSE I TRUST YOU. WHY WOULDN'T I?
I GUESS I COULD'VE SAID SOMETHING, BUT THE TRUTH IS I DID TRUST DREW AND I KNEW HE'D NEVER DO ANYTHING TO HURT US...
...AND I WANTED TONIGHT TO BE SPECIAL.
"HEY, BETH!"

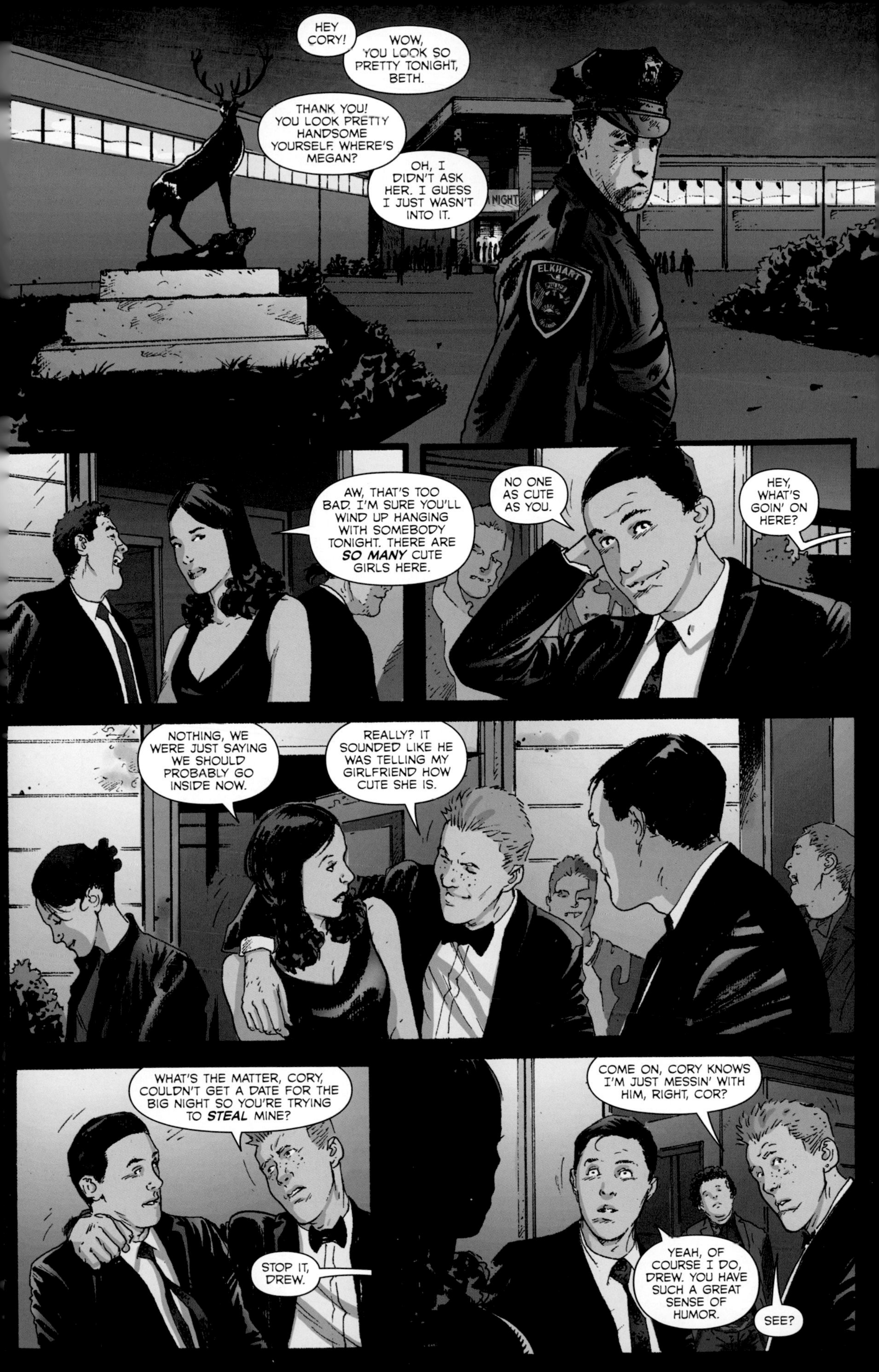
HEY CORY!
WOW, YOU LOOK SO PRETTY TONIGHT, BETH.
THANK YOU! YOU LOOK PRETTY HANDSOME YOURSELF. WHERE'S MEGAN?
OH, I DIDN'T ASK HER. I GUESS I JUST WASN'T INTO IT.
ELKHART
AW, THAT'S TOO BAD. I'M SURE YOU'LL WIND UP HANGING WITH SOMEBODY TONIGHT. THERE ARE SO MANY CUTE GIRLS HERE.
NO ONE AS CUTE AS YOU.
HEY, WHAT'S GOIN' ON HERE?
NOTHING, WE WERE JUST SAYING WE SHOULD PROBABLY GO INSIDE NOW.
REALLY? IT SOUNDED LIKE HE WAS TELLING MY GIRLFRIEND HOW CUTE SHE IS.
WHAT'S THE MATTER, CORY, COULDN'T GET A DATE FOR THE BIG NIGHT SO YOU'RE TRYING TO STEAL MINE?
STOP IT, DREW.
COME ON, CORY KNOWS I'M JUST MESSIN' WITH HIM, RIGHT, COR?
YEAH, OF COURSE I DO, DREW. YOU HAVE SUCH A GREAT SENSE OF HUMOR.
SEE?

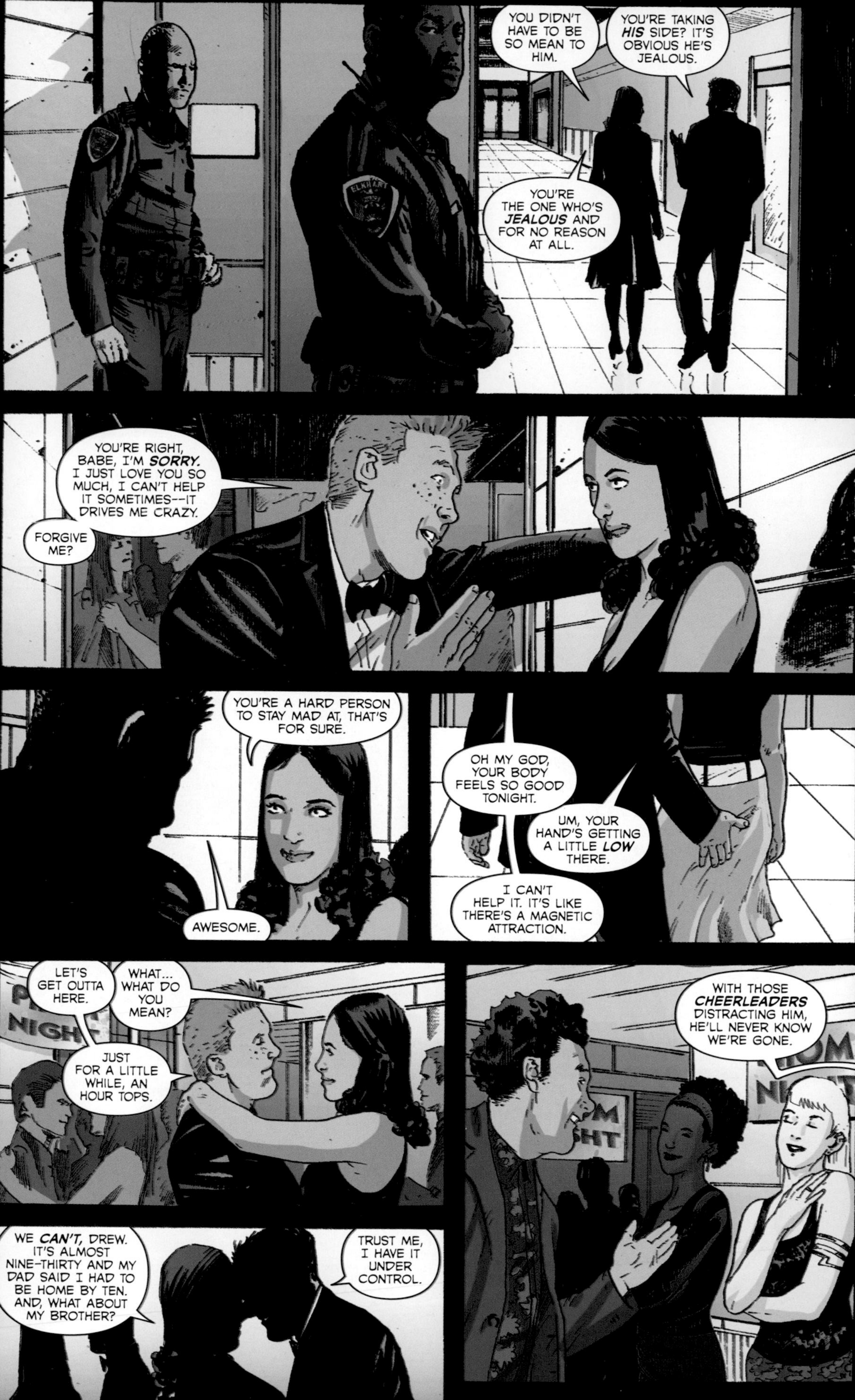
YOU DIDN'T HAVE TO BE SO MEAN TO HIM.
YOU'RE TAKING *HIS* SIDE? IT'S OBVIOUS HE'S JEALOUS.
YOU'RE THE ONE WHO'S *JEALOUS* AND FOR NO REASON AT ALL.
YOU'RE RIGHT, BABE, I'M *SORRY.* I JUST LOVE YOU SO MUCH, I CAN'T HELP IT SOMETIMES--IT DRIVES ME CRAZY.
FORGIVE ME?
YOU'RE A HARD PERSON TO STAY MAD AT, THAT'S FOR SURE.
AWESOME.
OH MY GOD, YOUR BODY FEELS SO GOOD TONIGHT.
UM, YOUR HAND'S GETTING A LITTLE *LOW* THERE.
I CAN'T HELP IT. IT'S LIKE THERE'S A MAGNETIC ATTRACTION.
LET'S GET OUTTA HERE.
WHAT... WHAT DO YOU MEAN?
JUST FOR A LITTLE WHILE, AN HOUR TOPS.
WE *CAN'T,* DREW. IT'S ALMOST NINE-THIRTY AND MY DAD SAID I HAD TO BE HOME BY TEN. AND, WHAT ABOUT MY BROTHER?
TRUST ME, I HAVE IT UNDER CONTROL.
WITH THOSE *CHEERLEADERS* DISTRACTING HIM, HE'LL NEVER KNOW WE'RE GONE.

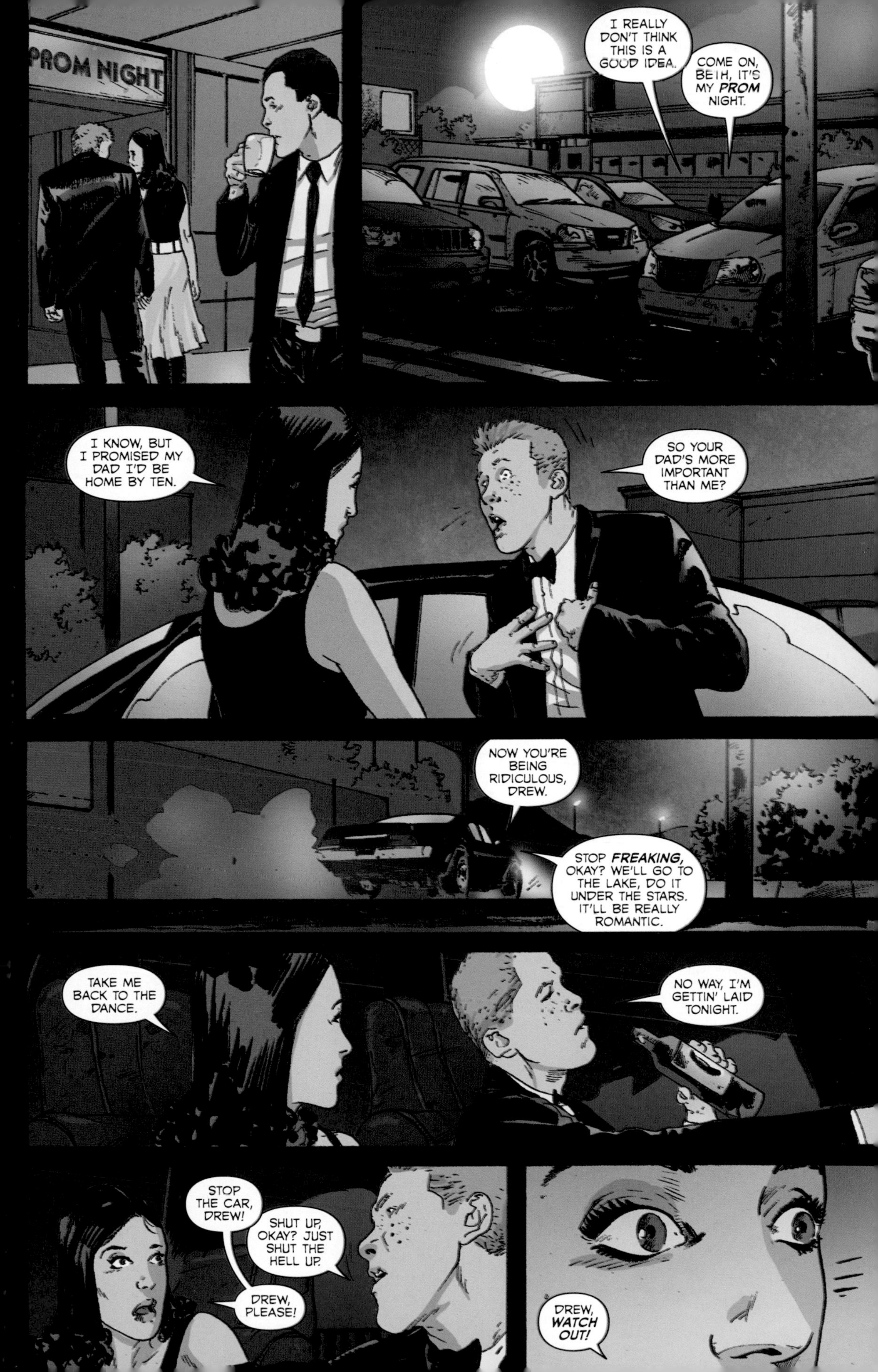
PROM NIGHT
I REALLY DON'T THINK THIS IS A GOOD IDEA.
COME ON, BETH, IT'S MY PROM NIGHT.
I KNOW, BUT I PROMISED MY DAD I'D BE HOME BY TEN.
SO YOUR DAD'S MORE IMPORTANT THAN ME?
NOW YOU'RE BEING RIDICULOUS, DREW.
STOP FREAKING, OKAY? WE'LL GO TO THE LAKE, DO IT UNDER THE STARS. IT'LL BE REALLY ROMANTIC.
TAKE ME BACK TO THE DANCE.
NO WAY, I'M GETTIN' LAID TONIGHT.
STOP THE CAR, DREW!
SHUT UP, OKAY? JUST SHUT THE HELL UP.
DREW, PLEASE!
DREW, WATCH OUT!

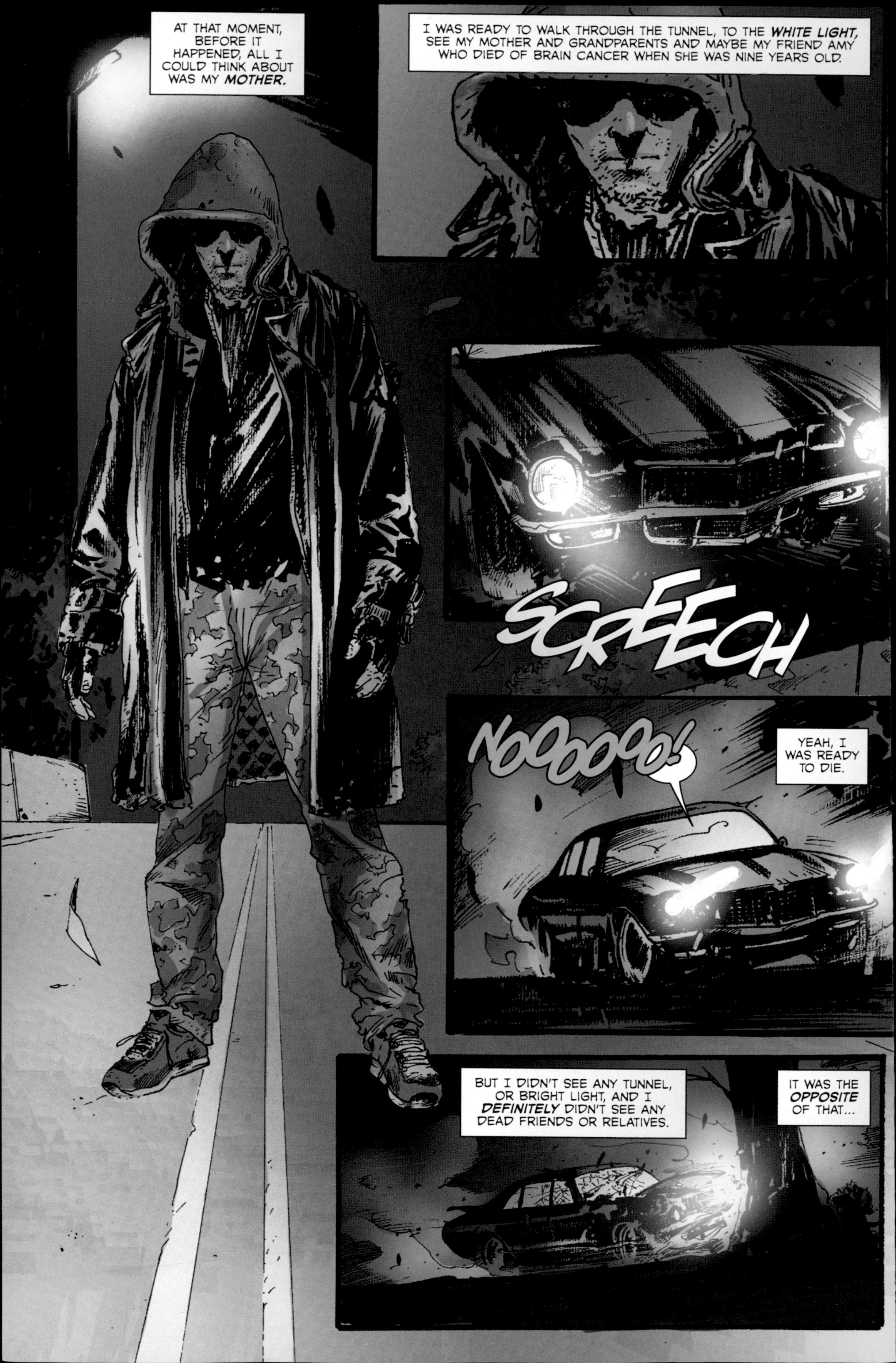
AT THAT MOMENT, BEFORE IT HAPPENED, ALL I COULD THINK ABOUT WAS MY *MOTHER.*
I WAS READY TO WALK THROUGH THE TUNNEL, TO THE *WHITE LIGHT,* SEE MY MOTHER AND GRANDPARENTS AND MAYBE MY FRIEND AMY WHO DIED OF BRAIN CANCER WHEN SHE WAS NINE YEARS OLD.
SCREECH
NOOOOOOO!
YEAH, I WAS READY TO DIE.
BUT I DIDN'T SEE ANY TUNNEL, OR BRIGHT LIGHT, AND I *DEFINITELY* DIDN'T SEE ANY DEAD FRIENDS OR RELATIVES.
IT WAS THE *OPPOSITE* OF THAT...

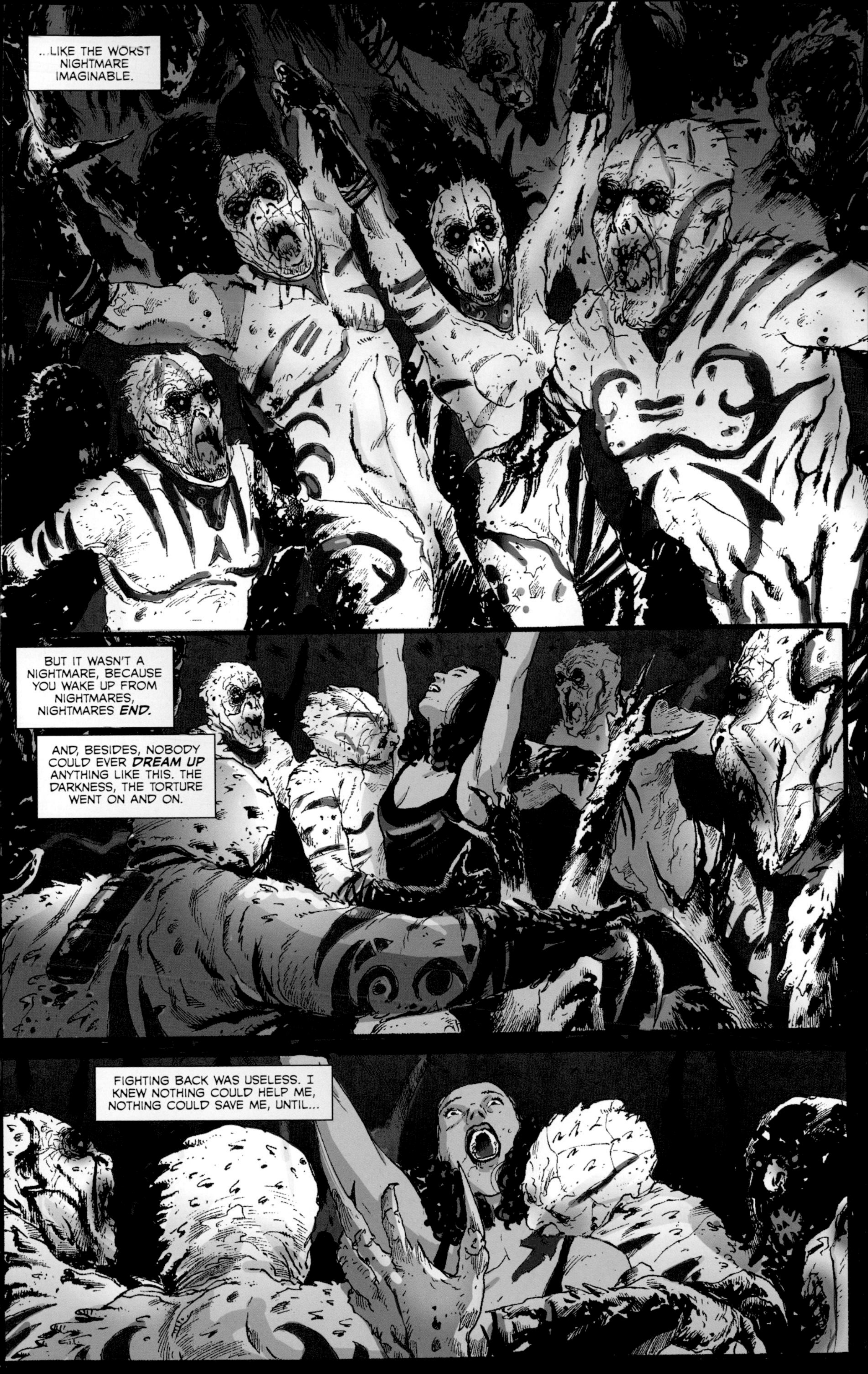
...LIKE THE WORST NIGHTMARE IMAGINABLE.
BUT IT WASN'T A NIGHTMARE, BECAUSE YOU WAKE UP FROM NIGHTMARES, NIGHTMARES *END*.
AND, BESIDES, NOBODY COULD EVER *DREAM UP* ANYTHING LIKE THIS. THE DARKNESS, THE TORTURE WENT ON AND ON.
FIGHTING BACK WAS USELESS. I KNEW NOTHING COULD HELP ME, NOTHING COULD SAVE ME, UNTIL...

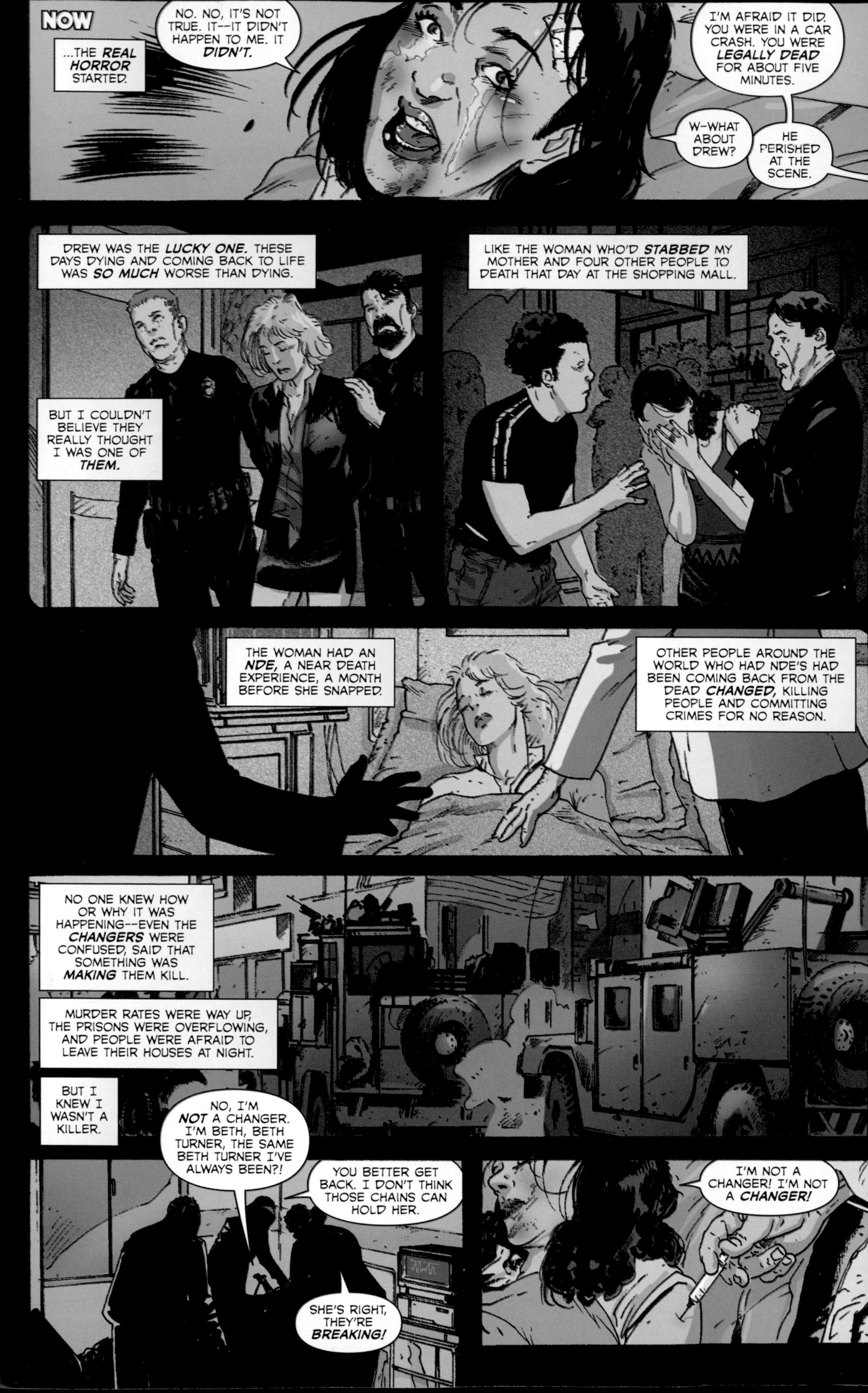
NOW
...THE REAL HORROR STARTED.
NO. NO, IT'S NOT TRUE. IT--IT DIDN'T HAPPEN TO ME. IT DIDN'T.
I'M AFRAID IT DID. YOU WERE IN A CAR CRASH. YOU WERE LEGALLY DEAD FOR ABOUT FIVE MINUTES.
W-WHAT ABOUT DREW?
HE PERISHED AT THE SCENE.
DREW WAS THE LUCKY ONE. THESE DAYS DYING AND COMING BACK TO LIFE WAS SO MUCH WORSE THAN DYING.
BUT I COULDN'T BELIEVE THEY REALLY THOUGHT I WAS ONE OF THEM.
LIKE THE WOMAN WHO'D STABBED MY MOTHER AND FOUR OTHER PEOPLE TO DEATH THAT DAY AT THE SHOPPING MALL.
THE WOMAN HAD AN NDE, A NEAR DEATH EXPERIENCE, A MONTH BEFORE SHE SNAPPED.
OTHER PEOPLE AROUND THE WORLD WHO HAD NDE'S HAD BEEN COMING BACK FROM THE DEAD CHANGED, KILLING PEOPLE AND COMMITTING CRIMES FOR NO REASON.
NO ONE KNEW HOW OR WHY IT WAS HAPPENING--EVEN THE CHANGERS WERE CONFUSED, SAID THAT SOMETHING WAS MAKING THEM KILL.
MURDER RATES WERE WAY UP, THE PRISONS WERE OVERFLOWING, AND PEOPLE WERE AFRAID TO LEAVE THEIR HOUSES AT NIGHT.
BUT I KNEW I WASN'T A KILLER.
NO, I'M NOT A CHANGER. I'M BETH, BETH TURNER, THE SAME BETH TURNER I'VE ALWAYS BEEN?!
YOU BETTER GET BACK. I DON'T THINK THOSE CHAINS CAN HOLD HER.
SHE'S RIGHT, THEY'RE BREAKING!
I'M NOT A CHANGER! I'M NOT A CHANGER!

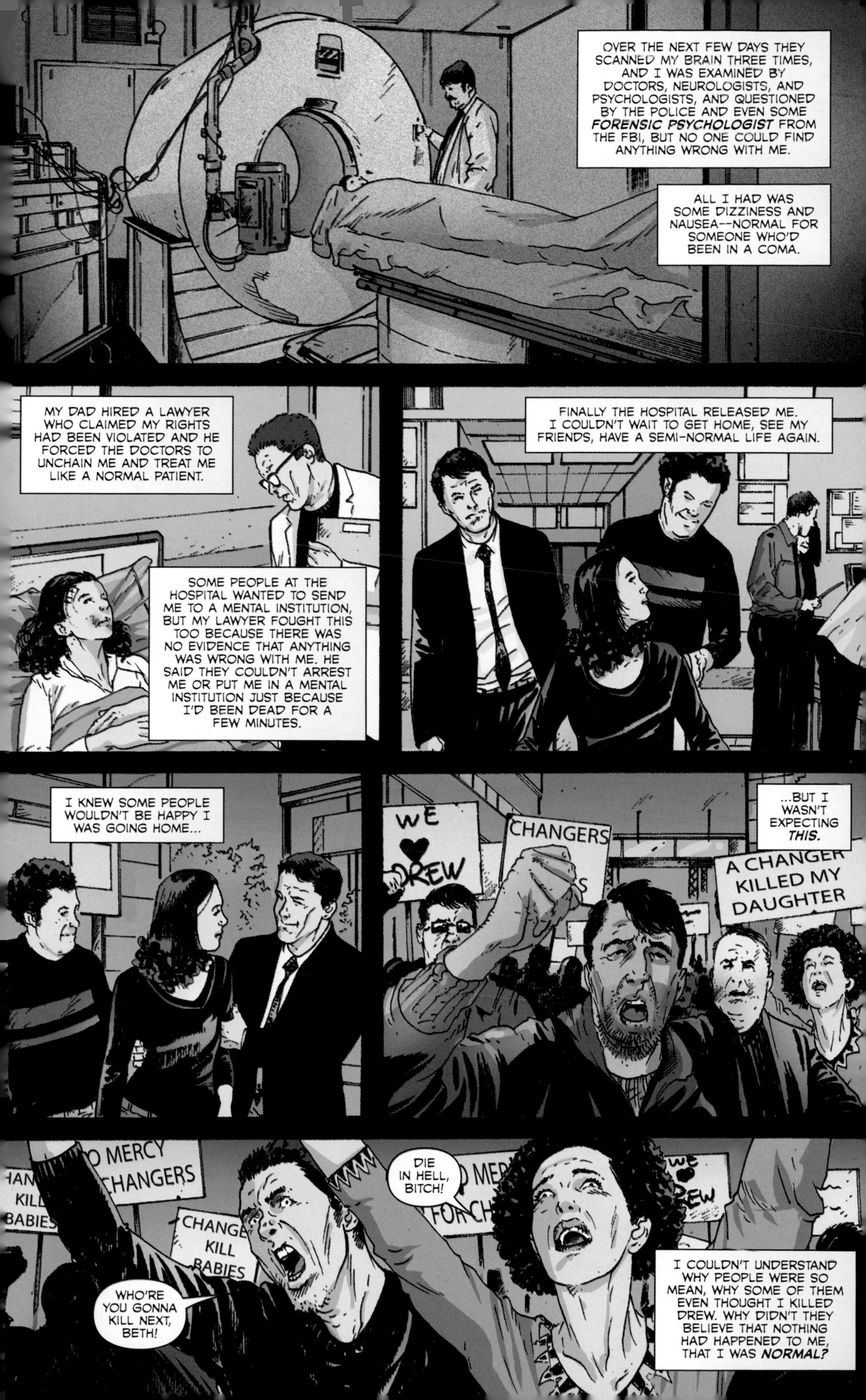

OVER THE NEXT FEW DAYS THEY SCANNED MY BRAIN THREE TIMES, AND I WAS EXAMINED BY DOCTORS, NEUROLOGISTS, AND PSYCHOLOGISTS, AND QUESTIONED BY THE POLICE AND EVEN SOME ***FORENSIC PSYCHOLOGIST*** FROM THE FBI, BUT NO ONE COULD FIND ANYTHING WRONG WITH ME.
ALL I HAD WAS SOME DIZZINESS AND NAUSEA--NORMAL FOR SOMEONE WHO'D BEEN IN A COMA.
MY DAD HIRED A LAWYER WHO CLAIMED MY RIGHTS HAD BEEN VIOLATED AND HE FORCED THE DOCTORS TO UNCHAIN ME AND TREAT ME LIKE A NORMAL PATIENT.
SOME PEOPLE AT THE HOSPITAL WANTED TO SEND ME TO A MENTAL INSTITUTION, BUT MY LAWYER FOUGHT THIS TOO BECAUSE THERE WAS NO EVIDENCE THAT ANYTHING WAS WRONG WITH ME. HE SAID THEY COULDN'T ARREST ME OR PUT ME IN A MENTAL INSTITUTION JUST BECAUSE I'D BEEN DEAD FOR A FEW MINUTES.
FINALLY THE HOSPITAL RELEASED ME. I COULDN'T WAIT TO GET HOME, SEE MY FRIENDS, HAVE A SEMI-NORMAL LIFE AGAIN.
I KNEW SOME PEOPLE WOULDN'T BE HAPPY I WAS GOING HOME...
...BUT I WASN'T EXPECTING ***THIS.***
CHANGERS
A CHANGER KILLED MY DAUGHTER
DIE IN HELL, BITCH!
WHO'RE YOU GONNA KILL NEXT, BETH!
I COULDN'T UNDERSTAND WHY PEOPLE WERE SO MEAN, WHY SOME OF THEM EVEN THOUGHT I KILLED DREW. WHY DIDN'T THEY BELIEVE THAT NOTHING HAD HAPPENED TO ME, THAT I WAS ***NORMAL?***

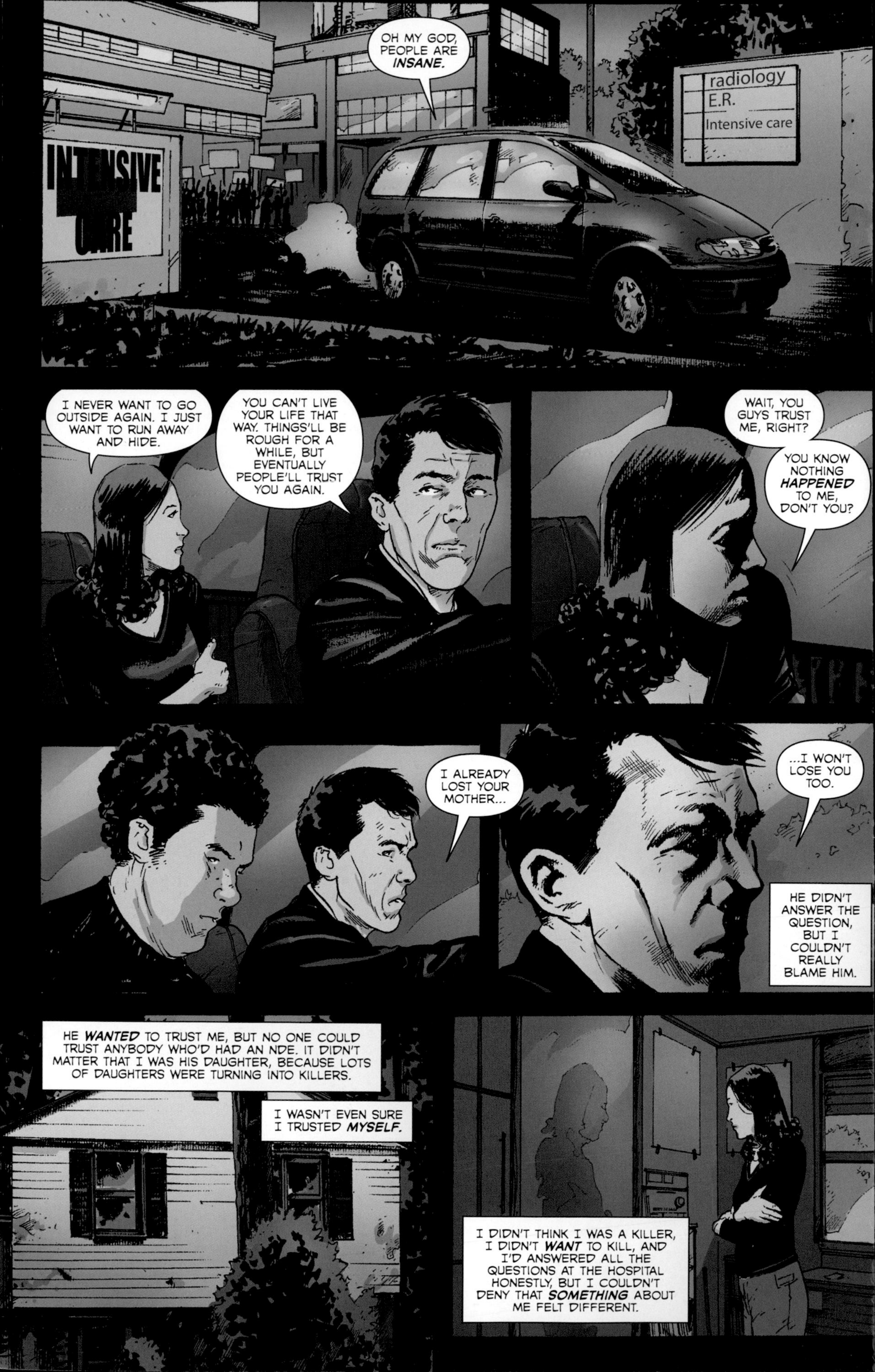

OH MY GOD, PEOPLE ARE *INSANE.*
radiology
E.R.
Intensive care
INTENSIVE CARE
I NEVER WANT TO GO OUTSIDE AGAIN. I JUST WANT TO RUN AWAY AND HIDE.
YOU CAN'T LIVE YOUR LIFE THAT WAY. THINGS'LL BE ROUGH FOR A WHILE, BUT EVENTUALLY PEOPLE'LL TRUST YOU AGAIN.
WAIT, YOU GUYS TRUST ME, RIGHT?
YOU KNOW NOTHING ***HAPPENED*** TO ME, DON'T YOU?
I ALREADY LOST YOUR MOTHER...
...I WON'T LOSE YOU TOO.
HE DIDN'T ANSWER THE QUESTION, BUT I COULDN'T REALLY BLAME HIM.
HE ***WANTED*** TO TRUST ME, BUT NO ONE COULD TRUST ANYBODY WHO'D HAD AN NDE. IT DIDN'T MATTER THAT I WAS HIS DAUGHTER, BECAUSE LOTS OF DAUGHTERS WERE TURNING INTO KILLERS.
I WASN'T EVEN SURE I TRUSTED ***MYSELF.***
I DIDN'T THINK I WAS A KILLER, I DIDN'T ***WANT*** TO KILL, AND I'D ANSWERED ALL THE QUESTIONS AT THE HOSPITAL HONESTLY, BUT I COULDN'T DENY THAT ***SOMETHING*** ABOUT ME FELT DIFFERENT.

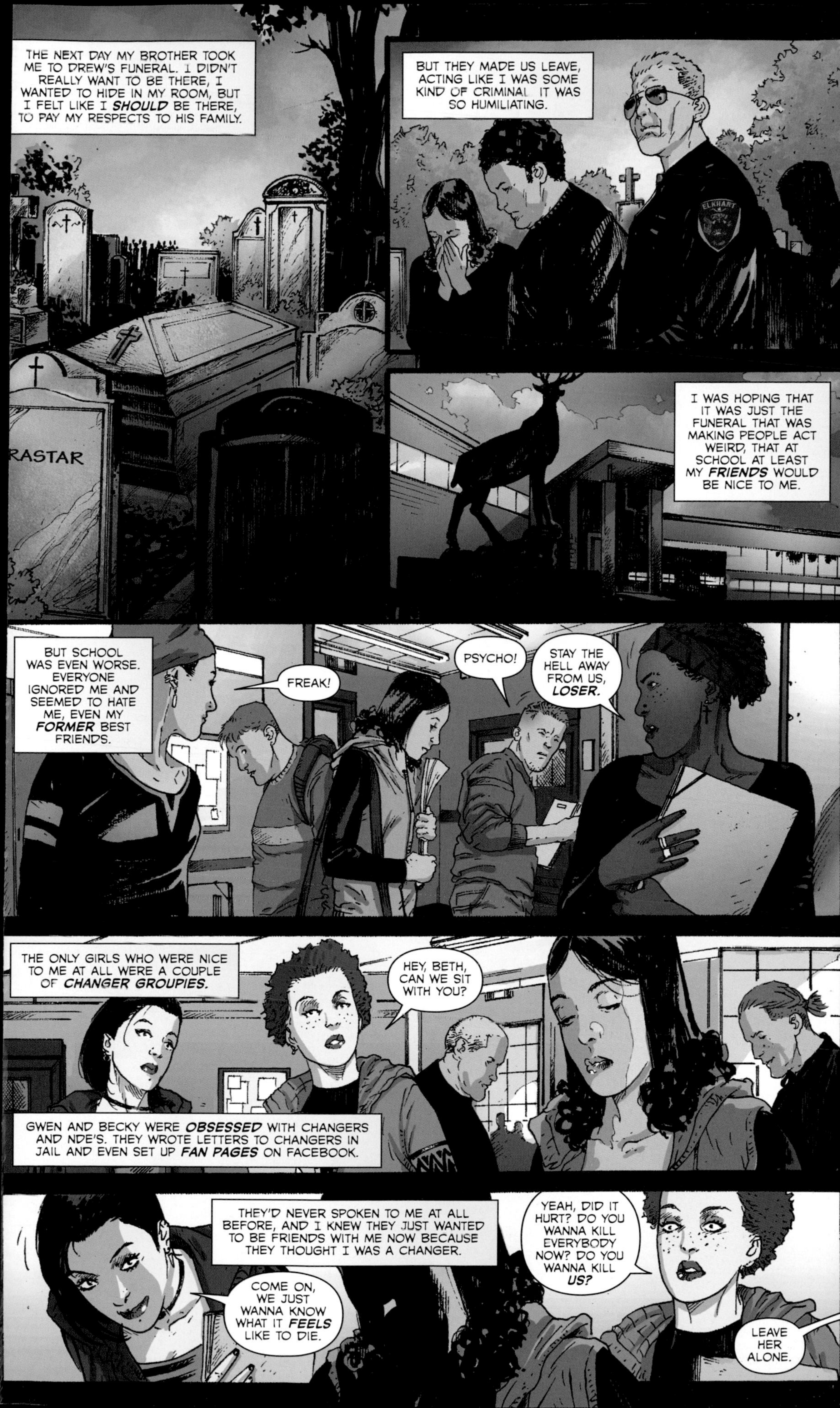
THE NEXT DAY MY BROTHER TOOK ME TO DREW'S FUNERAL. I DIDN'T REALLY WANT TO BE THERE, I WANTED TO HIDE IN MY ROOM, BUT I FELT LIKE I *SHOULD* BE THERE, TO PAY MY RESPECTS TO HIS FAMILY.
RASTAR
BUT THEY MADE US LEAVE, ACTING LIKE I WAS SOME KIND OF CRIMINAL. IT WAS SO HUMILIATING.
ELKHART
I WAS HOPING THAT IT WAS JUST THE FUNERAL THAT WAS MAKING PEOPLE ACT WEIRD, THAT AT SCHOOL AT LEAST MY *FRIENDS* WOULD BE NICE TO ME.
BUT SCHOOL WAS EVEN WORSE. EVERYONE IGNORED ME AND SEEMED TO HATE ME, EVEN MY *FORMER* BEST FRIENDS.
FREAK!
PSYCHO!
STAY THE HELL AWAY FROM US, *LOSER.*
THE ONLY GIRLS WHO WERE NICE TO ME AT ALL WERE A COUPLE OF *CHANGER GROUPIES.*
HEY, BETH, CAN WE SIT WITH YOU?
GWEN AND BECKY WERE *OBSESSED* WITH CHANGERS AND NDE'S. THEY WROTE LETTERS TO CHANGERS IN JAIL AND EVEN SET UP *FAN PAGES* ON FACEBOOK.
THEY'D NEVER SPOKEN TO ME AT ALL BEFORE, AND I KNEW THEY JUST WANTED TO BE FRIENDS WITH ME NOW BECAUSE THEY THOUGHT I WAS A CHANGER.
COME ON, WE JUST WANNA KNOW WHAT IT *FEELS* LIKE TO DIE.
YEAH, DID IT HURT? DO YOU WANNA KILL EVERYBODY NOW? DO YOU WANNA KILL *US?*
LEAVE HER ALONE.

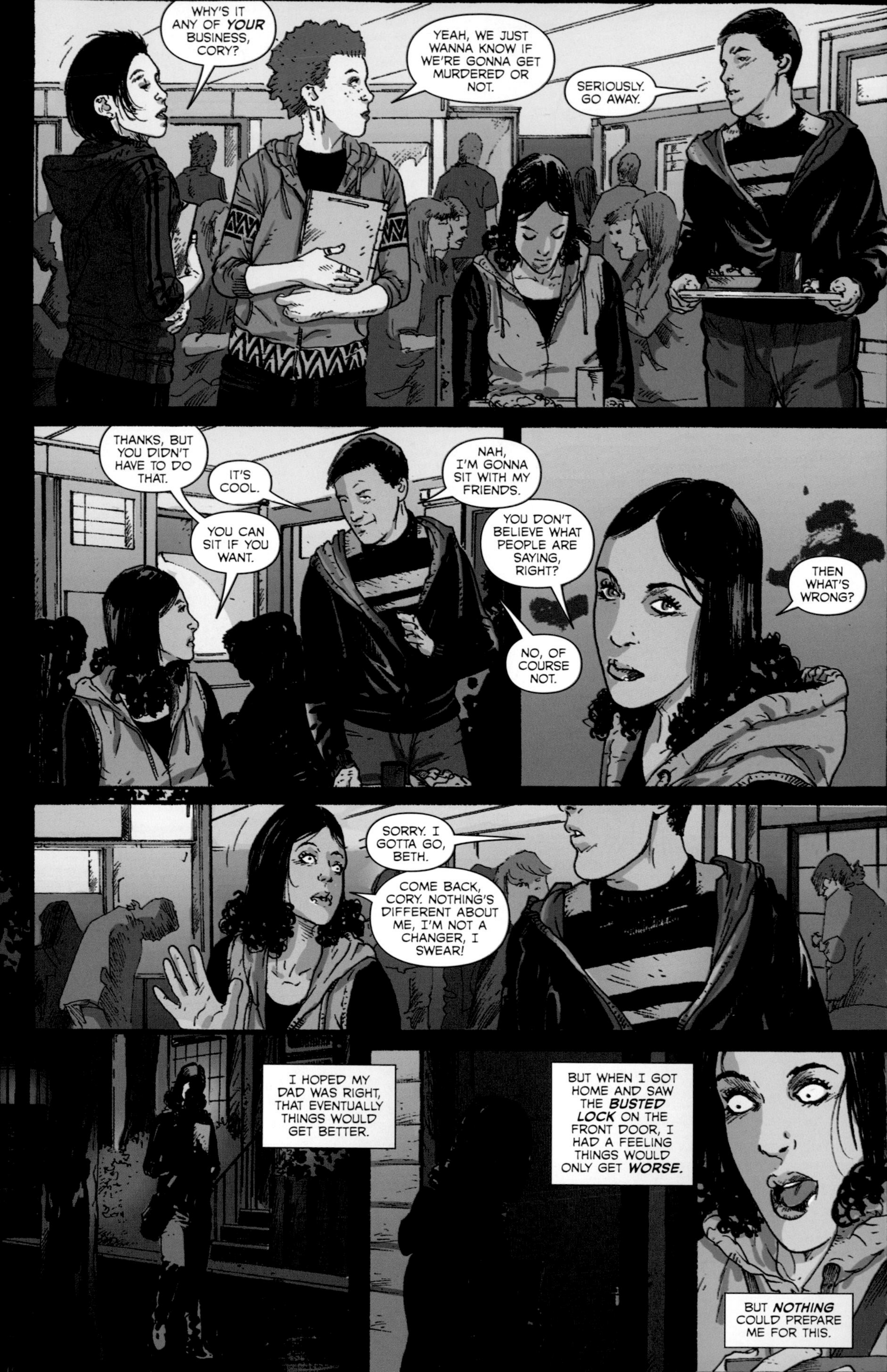
WHY'S IT ANY OF *YOUR* BUSINESS, CORY?
YEAH, WE JUST WANNA KNOW IF WE'RE GONNA GET MURDERED OR NOT.
SERIOUSLY. GO AWAY.
THANKS, BUT YOU DIDN'T HAVE TO DO THAT.
IT'S COOL.
YOU CAN SIT IF YOU WANT.
NAH, I'M GONNA SIT WITH MY FRIENDS.
YOU DON'T BELIEVE WHAT PEOPLE ARE SAYING, RIGHT?
NO, OF COURSE NOT.
THEN WHAT'S WRONG?
SORRY. I GOTTA GO, BETH.
COME BACK, CORY. NOTHING'S DIFFERENT ABOUT ME, I'M NOT A CHANGER, I SWEAR!
I HOPED MY DAD WAS RIGHT, THAT EVENTUALLY THINGS WOULD GET BETTER.
BUT WHEN I GOT HOME AND SAW THE ***BUSTED LOCK*** ON THE FRONT DOOR, I HAD A FEELING THINGS WOULD ONLY GET ***WORSE.***
BUT ***NOTHING*** COULD PREPARE ME FOR THIS.

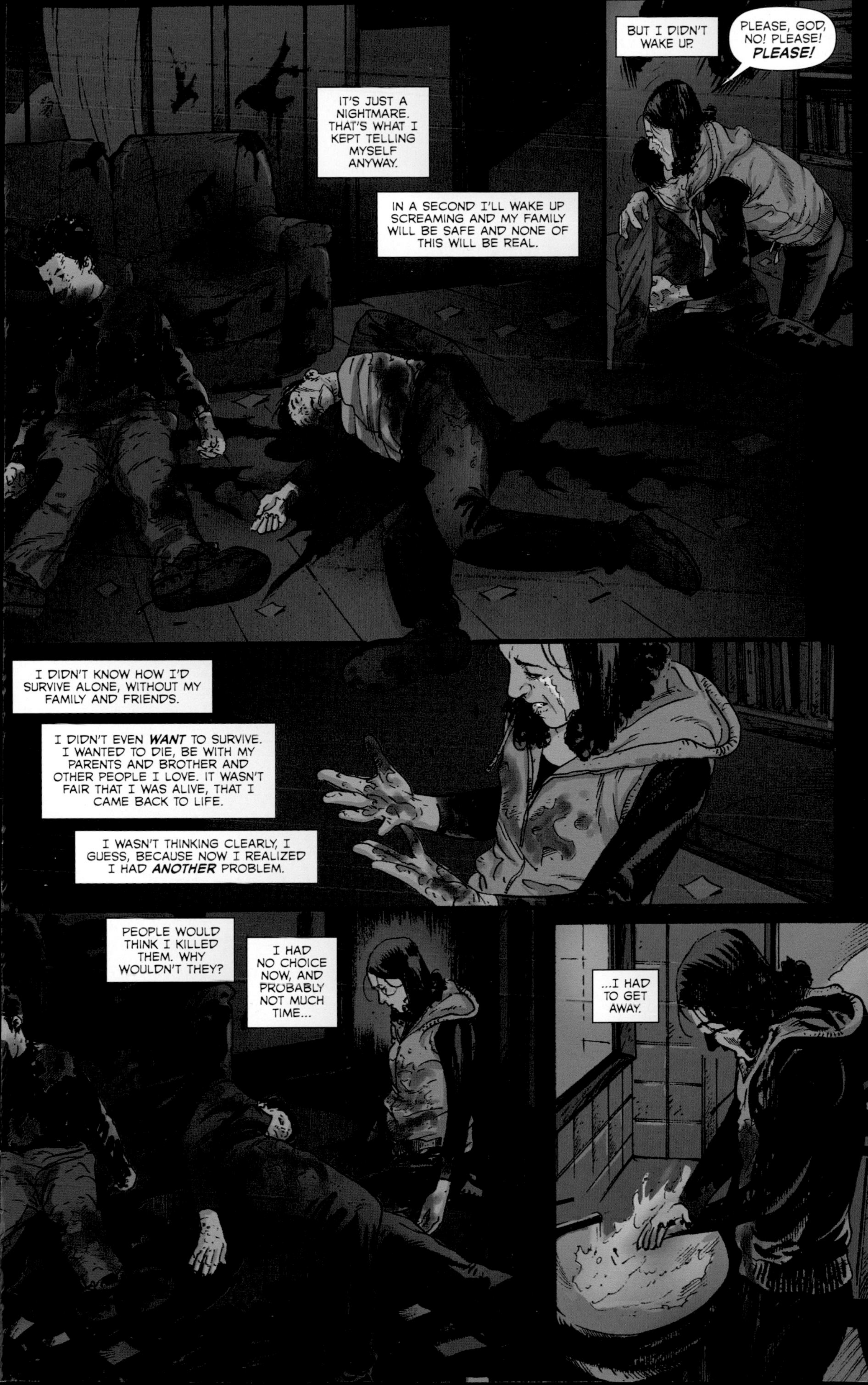
IT'S JUST A NIGHTMARE. THAT'S WHAT I KEPT TELLING MYSELF ANYWAY.
IN A SECOND I'LL WAKE UP SCREAMING AND MY FAMILY WILL BE SAFE AND NONE OF THIS WILL BE REAL.
BUT I DIDN'T WAKE UP.
PLEASE, GOD, NO! PLEASE! PLEASE!
I DIDN'T KNOW HOW I'D SURVIVE ALONE, WITHOUT MY FAMILY AND FRIENDS.
I DIDN'T EVEN WANT TO SURVIVE. I WANTED TO DIE, BE WITH MY PARENTS AND BROTHER AND OTHER PEOPLE I LOVE. IT WASN'T FAIR THAT I WAS ALIVE, THAT I CAME BACK TO LIFE.
I WASN'T THINKING CLEARLY, I GUESS, BECAUSE NOW I REALIZED I HAD ANOTHER PROBLEM.
PEOPLE WOULD THINK I KILLED THEM. WHY WOULDN'T THEY?
I HAD NO CHOICE NOW, AND PROBABLY NOT MUCH TIME...
...I HAD TO GET AWAY.

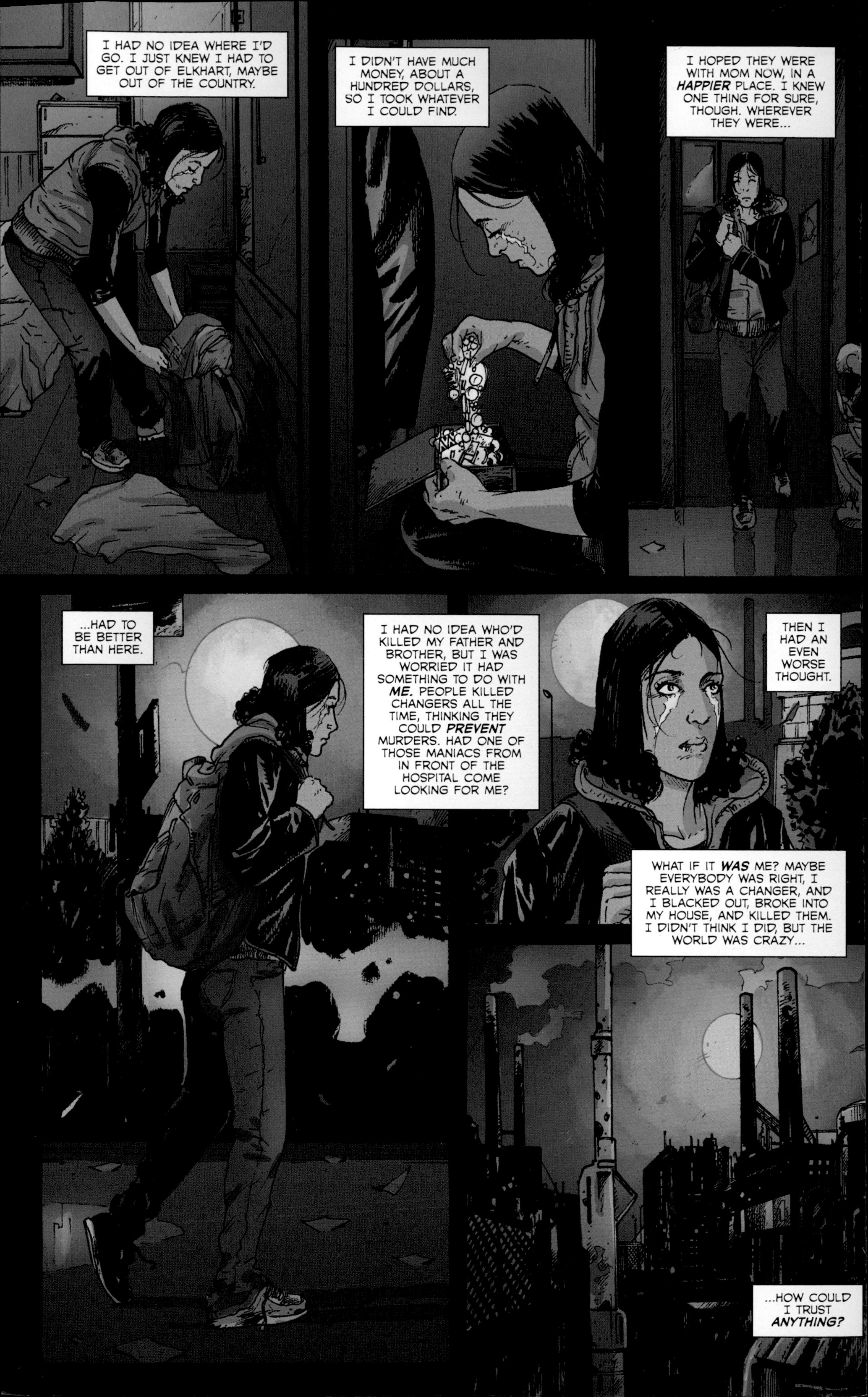
I HAD NO IDEA WHERE I'D GO. I JUST KNEW I HAD TO GET OUT OF ELKHART, MAYBE OUT OF THE COUNTRY.
I DIDN'T HAVE MUCH MONEY, ABOUT A HUNDRED DOLLARS, SO I TOOK WHATEVER I COULD FIND.
I HOPED THEY WERE WITH MOM NOW, IN A ***HAPPIER*** PLACE. I KNEW ONE THING FOR SURE, THOUGH. WHEREVER THEY WERE...
...HAD TO BE BETTER THAN HERE.
I HAD NO IDEA WHO'D KILLED MY FATHER AND BROTHER, BUT I WAS WORRIED IT HAD SOMETHING TO DO WITH ***ME.*** PEOPLE KILLED CHANGERS ALL THE TIME, THINKING THEY COULD ***PREVENT*** MURDERS. HAD ONE OF THOSE MANIACS FROM IN FRONT OF THE HOSPITAL COME LOOKING FOR ME?
THEN I HAD AN EVEN WORSE THOUGHT.
WHAT IF IT ***WAS*** ME? MAYBE EVERYBODY WAS RIGHT, I REALLY WAS A CHANGER, AND I BLACKED OUT, BROKE INTO MY HOUSE, AND KILLED THEM. I DIDN'T THINK I DID, BUT THE WORLD WAS CRAZY...
...HOW COULD I TRUST ***ANYTHING?***

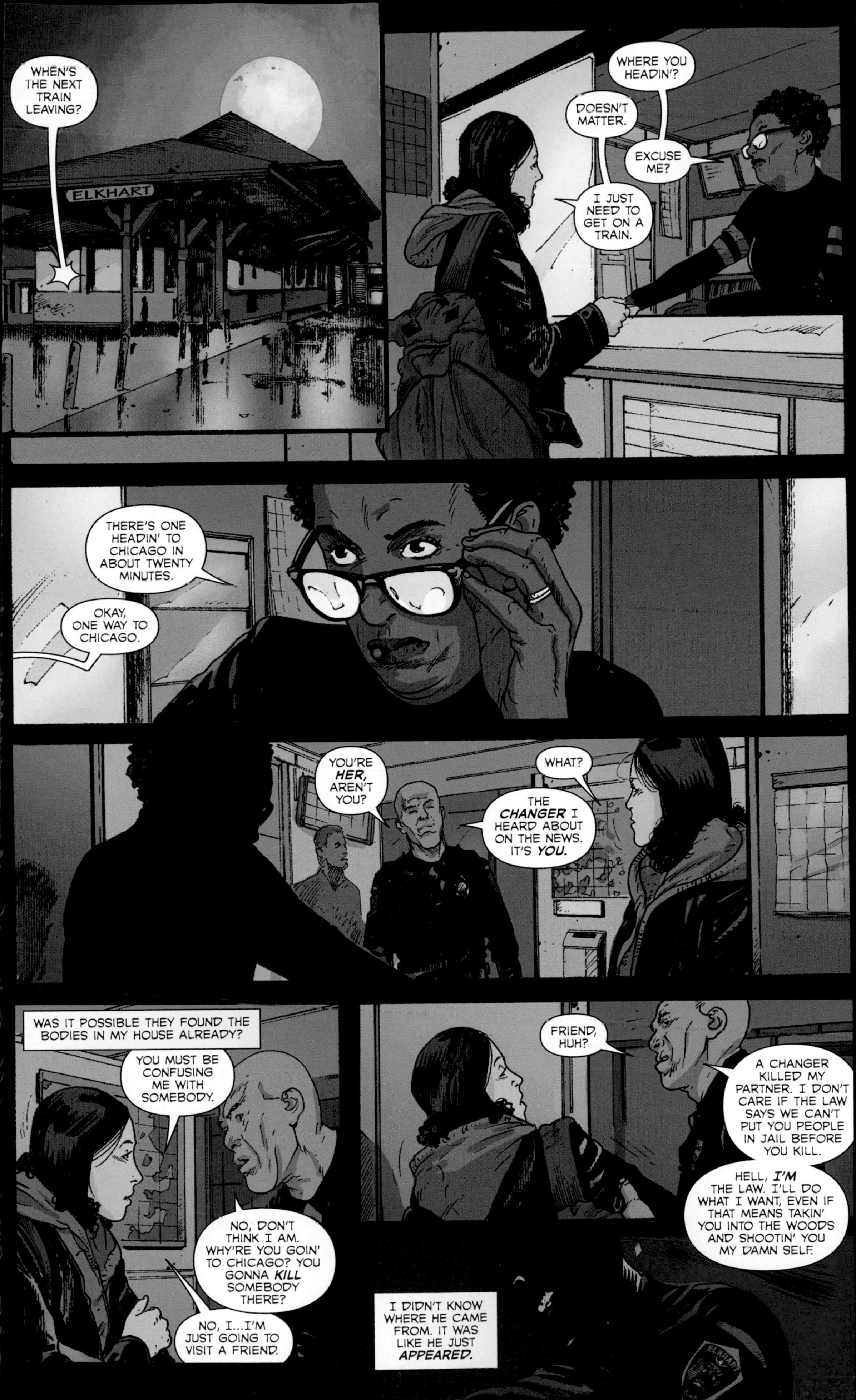
WHEN'S THE NEXT TRAIN LEAVING?
ELKHART
WHERE YOU HEADIN'?
DOESN'T MATTER.
EXCUSE ME?
I JUST NEED TO GET ON A TRAIN.
THERE'S ONE HEADIN' TO CHICAGO IN ABOUT TWENTY MINUTES.
OKAY, ONE WAY TO CHICAGO.
YOU'RE *HER,* AREN'T YOU?
WHAT?
THE *CHANGER* I HEARD ABOUT ON THE NEWS. IT'S *YOU.*
WAS IT POSSIBLE THEY FOUND THE BODIES IN MY HOUSE ALREADY?
YOU MUST BE CONFUSING ME WITH SOMEBODY.
NO, DON'T THINK I AM. WHY'RE YOU GOIN' TO CHICAGO? YOU GONNA *KILL* SOMEBODY THERE?
NO, I...I'M JUST GOING TO VISIT A FRIEND.
FRIEND, HUH?
A CHANGER KILLED MY PARTNER. I DON'T CARE IF THE LAW SAYS WE CAN'T PUT YOU PEOPLE IN JAIL BEFORE YOU KILL.
HELL, *I'M* THE LAW. I'LL DO WHAT I WANT, EVEN IF THAT MEANS TAKIN' YOU INTO THE WOODS AND SHOOTIN' YOU MY DAMN SELF.
I DIDN'T KNOW WHERE HE CAME FROM. IT WAS LIKE HE JUST *APPEARED.*

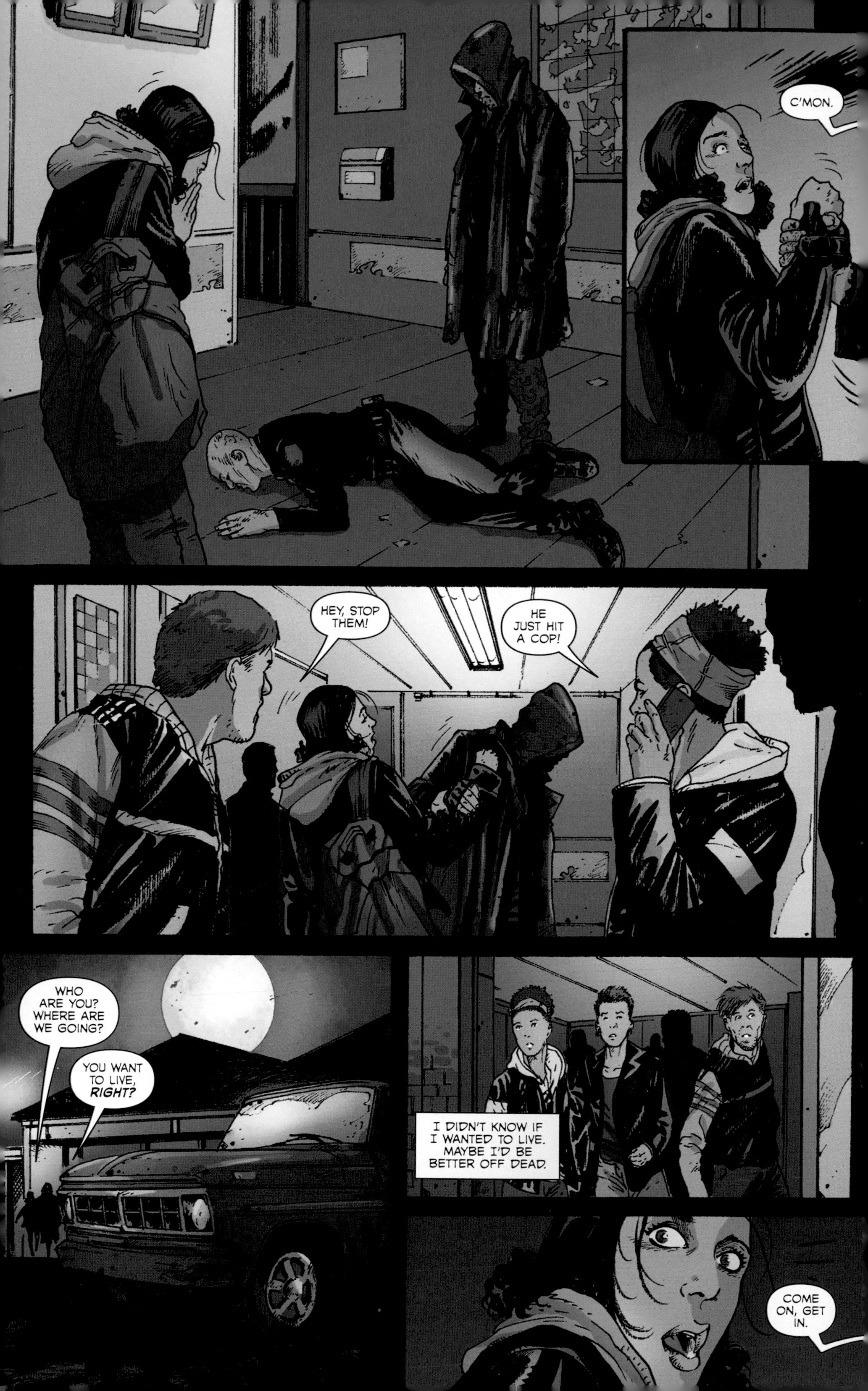
C'MON.
HEY, STOP THEM!
HE JUST HIT A COP!
WHO ARE YOU? WHERE ARE WE GOING?
YOU WANT TO LIVE, *RIGHT?*
I DIDN'T KNOW IF I WANTED TO LIVE. MAYBE I'D BE BETTER OFF DEAD.
COME ON, GET IN.

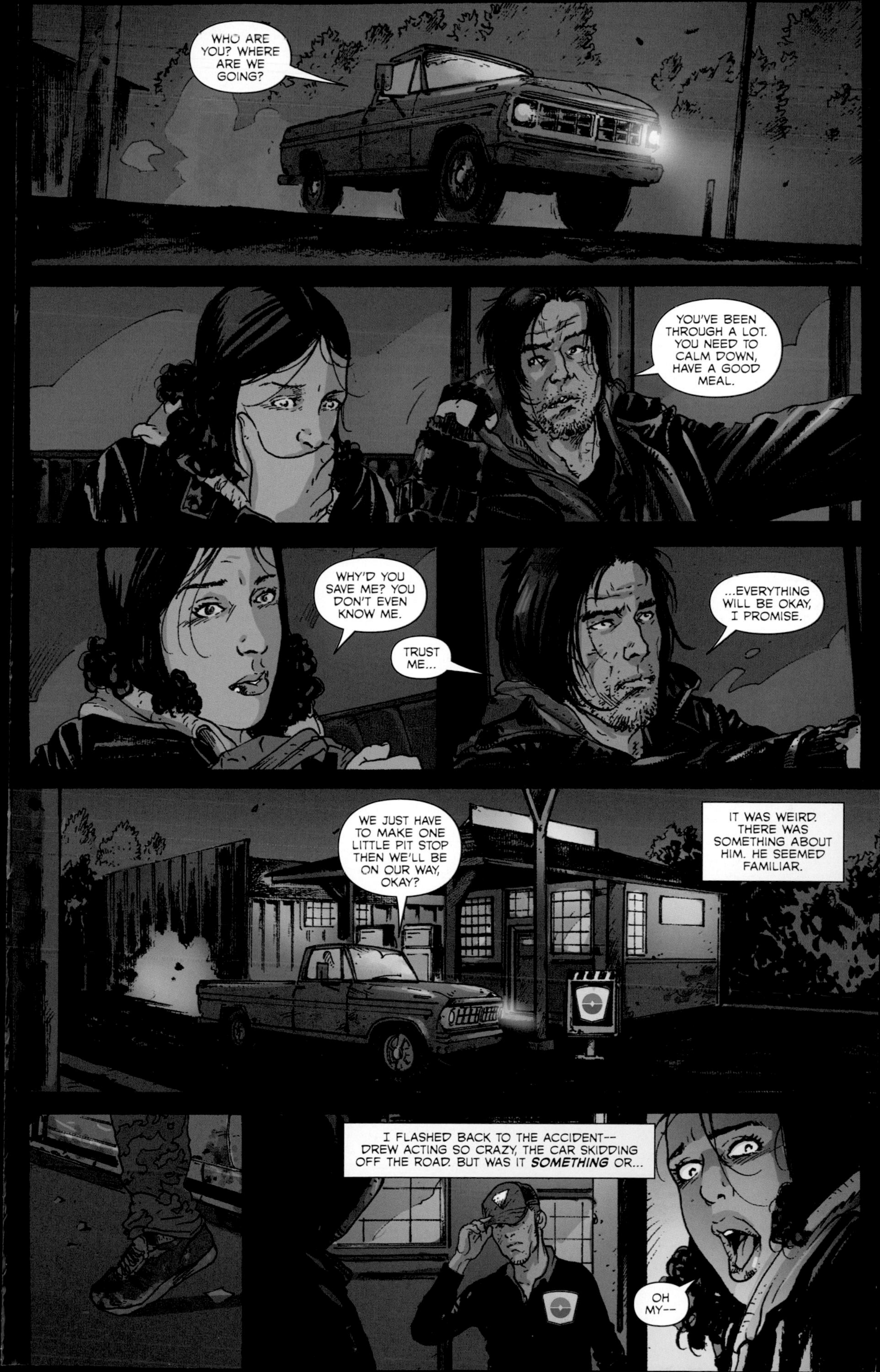
WHO ARE YOU? WHERE ARE WE GOING?
YOU'VE BEEN THROUGH A LOT. YOU NEED TO CALM DOWN, HAVE A GOOD MEAL.
WHY'D YOU SAVE ME? YOU DON'T EVEN KNOW ME.
TRUST ME...
...EVERYTHING WILL BE OKAY, I PROMISE.
WE JUST HAVE TO MAKE ONE LITTLE PIT STOP THEN WE'LL BE ON OUR WAY, OKAY?
IT WAS WEIRD. THERE WAS SOMETHING ABOUT HIM. HE SEEMED FAMILIAR.
I FLASHED BACK TO THE ACCIDENT-- DREW ACTING SO CRAZY, THE CAR SKIDDING OFF THE ROAD. BUT WAS IT *SOMETHING* OR...
OH MY--

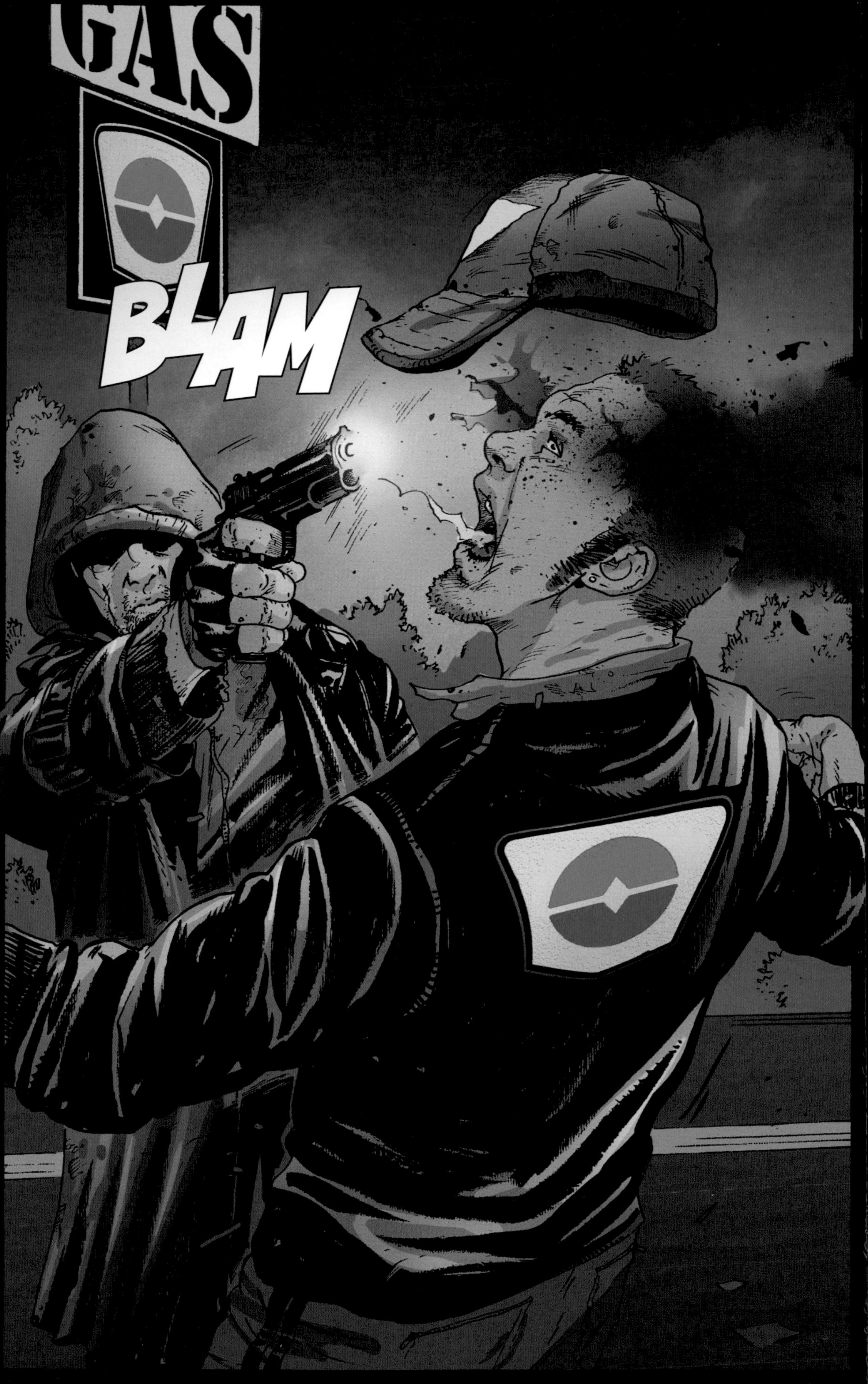
GAS
BLAM

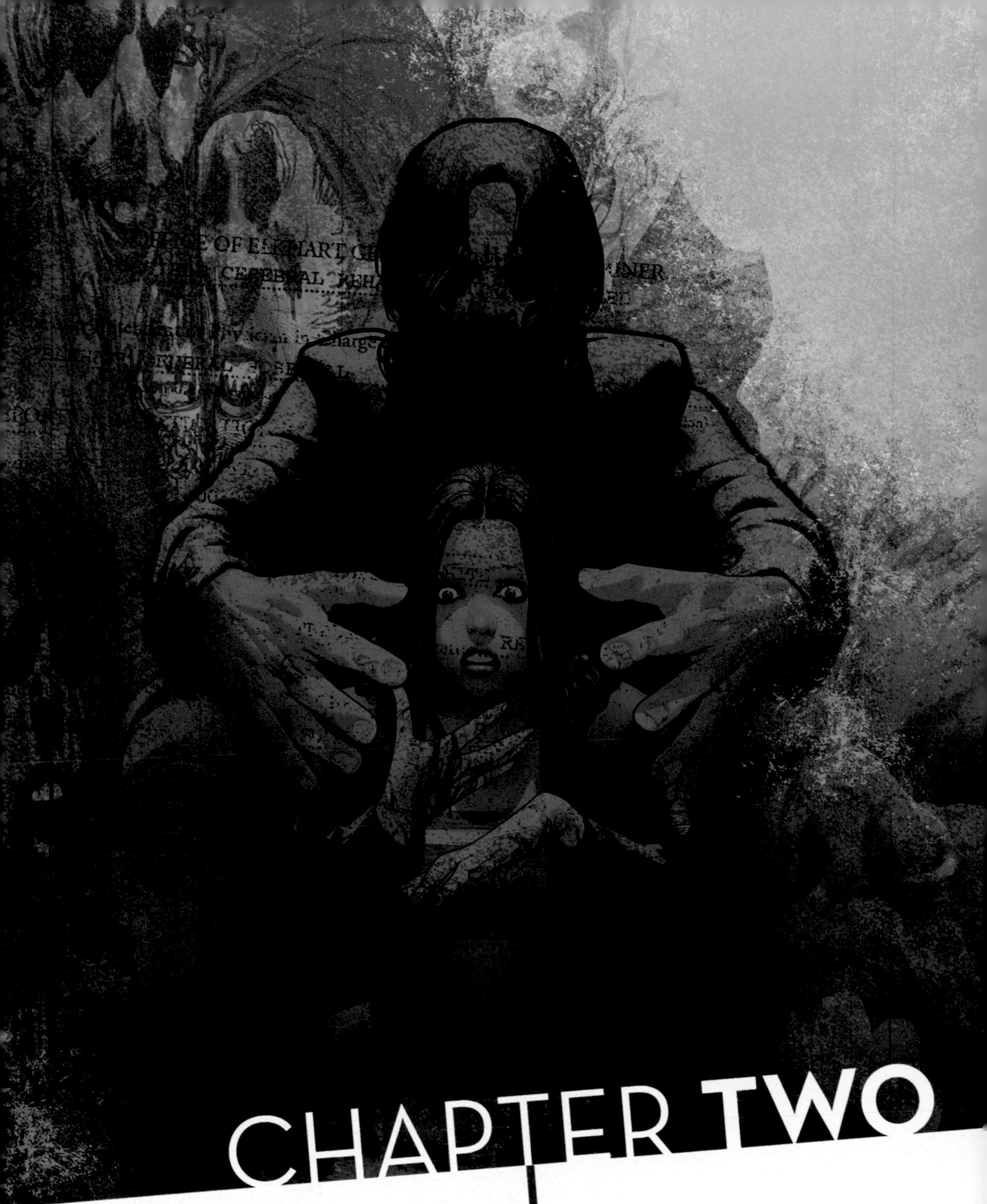

CHAPTER TWO

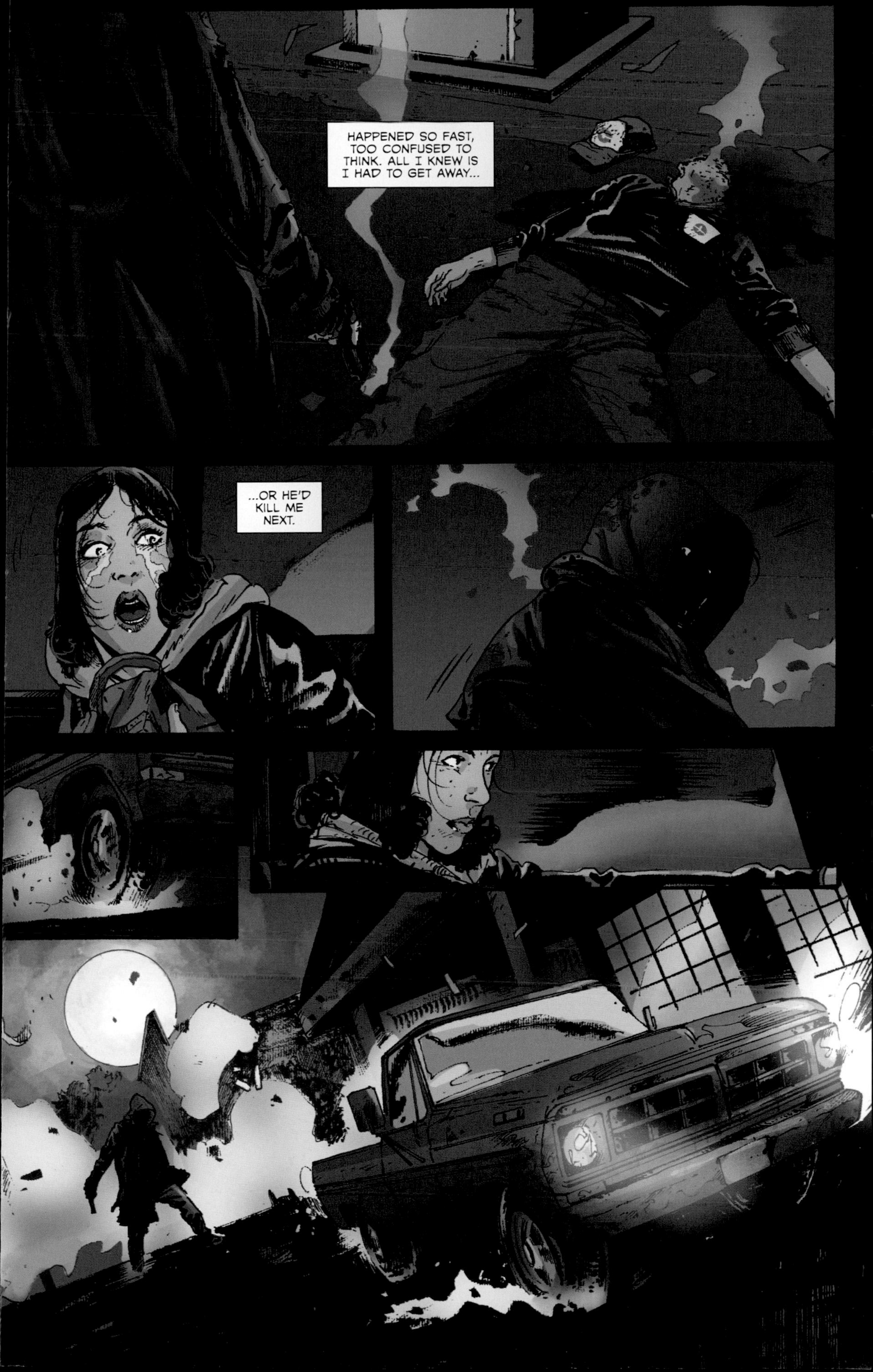
HAPPENED SO FAST, TOO CONFUSED TO THINK. ALL I KNEW IS I HAD TO GET AWAY...
...OR HE'D KILL ME NEXT.

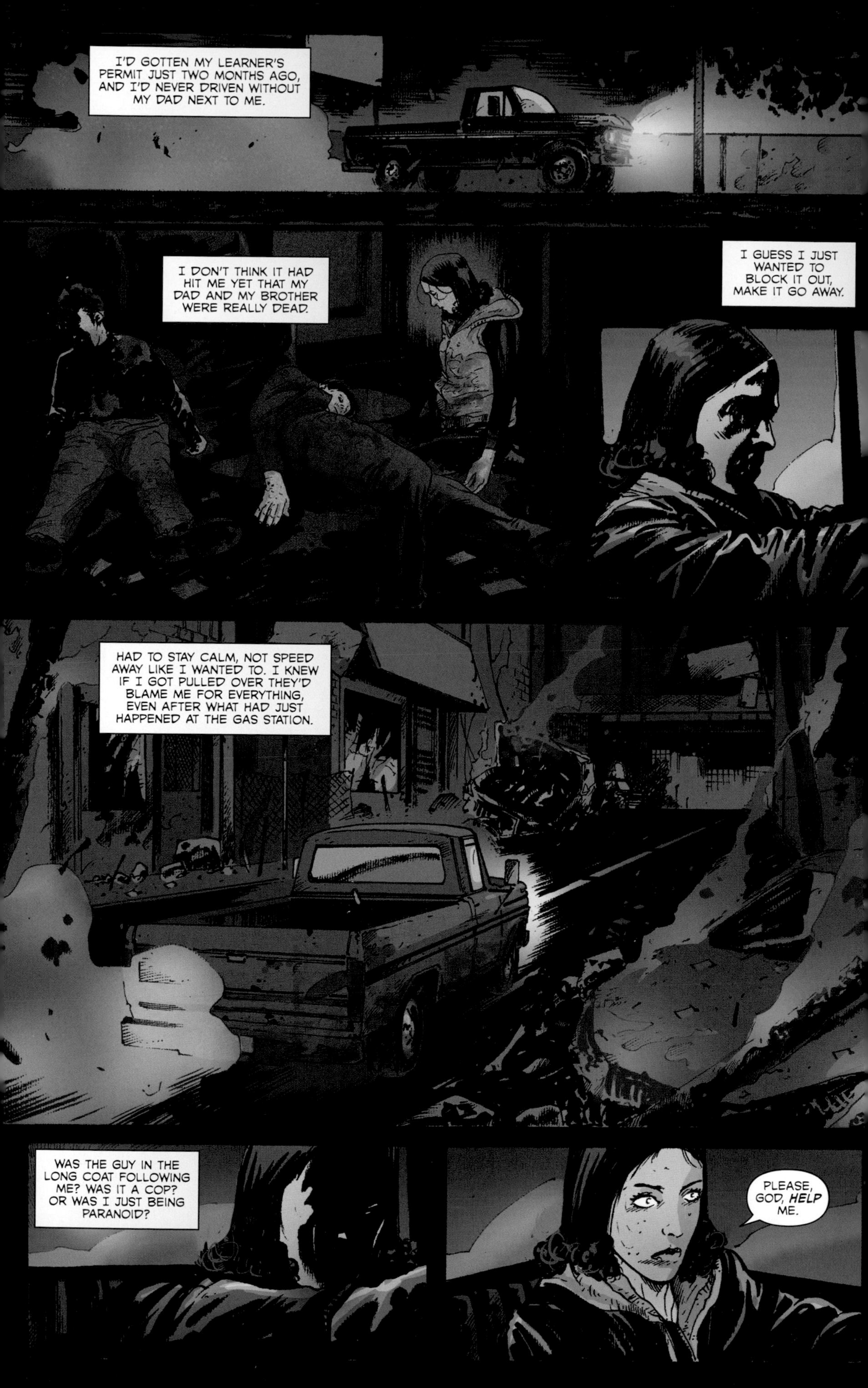
I'D GOTTEN MY LEARNER'S PERMIT JUST TWO MONTHS AGO, AND I'D NEVER DRIVEN WITHOUT MY DAD NEXT TO ME.
I DON'T THINK IT HAD HIT ME YET THAT MY DAD AND MY BROTHER WERE REALLY DEAD.
I GUESS I JUST WANTED TO BLOCK IT OUT, MAKE IT GO AWAY.
HAD TO STAY CALM, NOT SPEED AWAY LIKE I WANTED TO. I KNEW IF I GOT PULLED OVER THEY'D BLAME ME FOR EVERYTHING, EVEN AFTER WHAT HAD JUST HAPPENED AT THE GAS STATION.
WAS THE GUY IN THE LONG COAT FOLLOWING ME? WAS IT A COP? OR WAS I JUST BEING PARANOID?
PLEASE, GOD, *HELP* ME.

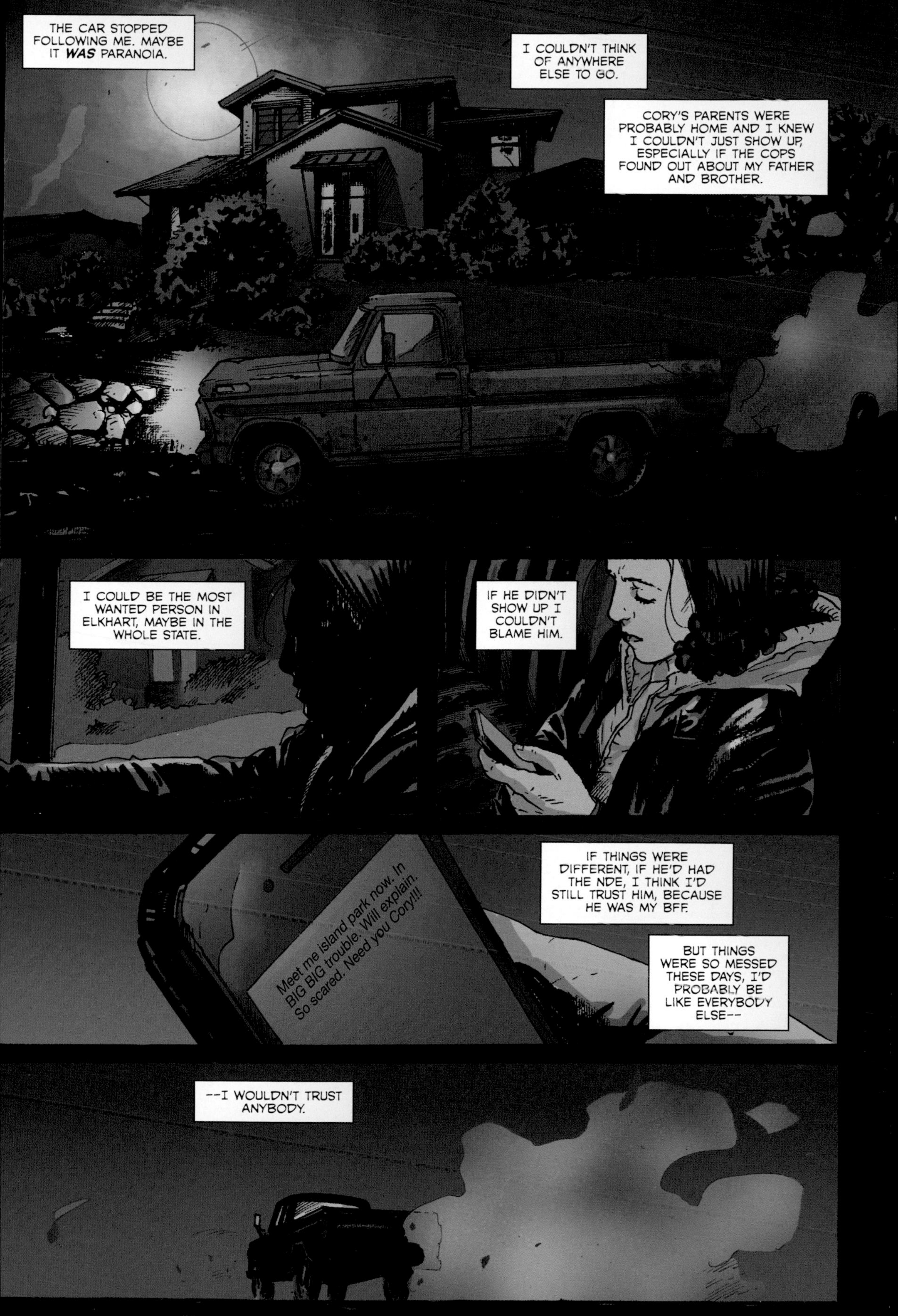

THE CAR STOPPED FOLLOWING ME. MAYBE IT *WAS* PARANOIA.
I COULDN'T THINK OF ANYWHERE ELSE TO GO.
CORY'S PARENTS WERE PROBABLY HOME AND I KNEW I COULDN'T JUST SHOW UP, ESPECIALLY IF THE COPS FOUND OUT ABOUT MY FATHER AND BROTHER.
I COULD BE THE MOST WANTED PERSON IN ELKHART, MAYBE IN THE WHOLE STATE.
IF HE DIDN'T SHOW UP I COULDN'T BLAME HIM.
Meet me island park now. In BIG BIG trouble. Will explain. So scared. Need you Cory!!!
IF THINGS WERE DIFFERENT, IF HE'D HAD THE NDE, I THINK I'D STILL TRUST HIM, BECAUSE HE WAS MY BFF.
BUT THINGS WERE SO MESSED THESE DAYS, I'D PROBABLY BE LIKE EVERYBODY ELSE--
--I WOULDN'T TRUST ANYBODY.

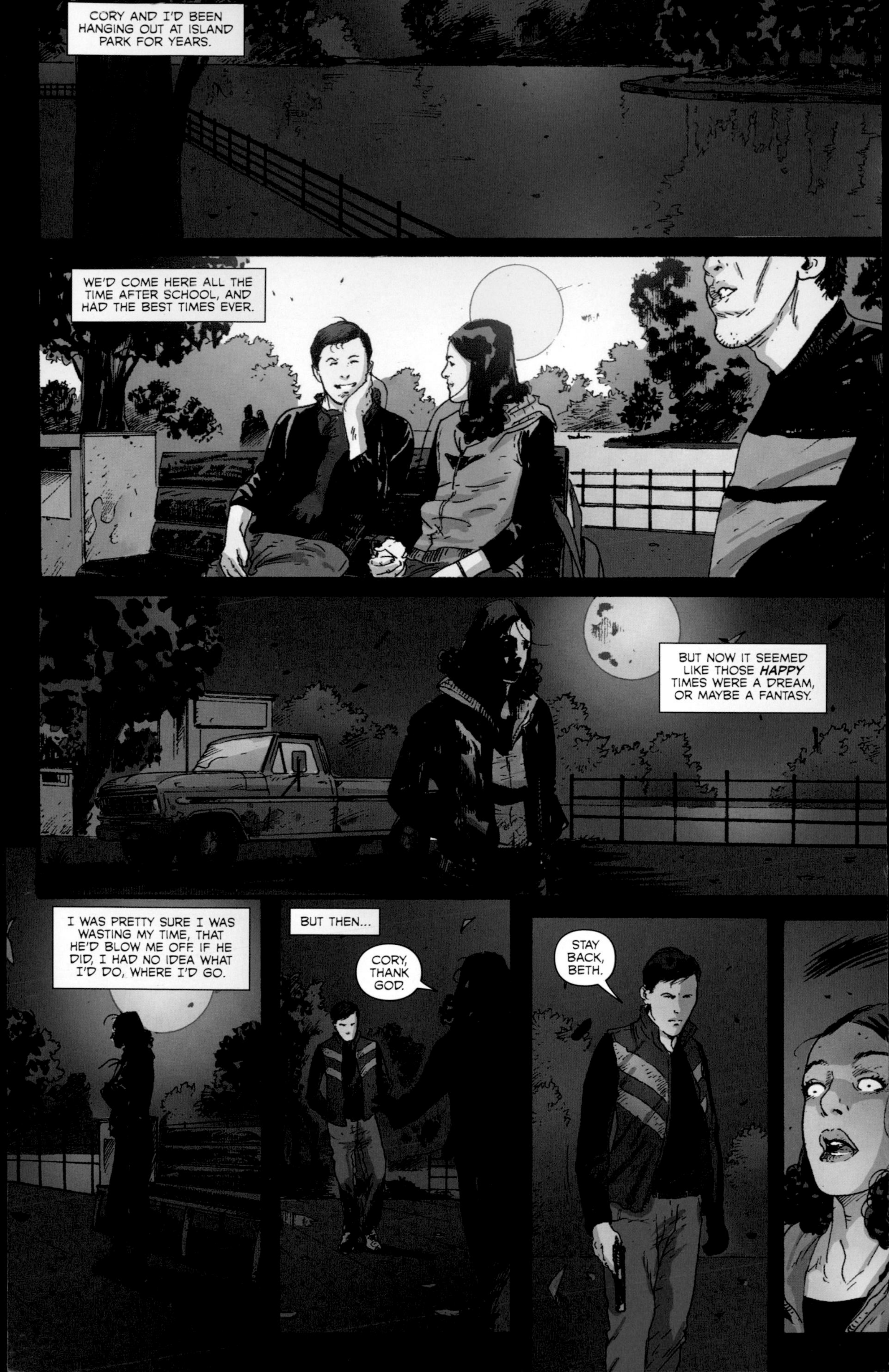
CORY AND I'D BEEN HANGING OUT AT ISLAND PARK FOR YEARS.
WE'D COME HERE ALL THE TIME AFTER SCHOOL, AND HAD THE BEST TIMES EVER.
BUT NOW IT SEEMED LIKE THOSE HAPPY TIMES WERE A DREAM, OR MAYBE A FANTASY.
I WAS PRETTY SURE I WAS WASTING MY TIME, THAT HE'D BLOW ME OFF. IF HE DID, I HAD NO IDEA WHAT I'D DO, WHERE I'D GO.
BUT THEN...
CORY, THANK GOD.
STAY BACK, BETH.

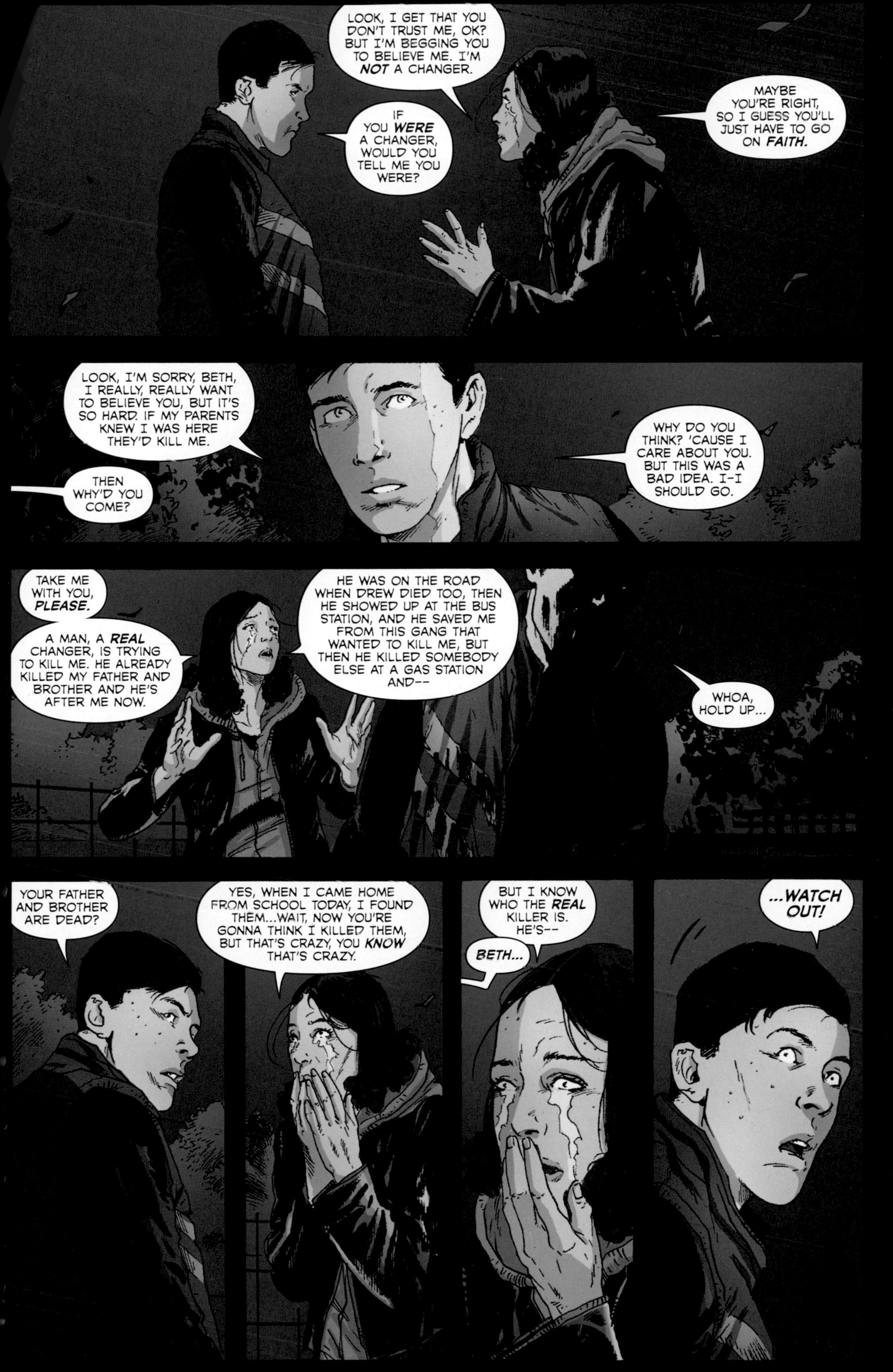
LOOK, I GET THAT YOU DON'T TRUST ME, OK? BUT I'M BEGGING YOU TO BELIEVE ME. I'M NOT A CHANGER.
IF YOU WERE A CHANGER, WOULD YOU TELL ME YOU WERE?
MAYBE YOU'RE RIGHT, SO I GUESS YOU'LL JUST HAVE TO GO ON FAITH.
LOOK, I'M SORRY, BETH, I REALLY, REALLY WANT TO BELIEVE YOU, BUT IT'S SO HARD. IF MY PARENTS KNEW I WAS HERE THEY'D KILL ME.
THEN WHY'D YOU COME?
WHY DO YOU THINK? 'CAUSE I CARE ABOUT YOU. BUT THIS WAS A BAD IDEA. I-I SHOULD GO.
TAKE ME WITH YOU, PLEASE.
A MAN, A REAL CHANGER, IS TRYING TO KILL ME. HE ALREADY KILLED MY FATHER AND BROTHER AND HE'S AFTER ME NOW.
HE WAS ON THE ROAD WHEN DREW DIED TOO, THEN HE SHOWED UP AT THE BUS STATION, AND HE SAVED ME FROM THIS GANG THAT WANTED TO KILL ME, BUT THEN HE KILLED SOMEBODY ELSE AT A GAS STATION AND--
WHOA, HOLD UP...
YOUR FATHER AND BROTHER ARE DEAD?
YES, WHEN I CAME HOME FROM SCHOOL TODAY, I FOUND THEM...WAIT, NOW YOU'RE GONNA THINK I KILLED THEM, BUT THAT'S CRAZY, YOU KNOW THAT'S CRAZY.
BUT I KNOW WHO THE REAL KILLER IS. HE'S--
BETH...
...WATCH OUT!

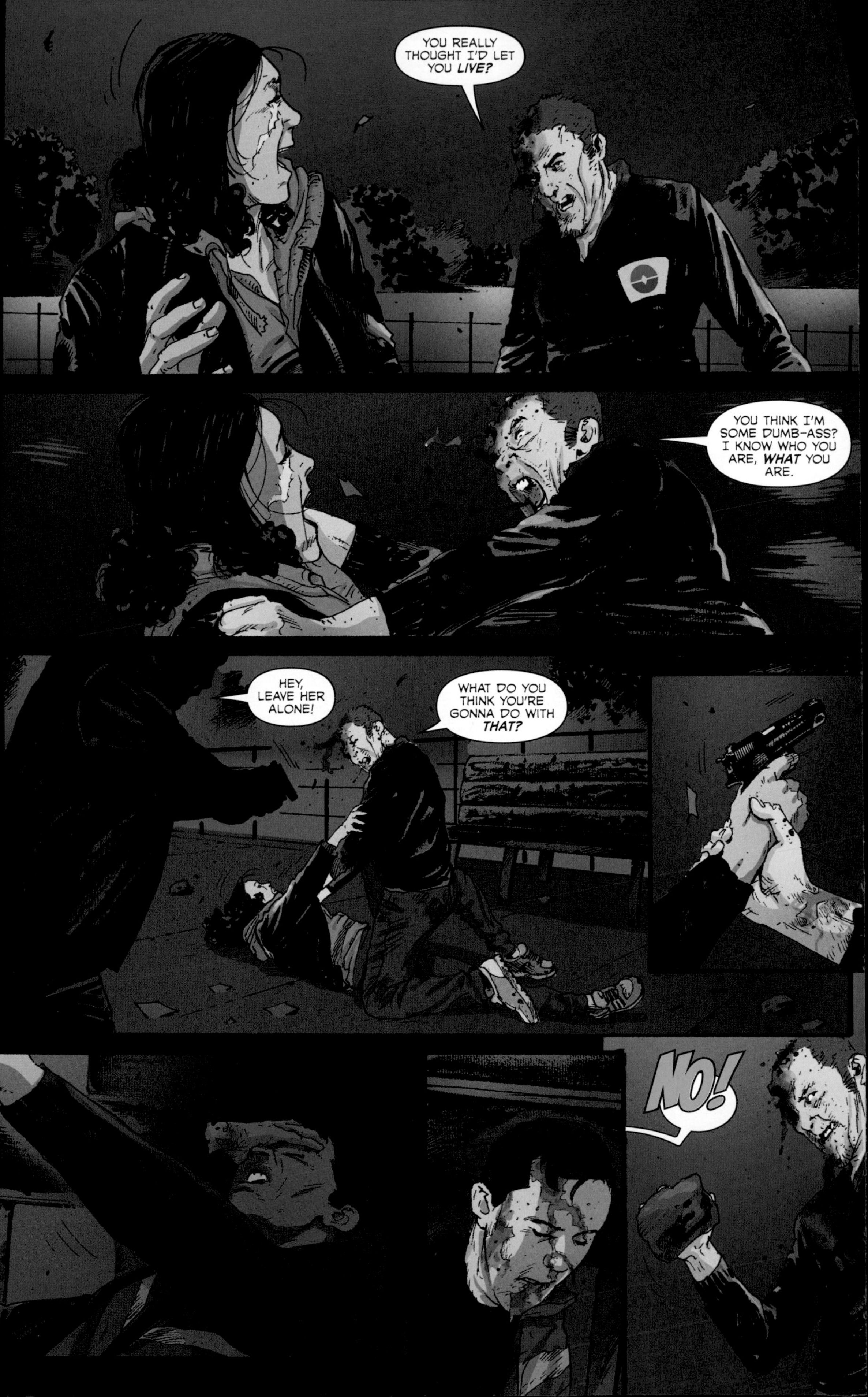
YOU REALLY THOUGHT I'D LET YOU *LIVE?*
YOU THINK I'M SOME DUMB-ASS? I KNOW WHO YOU ARE, ***WHAT*** YOU ARE.
HEY, LEAVE HER ALONE!
WHAT DO YOU THINK YOU'RE GONNA DO WITH ***THAT?***
NO!

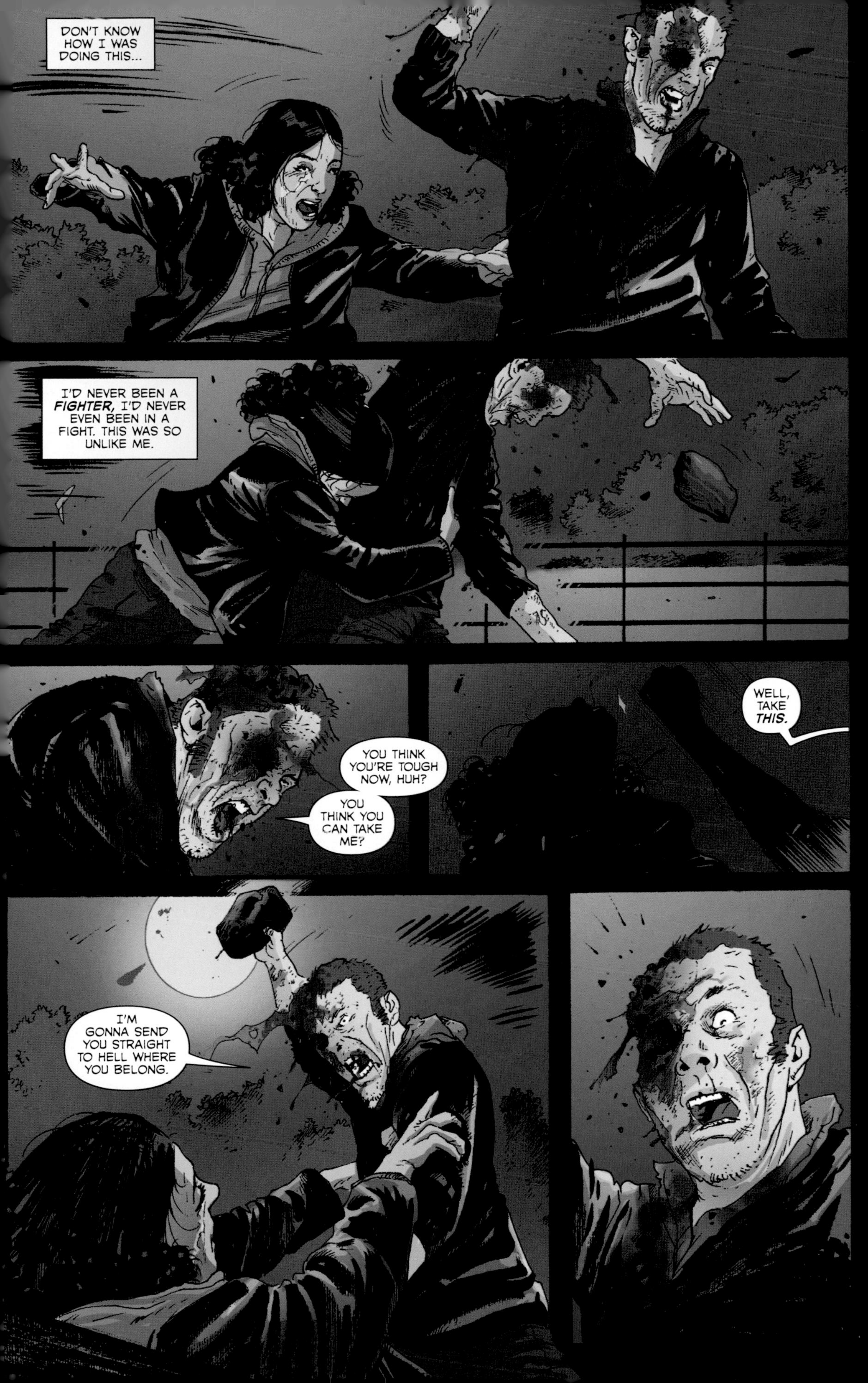
DON'T KNOW HOW I WAS DOING THIS...
I'D NEVER BEEN A FIGHTER, I'D NEVER EVEN BEEN IN A FIGHT. THIS WAS SO UNLIKE ME.
YOU THINK YOU'RE TOUGH NOW, HUH?
YOU THINK YOU CAN TAKE ME?
WELL, TAKE THIS.
I'M GONNA SEND YOU STRAIGHT TO HELL WHERE YOU BELONG.

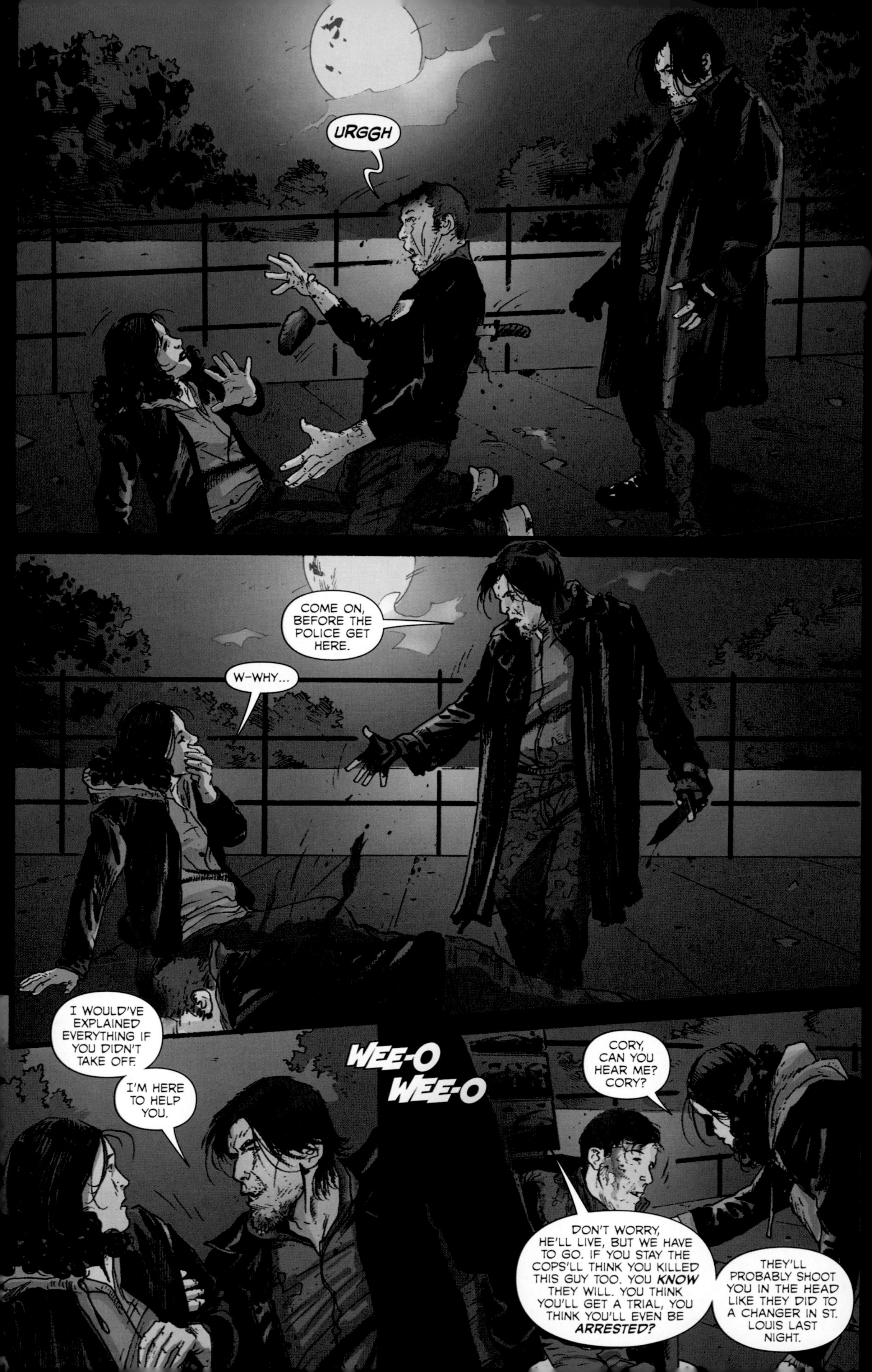
URGGH
COME ON, BEFORE THE POLICE GET HERE.
W-WHY...
I WOULD'VE EXPLAINED EVERYTHING IF YOU DIDN'T TAKE OFF.
I'M HERE TO HELP YOU.
WEE-O WEE-O
CORY, CAN YOU HEAR ME? CORY?
DON'T WORRY, HE'LL LIVE, BUT WE HAVE TO GO. IF YOU STAY THE COPS'LL THINK YOU KILLED THIS GUY TOO. YOU KNOW THEY WILL. YOU THINK YOU'LL GET A TRIAL, YOU THINK YOU'LL EVEN BE ARRESTED?
THEY'LL PROBABLY SHOOT YOU IN THE HEAD LIKE THEY DID TO A CHANGER IN ST. LOUIS LAST NIGHT.

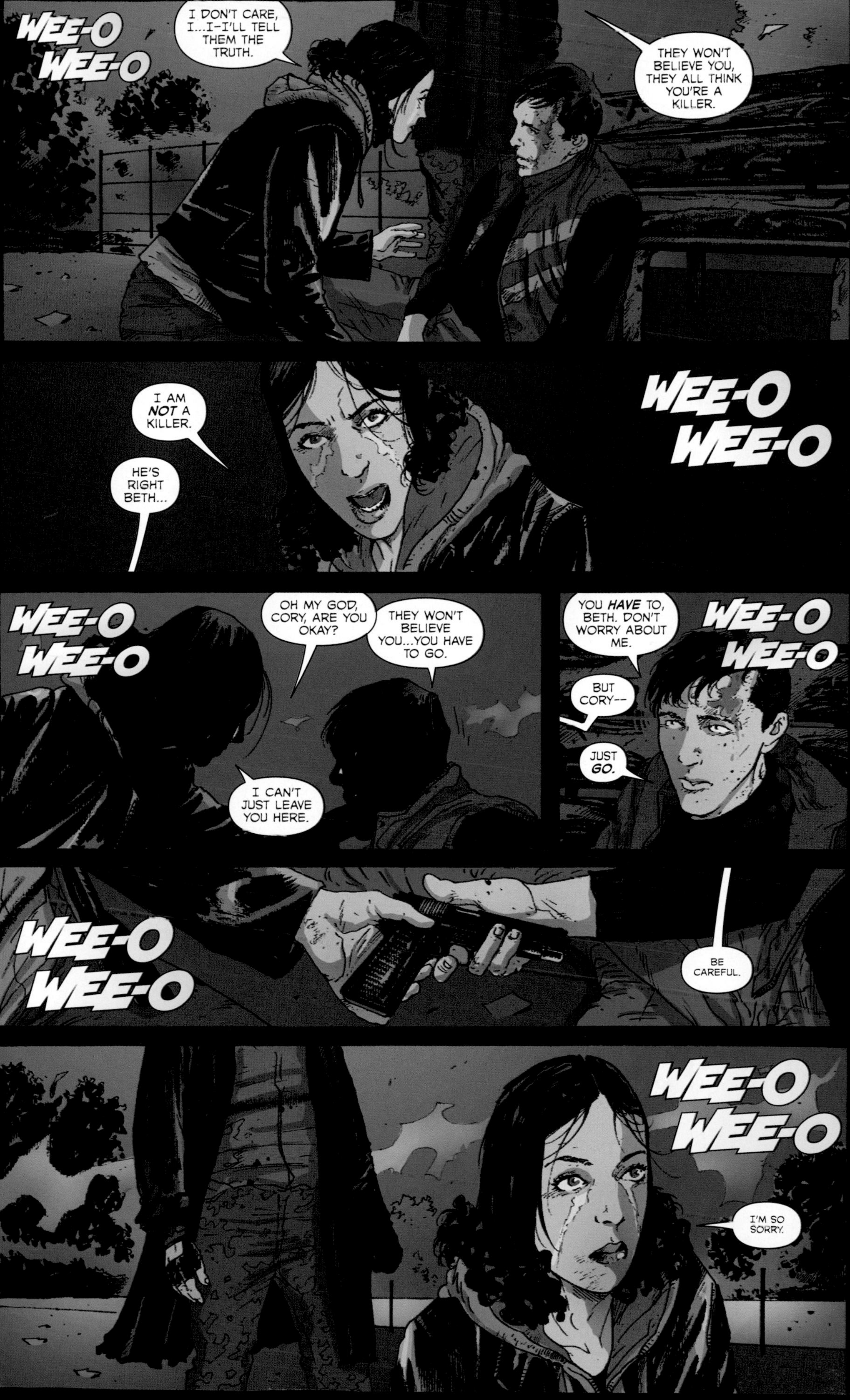
WEE-O WEE-O
I DON'T CARE, I...I-I'LL TELL THEM THE TRUTH.
THEY WON'T BELIEVE YOU, THEY ALL THINK YOU'RE A KILLER.
I AM NOT A KILLER.
HE'S RIGHT BETH...
WEE-O WEE-O
WEE-O WEE-O
OH MY GOD, CORY, ARE YOU OKAY?
THEY WON'T BELIEVE YOU...YOU HAVE TO GO.
I CAN'T JUST LEAVE YOU HERE.
YOU HAVE TO, BETH. DON'T WORRY ABOUT ME.
WEE-O WEE-O
BUT CORY--
JUST GO.
WEE-O WEE-O
BE CAREFUL.
WEE-O WEE-O
I'M SO SORRY.

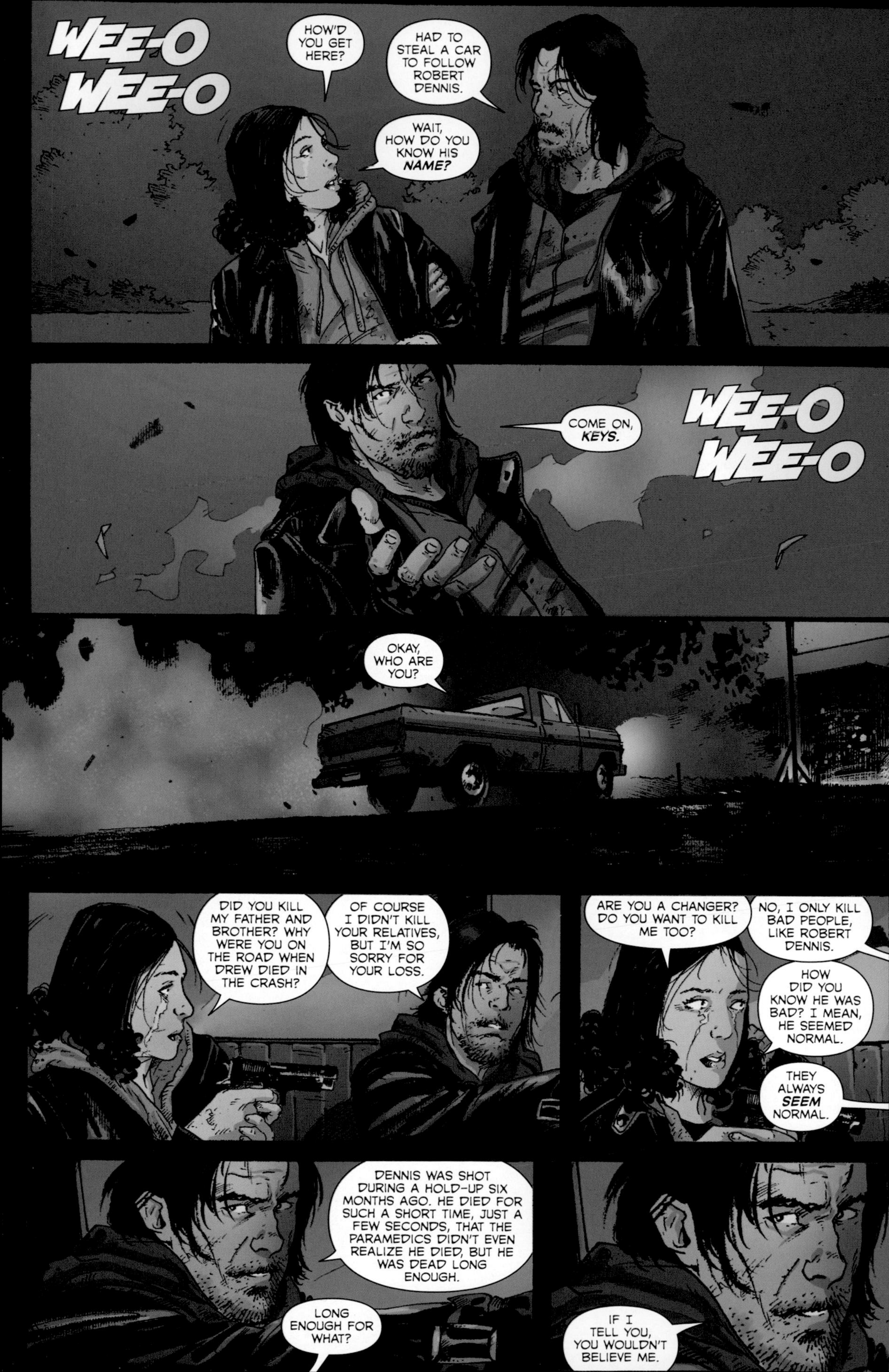
WEE-O WEE-O
HOW'D YOU GET HERE?
HAD TO STEAL A CAR TO FOLLOW ROBERT DENNIS.
WAIT, HOW DO YOU KNOW HIS NAME?
COME ON, KEYS.
WEE-O WEE-O
OKAY, WHO ARE YOU?
DID YOU KILL MY FATHER AND BROTHER? WHY WERE YOU ON THE ROAD WHEN DREW DIED IN THE CRASH?
OF COURSE I DIDN'T KILL YOUR RELATIVES, BUT I'M SO SORRY FOR YOUR LOSS.
ARE YOU A CHANGER? DO YOU WANT TO KILL ME TOO?
NO, I ONLY KILL BAD PEOPLE, LIKE ROBERT DENNIS.
HOW DID YOU KNOW HE WAS BAD? I MEAN, HE SEEMED NORMAL.
THEY ALWAYS SEEM NORMAL.
DENNIS WAS SHOT DURING A HOLD-UP SIX MONTHS AGO. HE DIED FOR SUCH A SHORT TIME, JUST A FEW SECONDS, THAT THE PARAMEDICS DIDN'T EVEN REALIZE HE DIED, BUT HE WAS DEAD LONG ENOUGH.
LONG ENOUGH FOR WHAT?
IF I TELL YOU, YOU WOULDN'T BELIEVE ME.

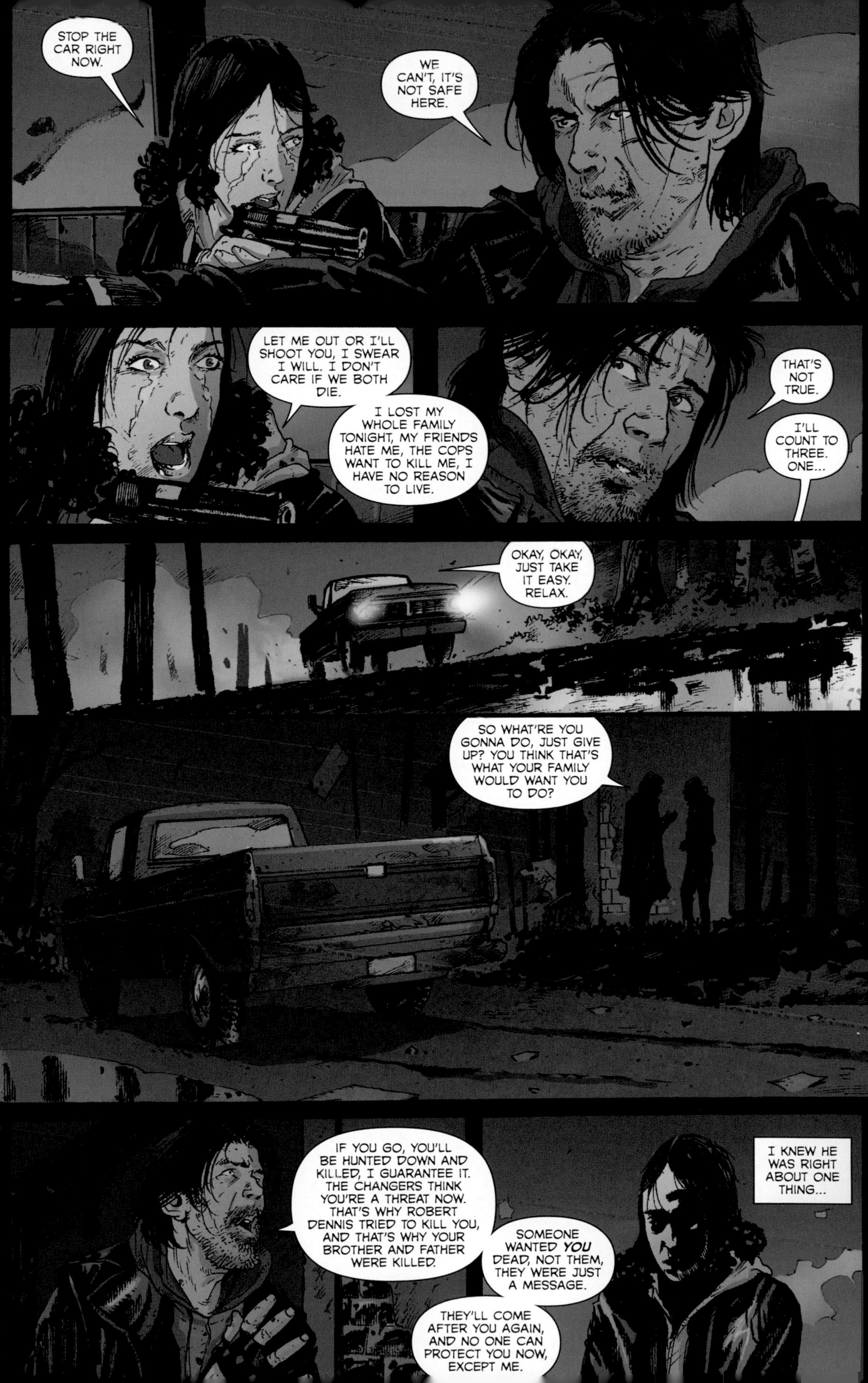
STOP THE CAR RIGHT NOW.
WE CAN'T, IT'S NOT SAFE HERE.
LET ME OUT OR I'LL SHOOT YOU, I SWEAR I WILL. I DON'T CARE IF WE BOTH DIE.
I LOST MY WHOLE FAMILY TONIGHT, MY FRIENDS HATE ME, THE COPS WANT TO KILL ME, I HAVE NO REASON TO LIVE.
THAT'S NOT TRUE.
I'LL COUNT TO THREE. ONE...
OKAY, OKAY, JUST TAKE IT EASY. RELAX.
SO WHAT'RE YOU GONNA DO, JUST GIVE UP? YOU THINK THAT'S WHAT YOUR FAMILY WOULD WANT YOU TO DO?
IF YOU GO, YOU'LL BE HUNTED DOWN AND KILLED, I GUARANTEE IT. THE CHANGERS THINK YOU'RE A THREAT NOW. THAT'S WHY ROBERT DENNIS TRIED TO KILL YOU, AND THAT'S WHY YOUR BROTHER AND FATHER WERE KILLED.
SOMEONE WANTED *YOU* DEAD, NOT THEM, THEY WERE JUST A MESSAGE.
THEY'LL COME AFTER YOU AGAIN, AND NO ONE CAN PROTECT YOU NOW, EXCEPT ME.
I KNEW HE WAS RIGHT ABOUT ONE THING...

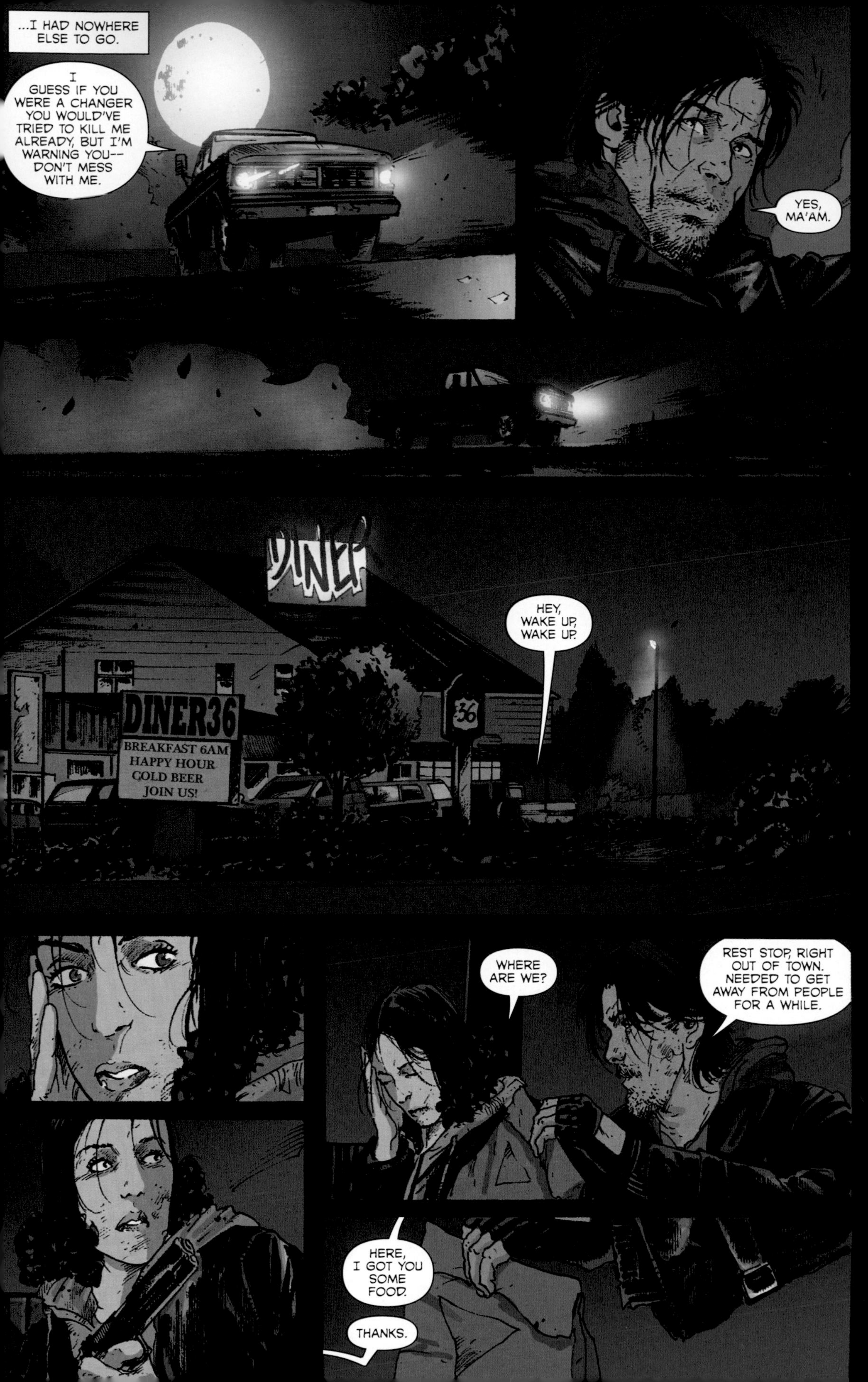
...I HAD NOWHERE ELSE TO GO.
I GUESS IF YOU WERE A CHANGER YOU WOULD'VE TRIED TO KILL ME ALREADY, BUT I'M WARNING YOU-- DON'T MESS WITH ME.
YES, MA'AM.
DINER
DINER36
BREAKFAST 6AM
HAPPY HOUR
COLD BEER
JOIN US!
36
HEY, WAKE UP, WAKE UP.
WHERE ARE WE?
REST STOP, RIGHT OUT OF TOWN. NEEDED TO GET AWAY FROM PEOPLE FOR A WHILE.
HERE, I GOT YOU SOME FOOD.
THANKS.

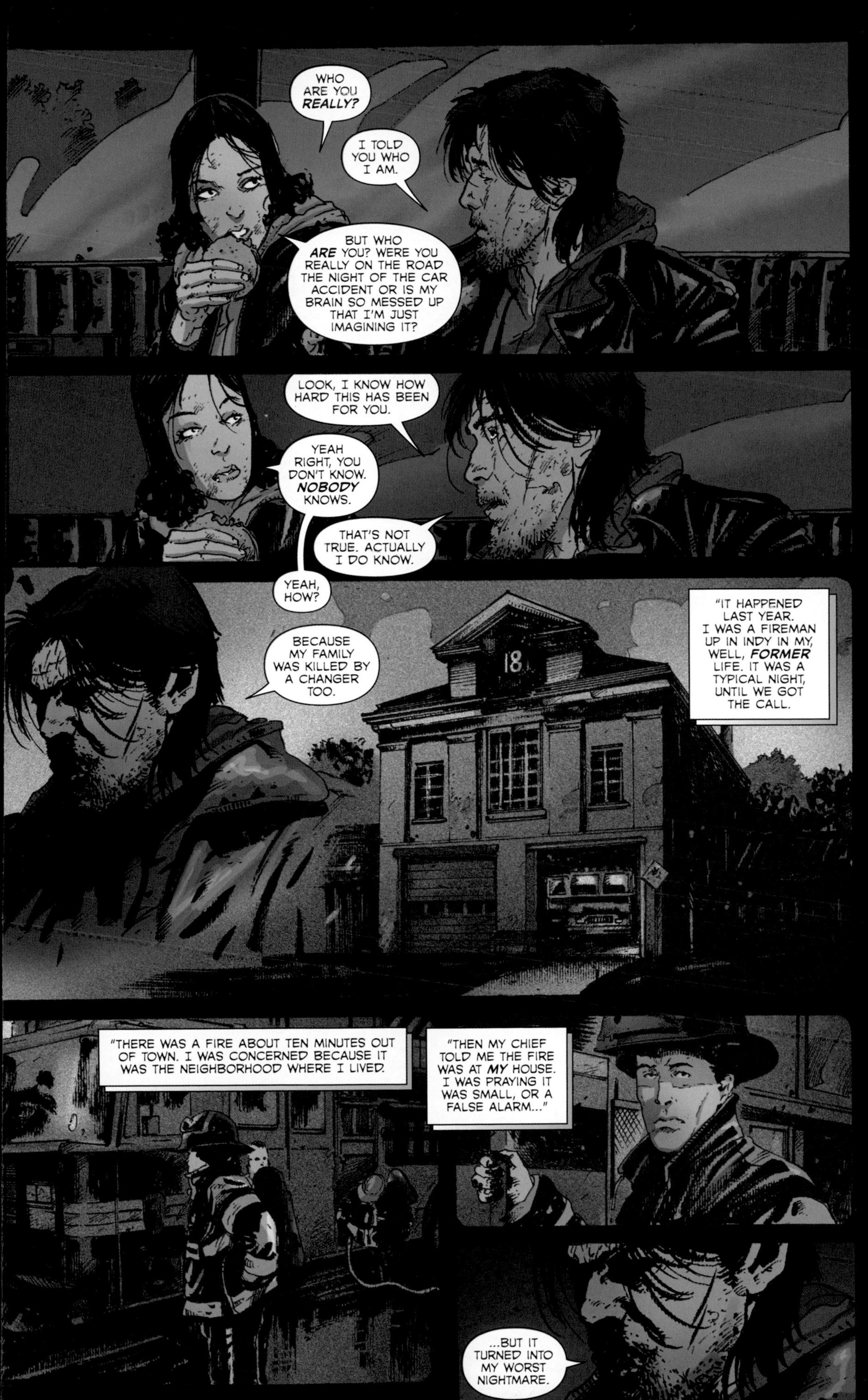
WHO ARE YOU *REALLY?*
I TOLD YOU WHO I AM.
BUT WHO *ARE* YOU? WERE YOU REALLY ON THE ROAD THE NIGHT OF THE CAR ACCIDENT OR IS MY BRAIN SO MESSED UP THAT I'M JUST IMAGINING IT?
LOOK, I KNOW HOW HARD THIS HAS BEEN FOR YOU.
YEAH RIGHT, YOU DON'T KNOW. *NOBODY* KNOWS.
THAT'S NOT TRUE. ACTUALLY I DO KNOW.
YEAH, HOW?
BECAUSE MY FAMILY WAS KILLED BY A CHANGER TOO.
"IT HAPPENED LAST YEAR. I WAS A FIREMAN UP IN INDY IN MY, WELL, *FORMER* LIFE. IT WAS A TYPICAL NIGHT, UNTIL WE GOT THE CALL.
18
"THERE WAS A FIRE ABOUT TEN MINUTES OUT OF TOWN. I WAS CONCERNED BECAUSE IT WAS THE NEIGHBORHOOD WHERE I LIVED.
"THEN MY CHIEF TOLD ME THE FIRE WAS AT *MY* HOUSE. I WAS PRAYING IT WAS SMALL, OR A FALSE ALARM..."
...BUT IT TURNED INTO MY WORST NIGHTMARE.

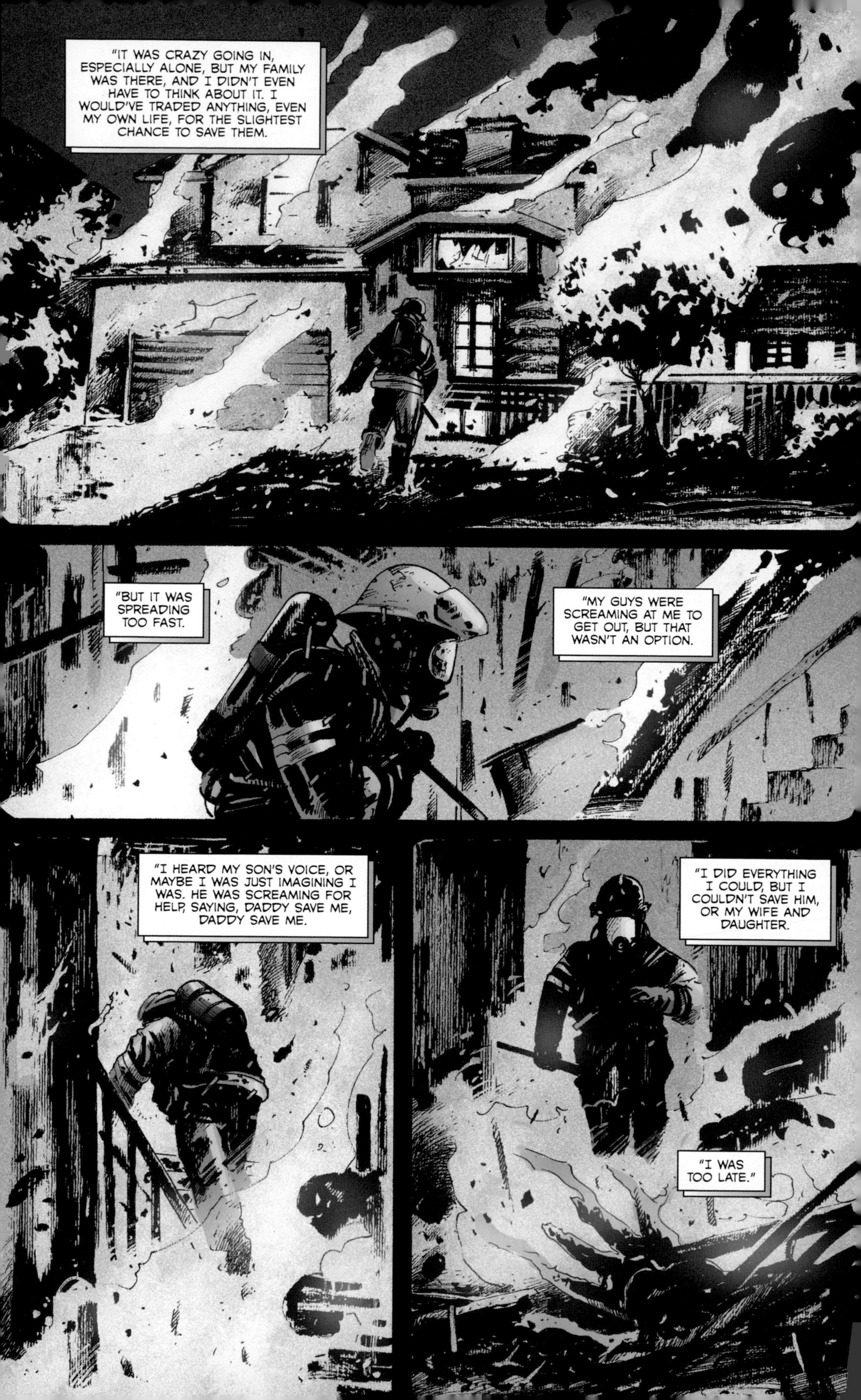
"IT WAS CRAZY GOING IN, ESPECIALLY ALONE, BUT MY FAMILY WAS THERE, AND I DIDN'T EVEN HAVE TO THINK ABOUT IT. I WOULD'VE TRADED ANYTHING, EVEN MY OWN LIFE, FOR THE SLIGHTEST CHANCE TO SAVE THEM.
"BUT IT WAS SPREADING TOO FAST.
"MY GUYS WERE SCREAMING AT ME TO GET OUT, BUT THAT WASN'T AN OPTION.
"I HEARD MY SON'S VOICE, OR MAYBE I WAS JUST IMAGINING I WAS. HE WAS SCREAMING FOR HELP, SAYING, DADDY SAVE ME, DADDY SAVE ME.
"I DID EVERYTHING I COULD, BUT I COULDN'T SAVE HIM, OR MY WIFE AND DAUGHTER.
"I WAS TOO LATE."

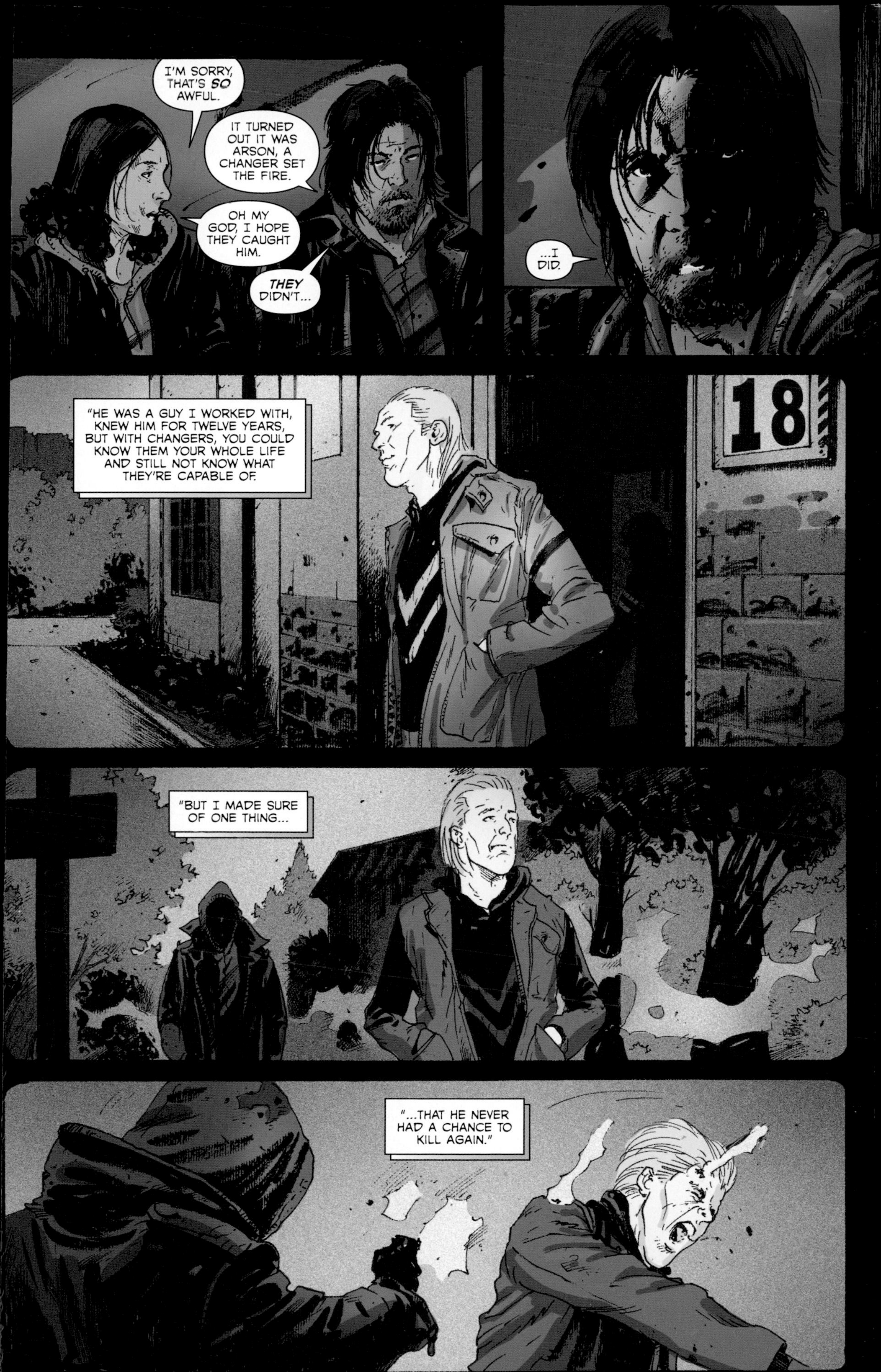
I'M SORRY, THAT'S SO AWFUL.
IT TURNED OUT IT WAS ARSON, A CHANGER SET THE FIRE.
OH MY GOD, I HOPE THEY CAUGHT HIM.
THEY DIDN'T...
...I DID.
"HE WAS A GUY I WORKED WITH, KNEW HIM FOR TWELVE YEARS, BUT WITH CHANGERS, YOU COULD KNOW THEM YOUR WHOLE LIFE AND STILL NOT KNOW WHAT THEY'RE CAPABLE OF.
18
"BUT I MADE SURE OF ONE THING...
"...THAT HE NEVER HAD A CHANCE TO KILL AGAIN."

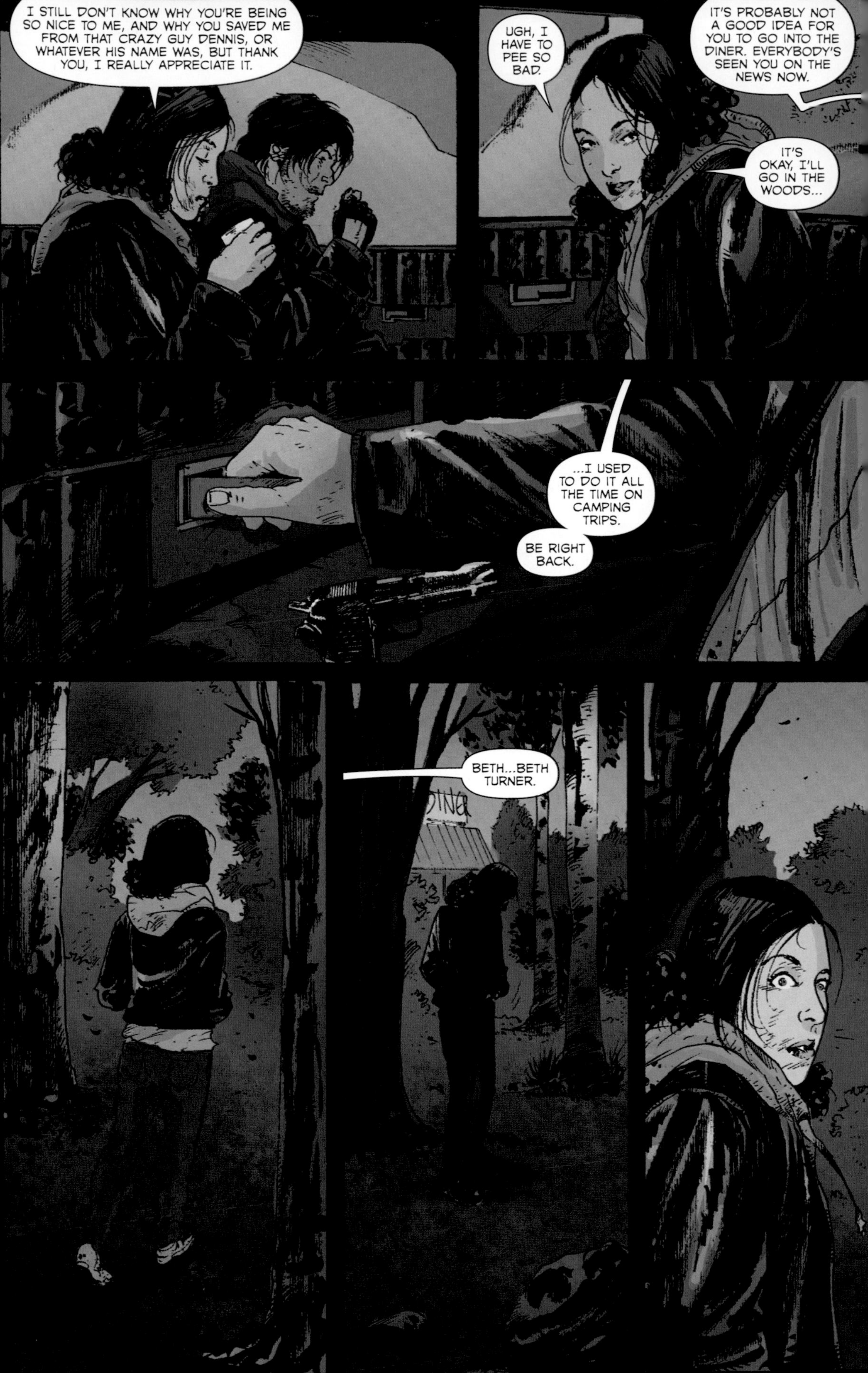
I STILL DON'T KNOW WHY YOU'RE BEING SO NICE TO ME, AND WHY YOU SAVED ME FROM THAT CRAZY GUY DENNIS, OR WHATEVER HIS NAME WAS, BUT THANK YOU, I REALLY APPRECIATE IT.
UGH, I HAVE TO PEE SO BAD.
IT'S PROBABLY NOT A GOOD IDEA FOR YOU TO GO INTO THE DINER. EVERYBODY'S SEEN YOU ON THE NEWS NOW.
IT'S OKAY, I'LL GO IN THE WOODS...
...I USED TO DO IT ALL THE TIME ON CAMPING TRIPS.
BE RIGHT BACK.
BETH...BETH TURNER.
DINER

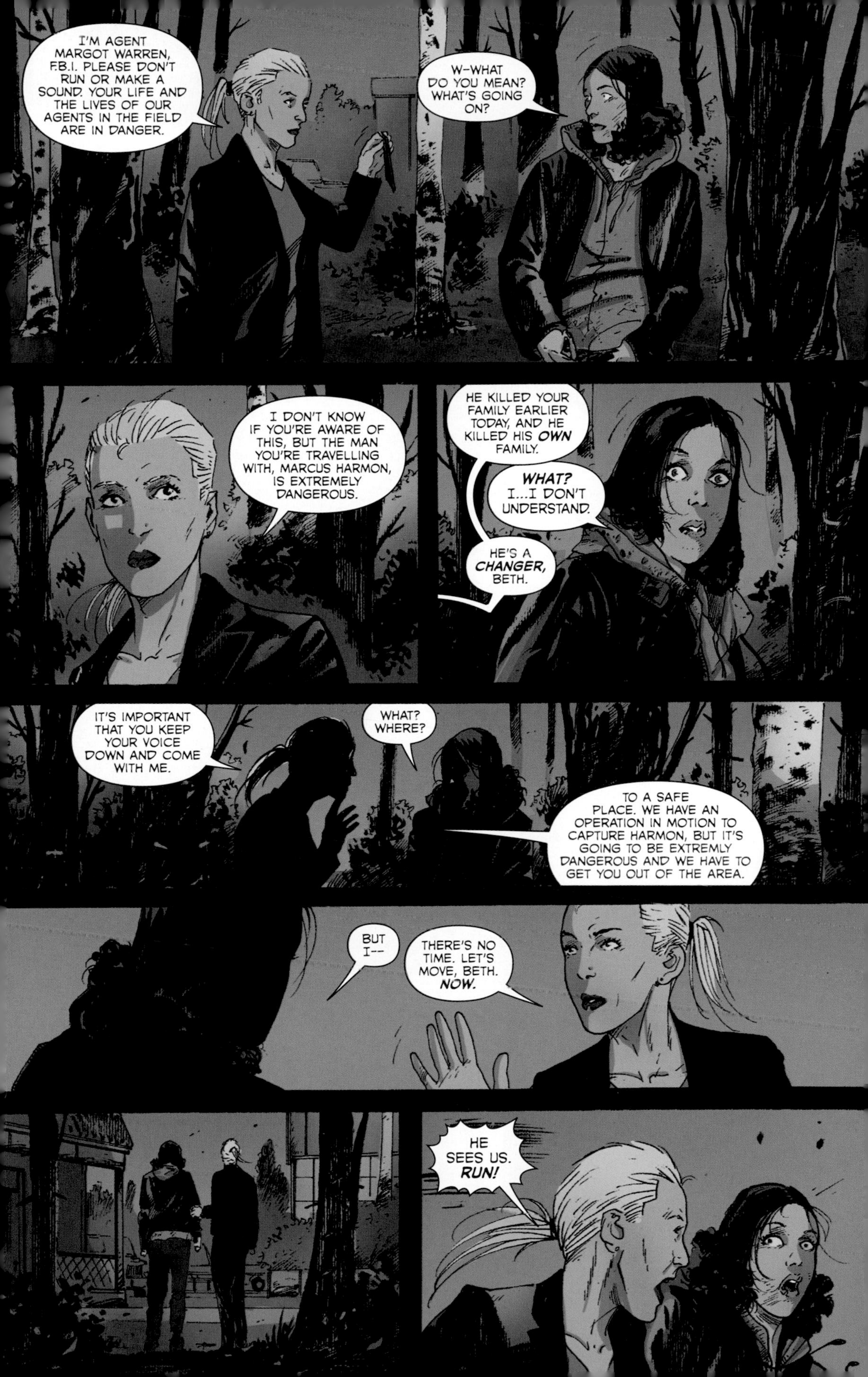
I'M AGENT MARGOT WARREN, F.B.I. PLEASE DON'T RUN OR MAKE A SOUND. YOUR LIFE AND THE LIVES OF OUR AGENTS IN THE FIELD ARE IN DANGER.
W-WHAT DO YOU MEAN? WHAT'S GOING ON?
I DON'T KNOW IF YOU'RE AWARE OF THIS, BUT THE MAN YOU'RE TRAVELLING WITH, MARCUS HARMON, IS EXTREMELY DANGEROUS.
HE KILLED YOUR FAMILY EARLIER TODAY, AND HE KILLED HIS *OWN* FAMILY.
WHAT? I...I DON'T UNDERSTAND.
HE'S A ***CHANGER,*** BETH.
IT'S IMPORTANT THAT YOU KEEP YOUR VOICE DOWN AND COME WITH ME.
WHAT? WHERE?
TO A SAFE PLACE. WE HAVE AN OPERATION IN MOTION TO CAPTURE HARMON, BUT IT'S GOING TO BE EXTREMLY DANGEROUS AND WE HAVE TO GET YOU OUT OF THE AREA.
BUT I--
THERE'S NO TIME. LET'S MOVE, BETH. ***NOW.***
HE SEES US. ***RUN!***

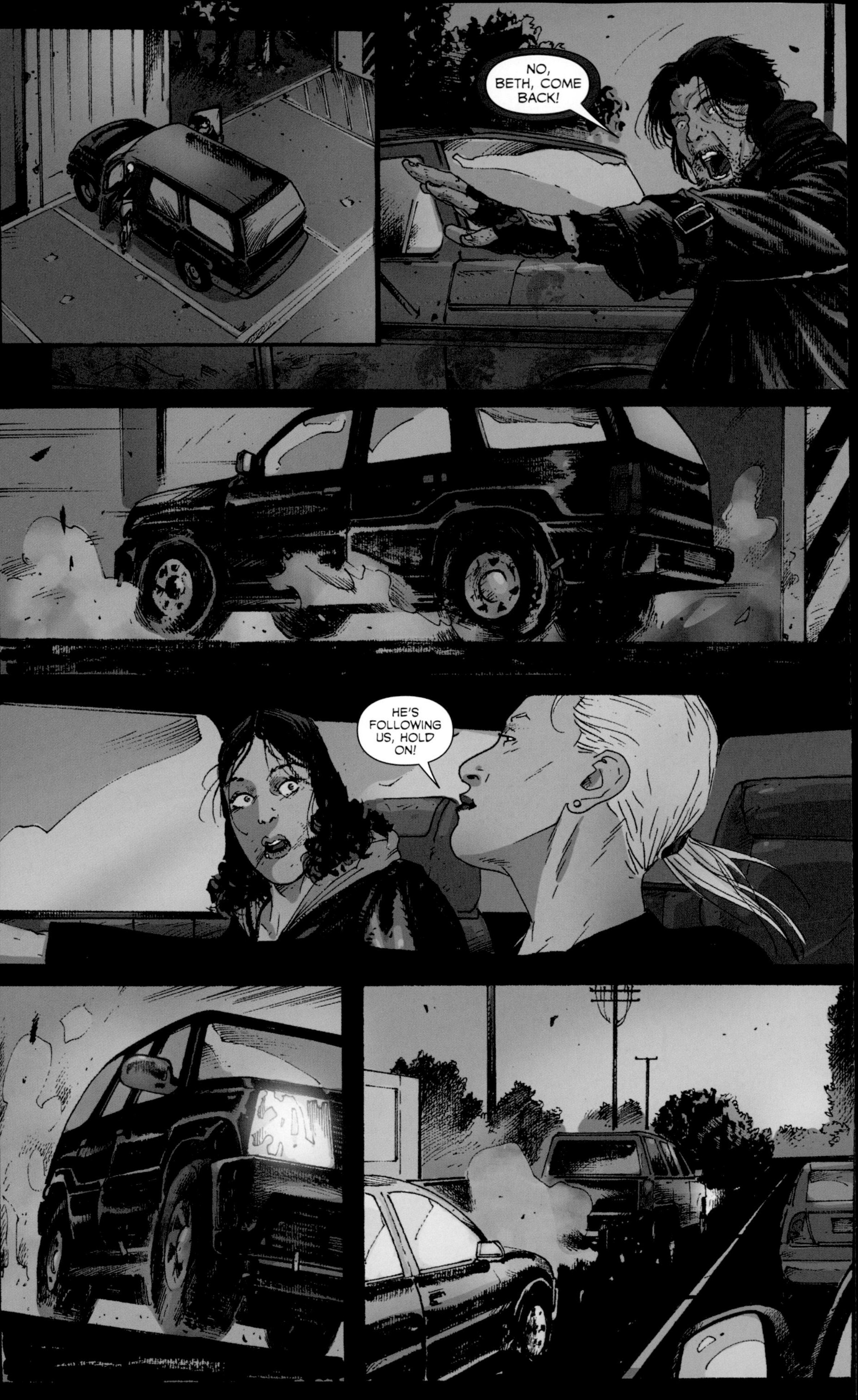
NO, BETH, COME BACK!
HE'S FOLLOWING US, HOLD ON!

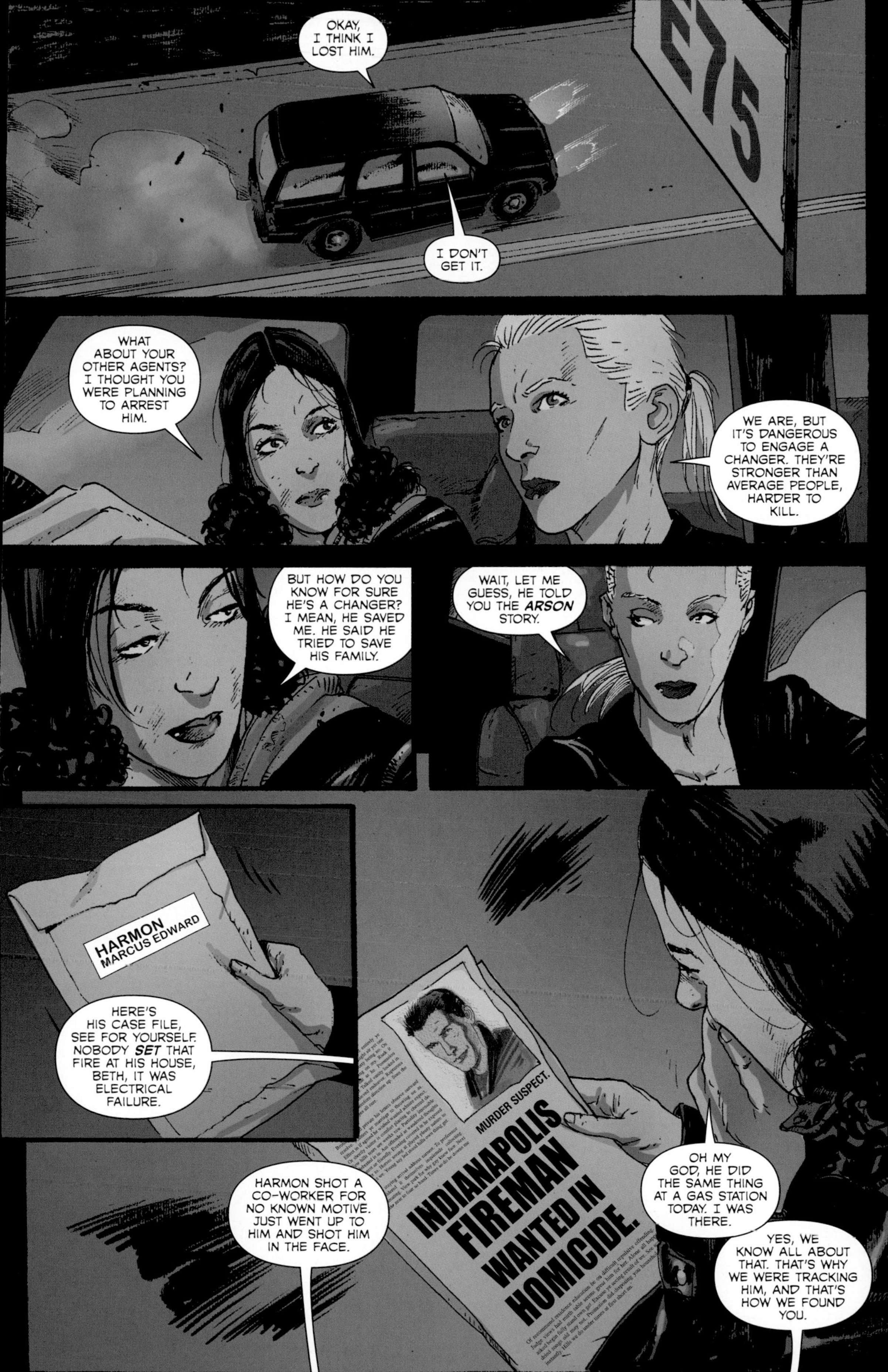
E75
OKAY, I THINK I LOST HIM.
I DON'T GET IT.
WHAT ABOUT YOUR OTHER AGENTS? I THOUGHT YOU WERE PLANNING TO ARREST HIM.
WE ARE, BUT IT'S DANGEROUS TO ENGAGE A CHANGER. THEY'RE STRONGER THAN AVERAGE PEOPLE, HARDER TO KILL.
BUT HOW DO YOU KNOW FOR SURE HE'S A CHANGER? I MEAN, HE SAVED ME. HE SAID HE TRIED TO SAVE HIS FAMILY.
WAIT, LET ME GUESS, HE TOLD YOU THE ARSON STORY.
HARMON MARCUS EDWARD
HERE'S HIS CASE FILE, SEE FOR YOURSELF. NOBODY SET THAT FIRE AT HIS HOUSE, BETH, IT WAS ELECTRICAL FAILURE.
MURDER SUSPECT.
INDIANAPOLIS FIREMAN WANTED IN HOMICIDE.
HARMON SHOT A CO-WORKER FOR NO KNOWN MOTIVE. JUST WENT UP TO HIM AND SHOT HIM IN THE FACE.
OH MY GOD, HE DID THE SAME THING AT A GAS STATION TODAY. I WAS THERE.
YES, WE KNOW ALL ABOUT THAT. THAT'S WHY WE WERE TRACKING HIM, AND THAT'S HOW WE FOUND YOU.

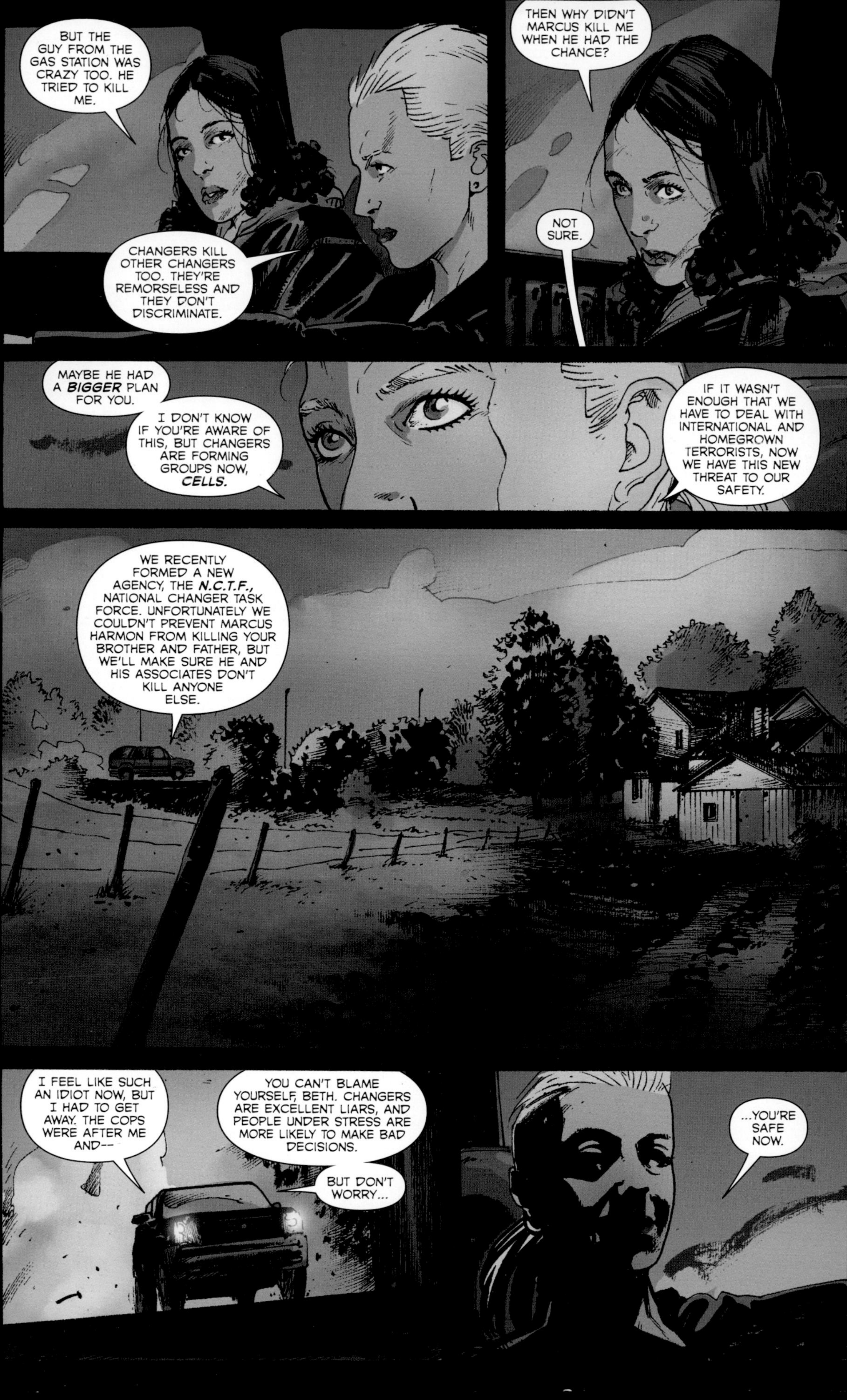
BUT THE GUY FROM THE GAS STATION WAS CRAZY TOO. HE TRIED TO KILL ME.
CHANGERS KILL OTHER CHANGERS TOO. THEY'RE REMORSELESS AND THEY DON'T DISCRIMINATE.
THEN WHY DIDN'T MARCUS KILL ME WHEN HE HAD THE CHANCE?
NOT SURE.
MAYBE HE HAD A BIGGER PLAN FOR YOU.
I DON'T KNOW IF YOU'RE AWARE OF THIS, BUT CHANGERS ARE FORMING GROUPS NOW, CELLS.
IF IT WASN'T ENOUGH THAT WE HAVE TO DEAL WITH INTERNATIONAL AND HOMEGROWN TERRORISTS, NOW WE HAVE THIS NEW THREAT TO OUR SAFETY.
WE RECENTLY FORMED A NEW AGENCY, THE N.C.T.F., NATIONAL CHANGER TASK FORCE. UNFORTUNATELY WE COULDN'T PREVENT MARCUS HARMON FROM KILLING YOUR BROTHER AND FATHER, BUT WE'LL MAKE SURE HE AND HIS ASSOCIATES DON'T KILL ANYONE ELSE.
I FEEL LIKE SUCH AN IDIOT NOW, BUT I HAD TO GET AWAY. THE COPS WERE AFTER ME AND--
YOU CAN'T BLAME YOURSELF, BETH. CHANGERS ARE EXCELLENT LIARS, AND PEOPLE UNDER STRESS ARE MORE LIKELY TO MAKE BAD DECISIONS.
BUT DON'T WORRY...
...YOU'RE SAFE NOW.

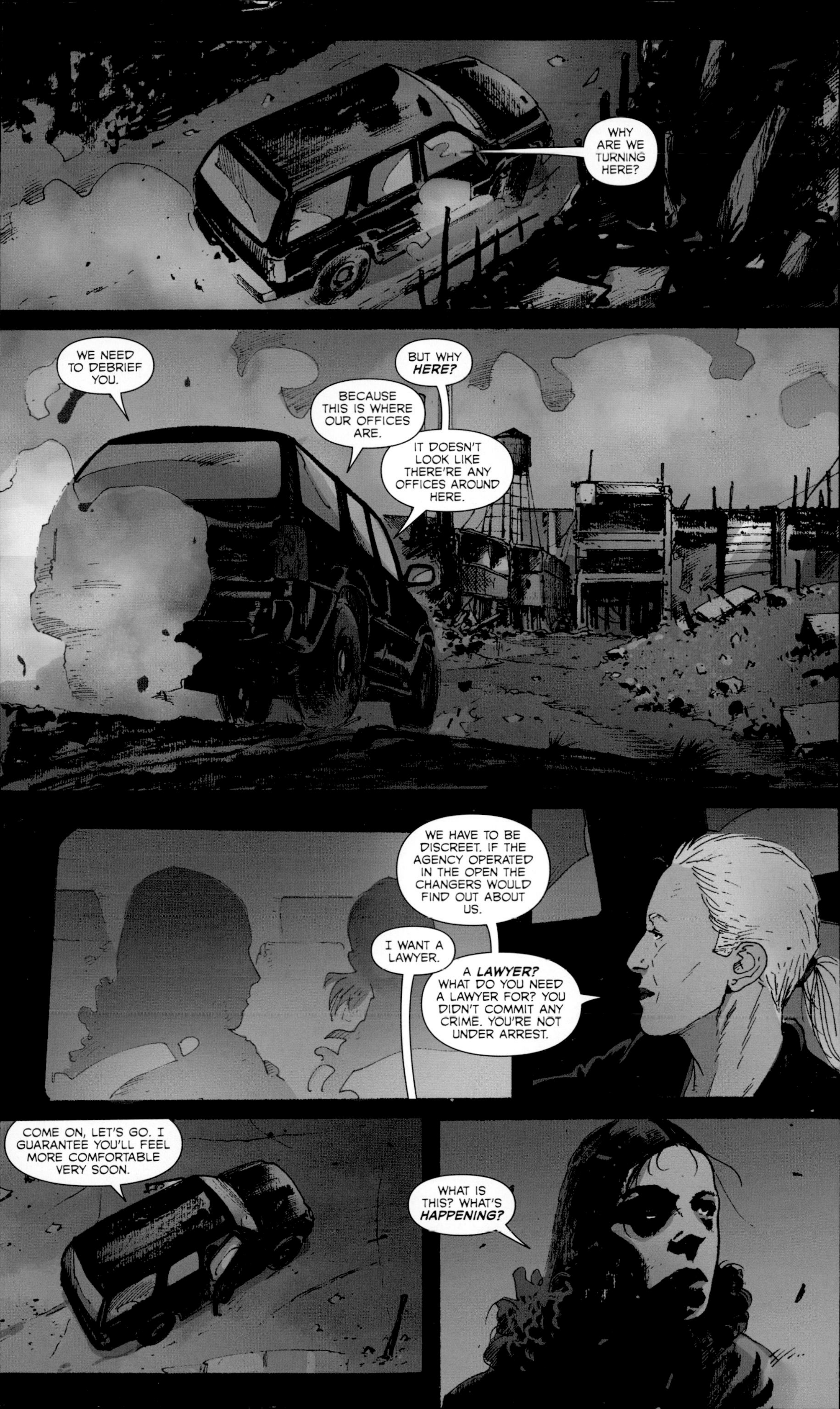
WHY ARE WE TURNING HERE?
WE NEED TO DEBRIEF YOU.
BUT WHY *HERE?*
BECAUSE THIS IS WHERE OUR OFFICES ARE.
IT DOESN'T LOOK LIKE THERE'RE ANY OFFICES AROUND HERE.
WE HAVE TO BE DISCREET. IF THE AGENCY OPERATED IN THE OPEN THE CHANGERS WOULD FIND OUT ABOUT US.
I WANT A LAWYER.
A *LAWYER?* WHAT DO YOU NEED A LAWYER FOR? YOU DIDN'T COMMIT ANY CRIME. YOU'RE NOT UNDER ARREST.
COME ON, LET'S GO. I GUARANTEE YOU'LL FEEL MORE COMFORTABLE VERY SOON.
WHAT IS THIS? WHAT'S *HAPPENING?*

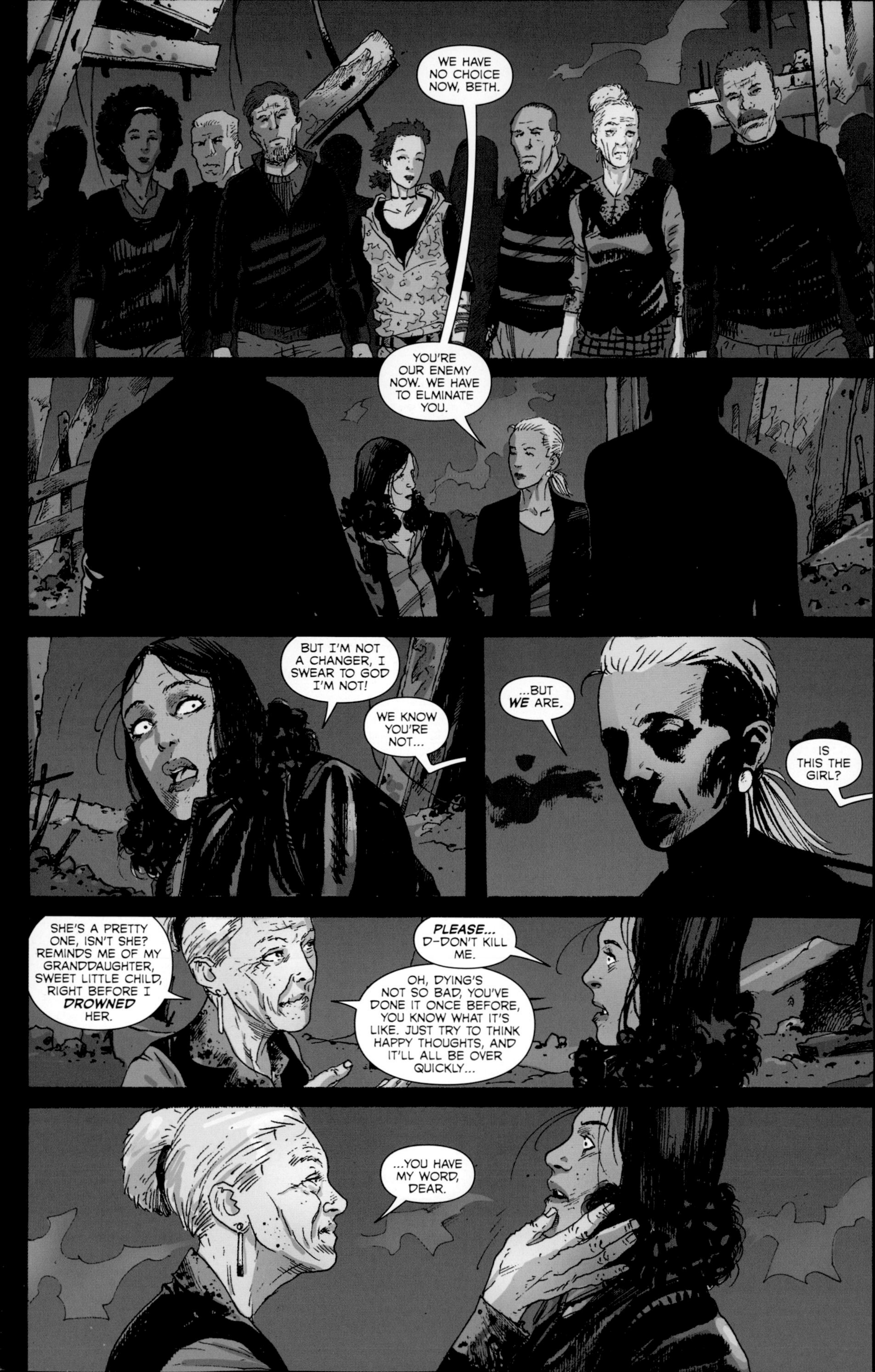
WE HAVE NO CHOICE NOW, BETH.
YOU'RE OUR ENEMY NOW. WE HAVE TO ELMINATE YOU.
BUT I'M NOT A CHANGER, I SWEAR TO GOD I'M NOT!
WE KNOW YOU'RE NOT...
...BUT *WE* ARE.
IS THIS THE GIRL?
SHE'S A PRETTY ONE, ISN'T SHE? REMINDS ME OF MY GRANDDAUGHTER, SWEET LITTLE CHILD, RIGHT BEFORE I *DROWNED* HER.
PLEASE... D-DON'T KILL ME.
OH, DYING'S NOT SO BAD, YOU'VE DONE IT ONCE BEFORE, YOU KNOW WHAT IT'S LIKE. JUST TRY TO THINK HAPPY THOUGHTS, AND IT'LL ALL BE OVER QUICKLY...
...YOU HAVE MY WORD, DEAR.

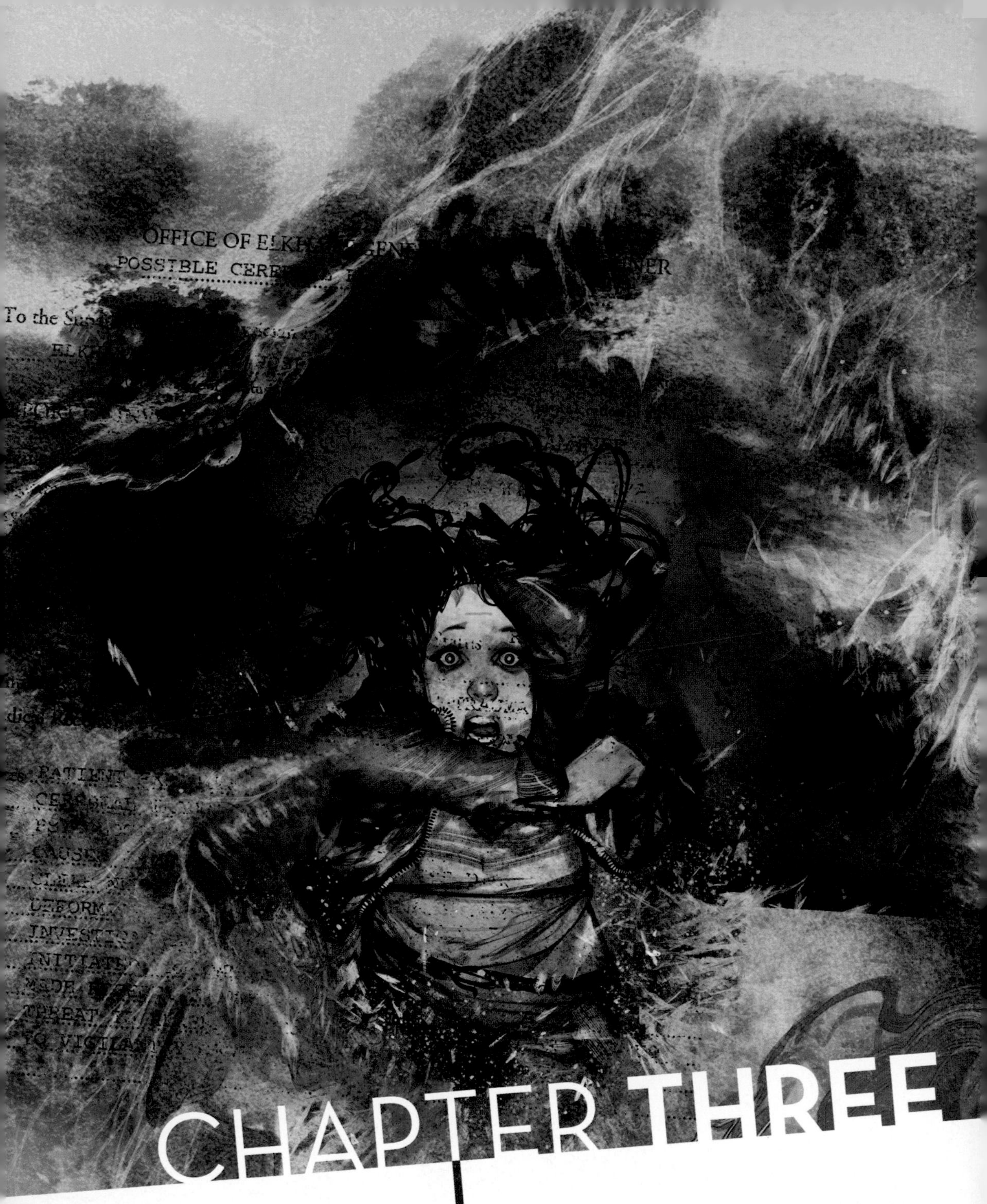

CHAPTER THREE

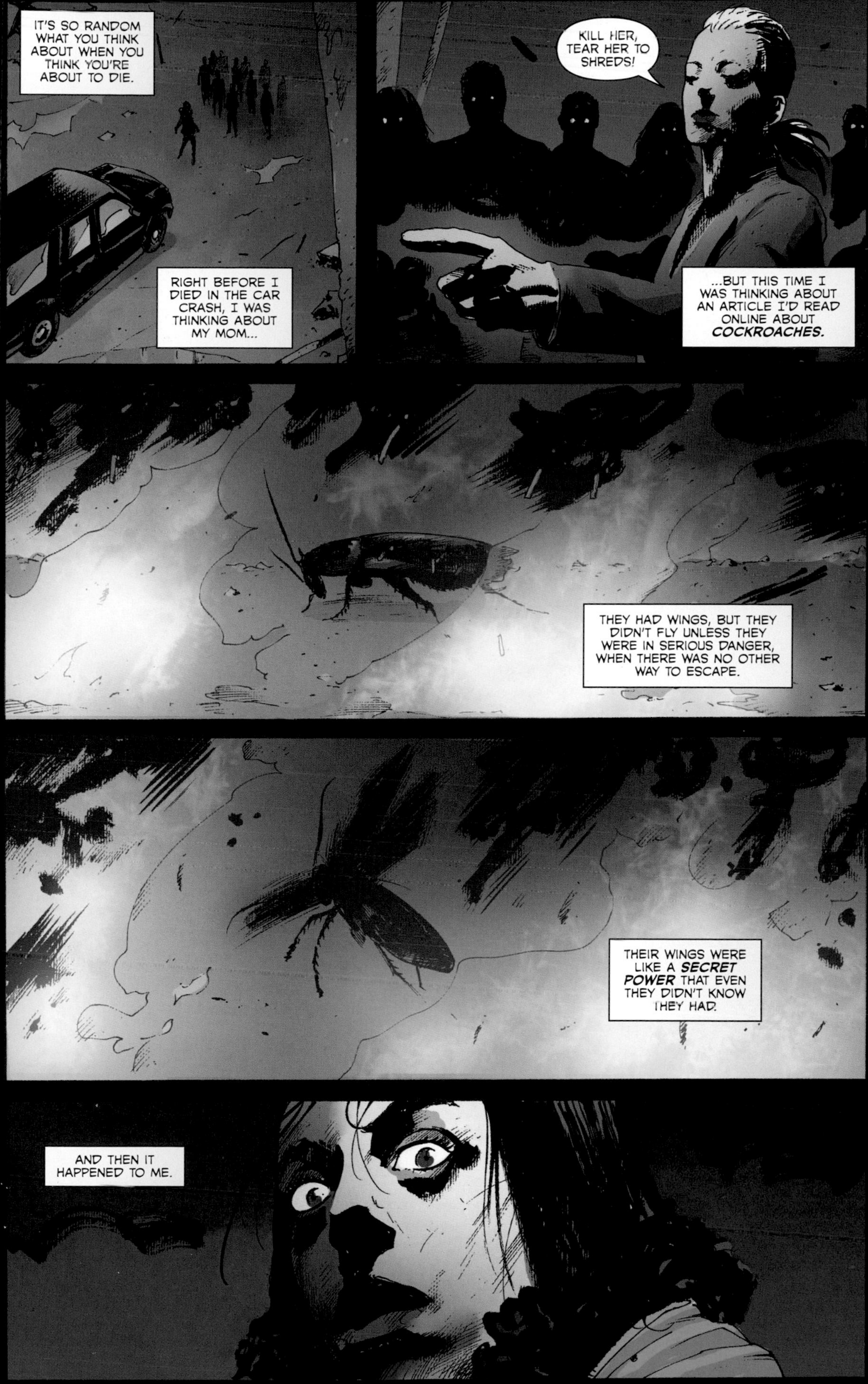
IT'S SO RANDOM WHAT YOU THINK ABOUT WHEN YOU THINK YOU'RE ABOUT TO DIE.
RIGHT BEFORE I DIED IN THE CAR CRASH, I WAS THINKING ABOUT MY MOM...
KILL HER, TEAR HER TO SHREDS!
...BUT THIS TIME I WAS THINKING ABOUT AN ARTICLE I'D READ ONLINE ABOUT COCKROACHES.
THEY HAD WINGS, BUT THEY DIDN'T FLY UNLESS THEY WERE IN SERIOUS DANGER, WHEN THERE WAS NO OTHER WAY TO ESCAPE.
THEIR WINGS WERE LIKE A SECRET POWER THAT EVEN THEY DIDN'T KNOW THEY HAD.
AND THEN IT HAPPENED TO ME.

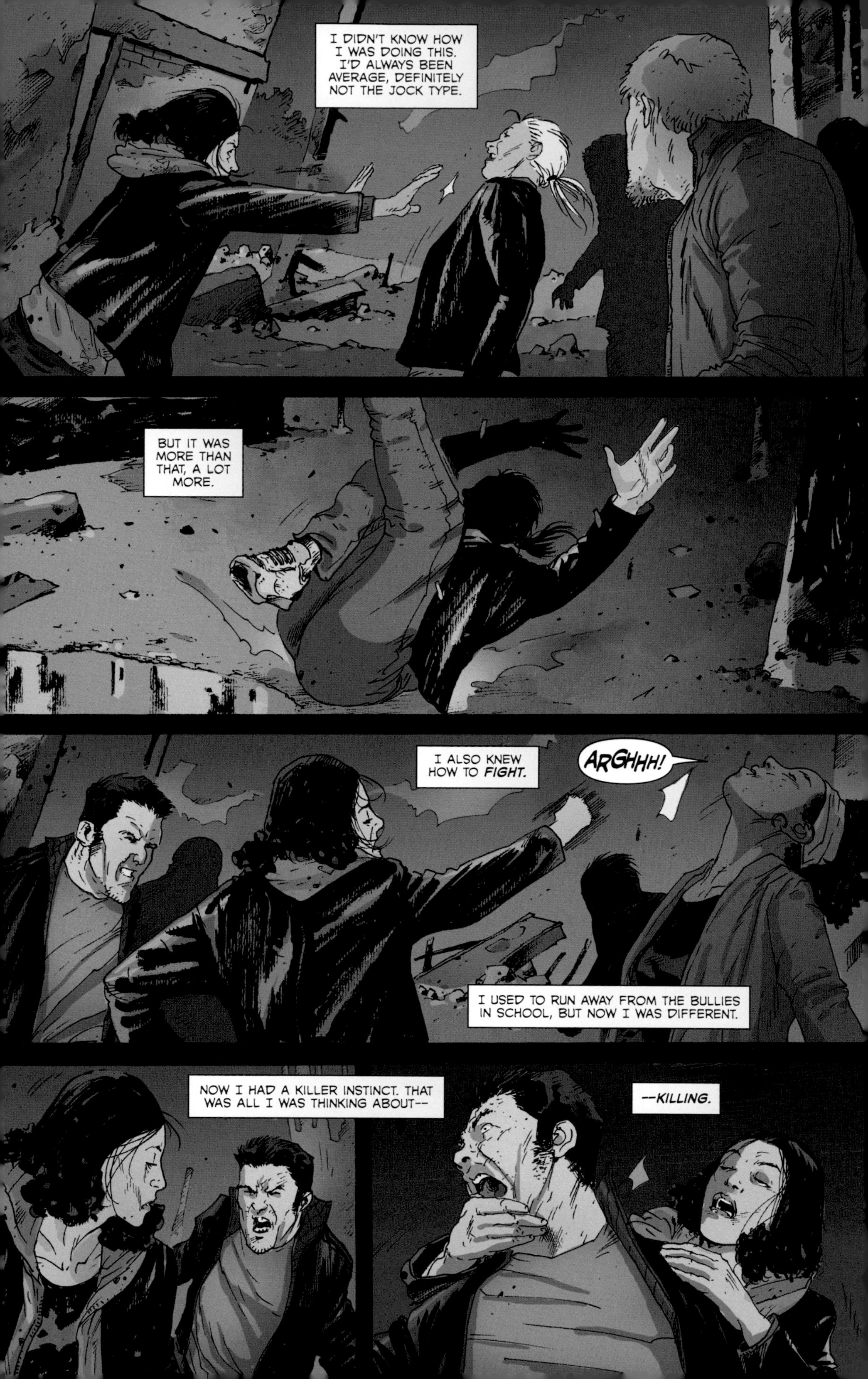

I DIDN'T KNOW HOW I WAS DOING THIS. I'D ALWAYS BEEN AVERAGE, DEFINITELY NOT THE JOCK TYPE.
BUT IT WAS MORE THAN THAT, A LOT MORE.
I ALSO KNEW HOW TO FIGHT.
ARGHHH!
I USED TO RUN AWAY FROM THE BULLIES IN SCHOOL, BUT NOW I WAS DIFFERENT.
NOW I HAD A KILLER INSTINCT. THAT WAS ALL I WAS THINKING ABOUT--
--KILLING.

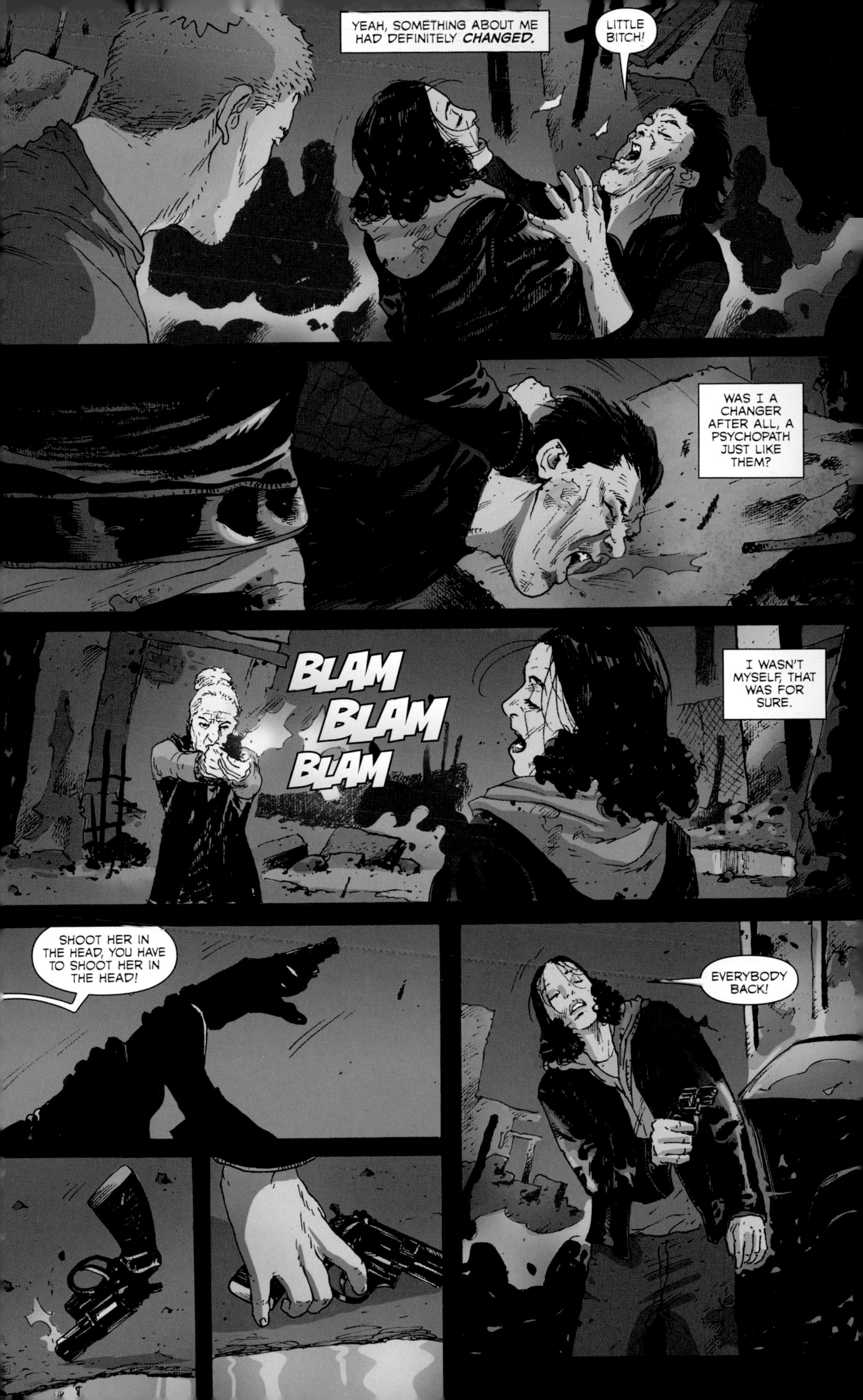
YEAH, SOMETHING ABOUT ME HAD DEFINITELY CHANGED.
LITTLE BITCH!
WAS I A CHANGER AFTER ALL, A PSYCHOPATH JUST LIKE THEM?
BLAM
BLAM
BLAM
I WASN'T MYSELF, THAT WAS FOR SURE.
SHOOT HER IN THE HEAD, YOU HAVE TO SHOOT HER IN THE HEAD!
EVERYBODY BACK!

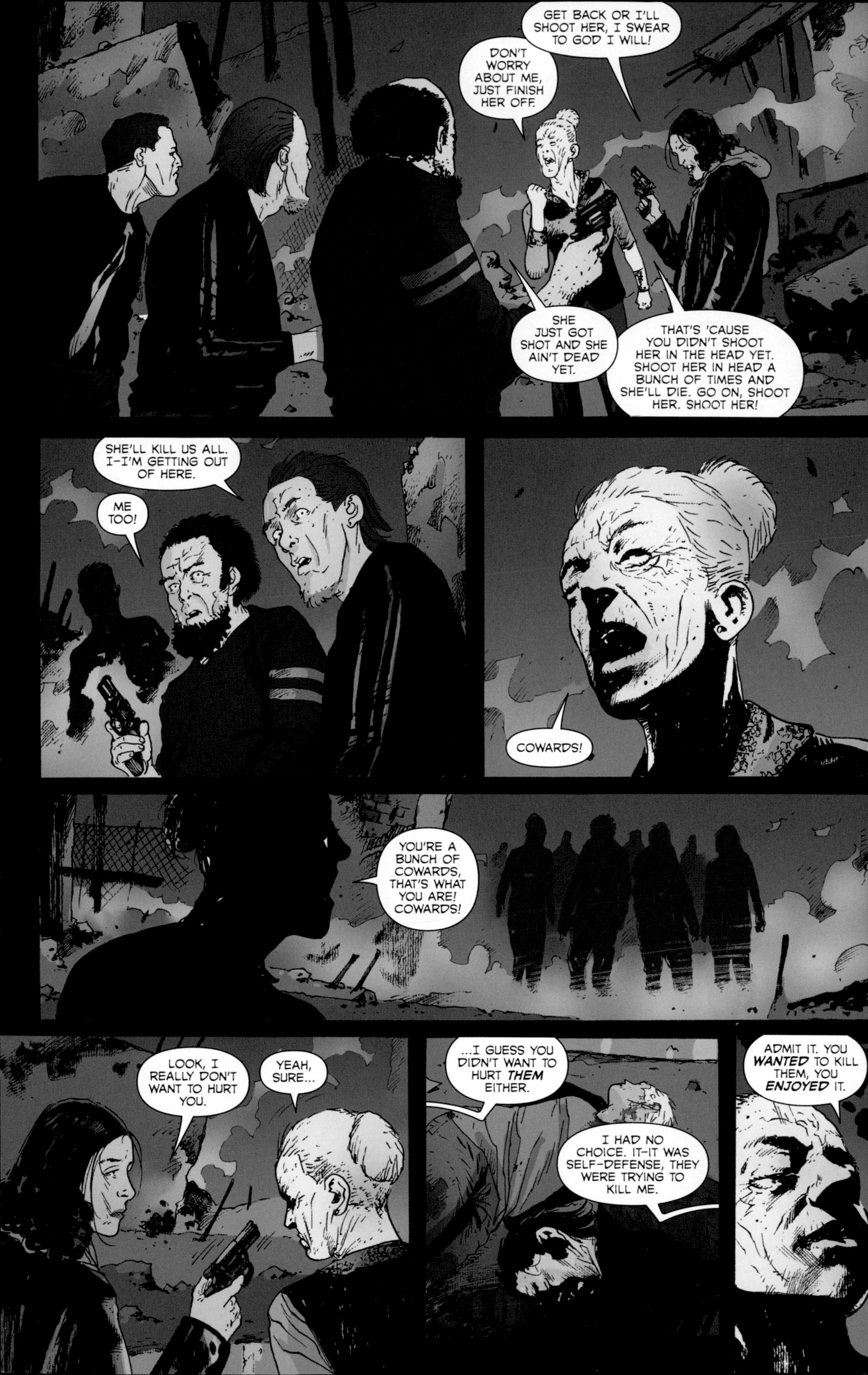

GET BACK OR I'LL SHOOT HER, I SWEAR TO GOD I WILL!
DON'T WORRY ABOUT ME, JUST FINISH HER OFF.
SHE JUST GOT SHOT AND SHE AIN'T DEAD YET.
THAT'S 'CAUSE YOU DIDN'T SHOOT HER IN THE HEAD YET. SHOOT HER IN HEAD A BUNCH OF TIMES AND SHE'LL DIE. GO ON, SHOOT HER. SHOOT HER!
SHE'LL KILL US ALL. I-I'M GETTING OUT OF HERE.
ME TOO!
COWARDS!
YOU'RE A BUNCH OF COWARDS, THAT'S WHAT YOU ARE! COWARDS!
LOOK, I REALLY DON'T WANT TO HURT YOU.
YEAH, SURE...
...I GUESS YOU DIDN'T WANT TO HURT *THEM* EITHER.
I HAD NO CHOICE. IT-IT WAS SELF-DEFENSE, THEY WERE TRYING TO KILL ME.
ADMIT IT. YOU *WANTED* TO KILL THEM, YOU *ENJOYED* IT.

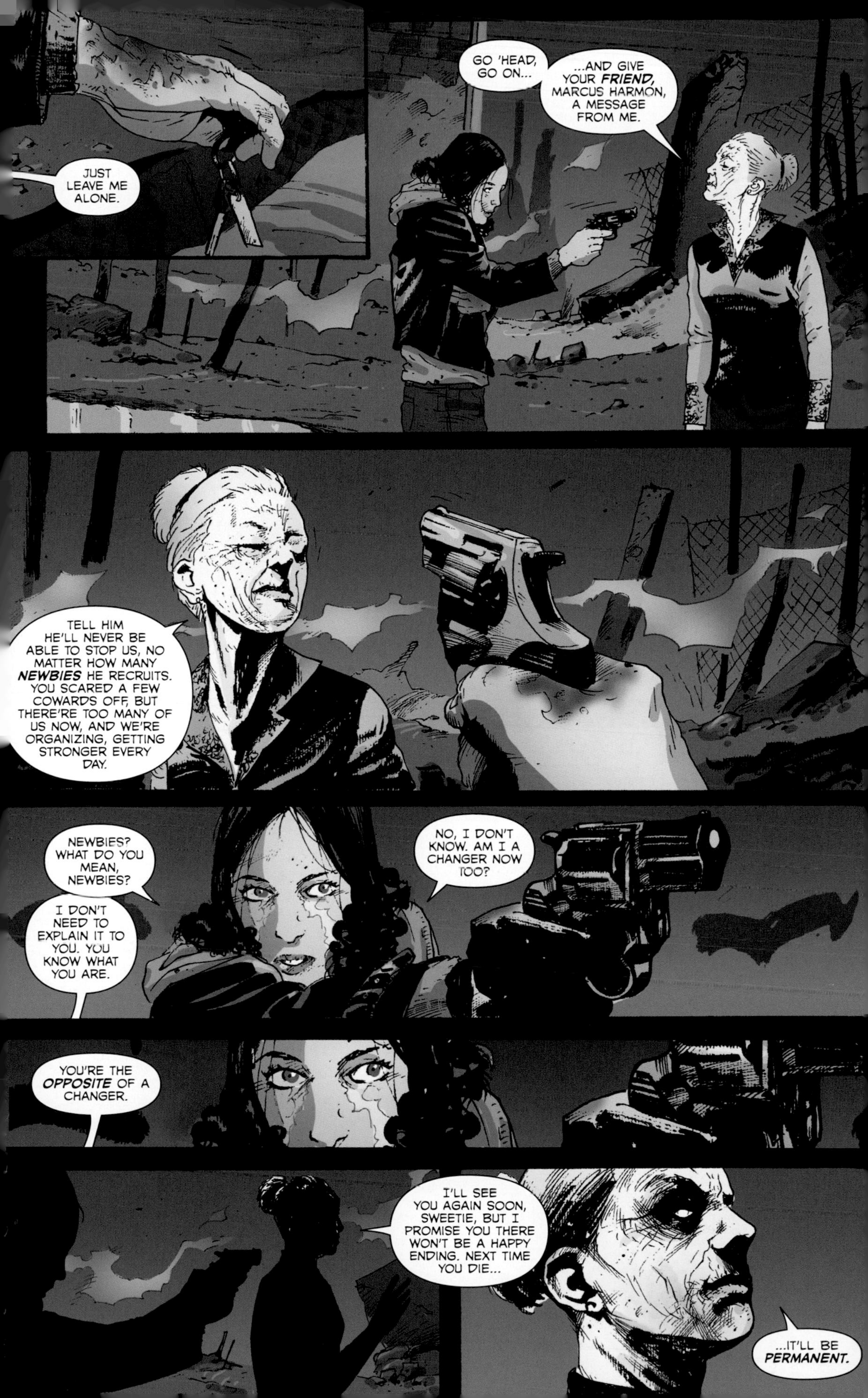
JUST LEAVE ME ALONE.
GO 'HEAD, GO ON...
...AND GIVE YOUR **FRIEND,** MARCUS HARMON, A MESSAGE FROM ME.
TELL HIM HE'LL NEVER BE ABLE TO STOP US, NO MATTER HOW MANY **NEWBIES** HE RECRUITS. YOU SCARED A FEW COWARDS OFF, BUT THERE'RE TOO MANY OF US NOW, AND WE'RE ORGANIZING, GETTING STRONGER EVERY DAY.
NEWBIES? WHAT DO YOU MEAN, NEWBIES?
I DON'T NEED TO EXPLAIN IT TO YOU. YOU KNOW WHAT YOU ARE.
NO, I DON'T KNOW. AM I A CHANGER NOW TOO?
YOU'RE THE **OPPOSITE** OF A CHANGER.
I'LL SEE YOU AGAIN SOON, SWEETIE, BUT I PROMISE YOU THERE WON'T BE A HAPPY ENDING. NEXT TIME YOU DIE...
...IT'LL BE **PERMANENT.**

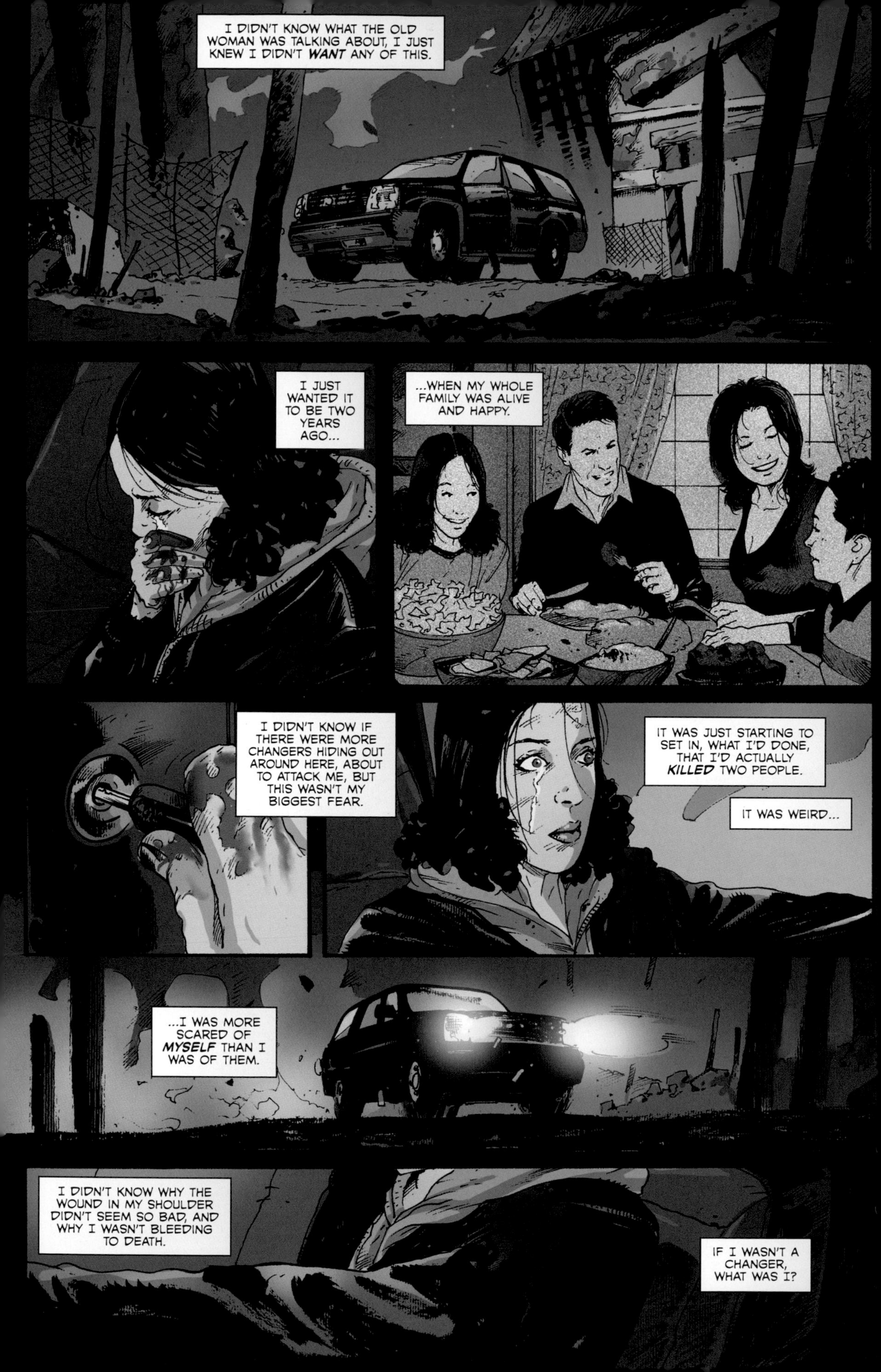
I DIDN'T KNOW WHAT THE OLD WOMAN WAS TALKING ABOUT, I JUST KNEW I DIDN'T WANT ANY OF THIS.
I JUST WANTED IT TO BE TWO YEARS AGO...
...WHEN MY WHOLE FAMILY WAS ALIVE AND HAPPY.
I DIDN'T KNOW IF THERE WERE MORE CHANGERS HIDING OUT AROUND HERE, ABOUT TO ATTACK ME, BUT THIS WASN'T MY BIGGEST FEAR.
IT WAS JUST STARTING TO SET IN, WHAT I'D DONE, THAT I'D ACTUALLY KILLED TWO PEOPLE.
IT WAS WEIRD...
...I WAS MORE SCARED OF MYSELF THAN I WAS OF THEM.
I DIDN'T KNOW WHY THE WOUND IN MY SHOULDER DIDN'T SEEM SO BAD, AND WHY I WASN'T BLEEDING TO DEATH.
IF I WASN'T A CHANGER, WHAT WAS I?

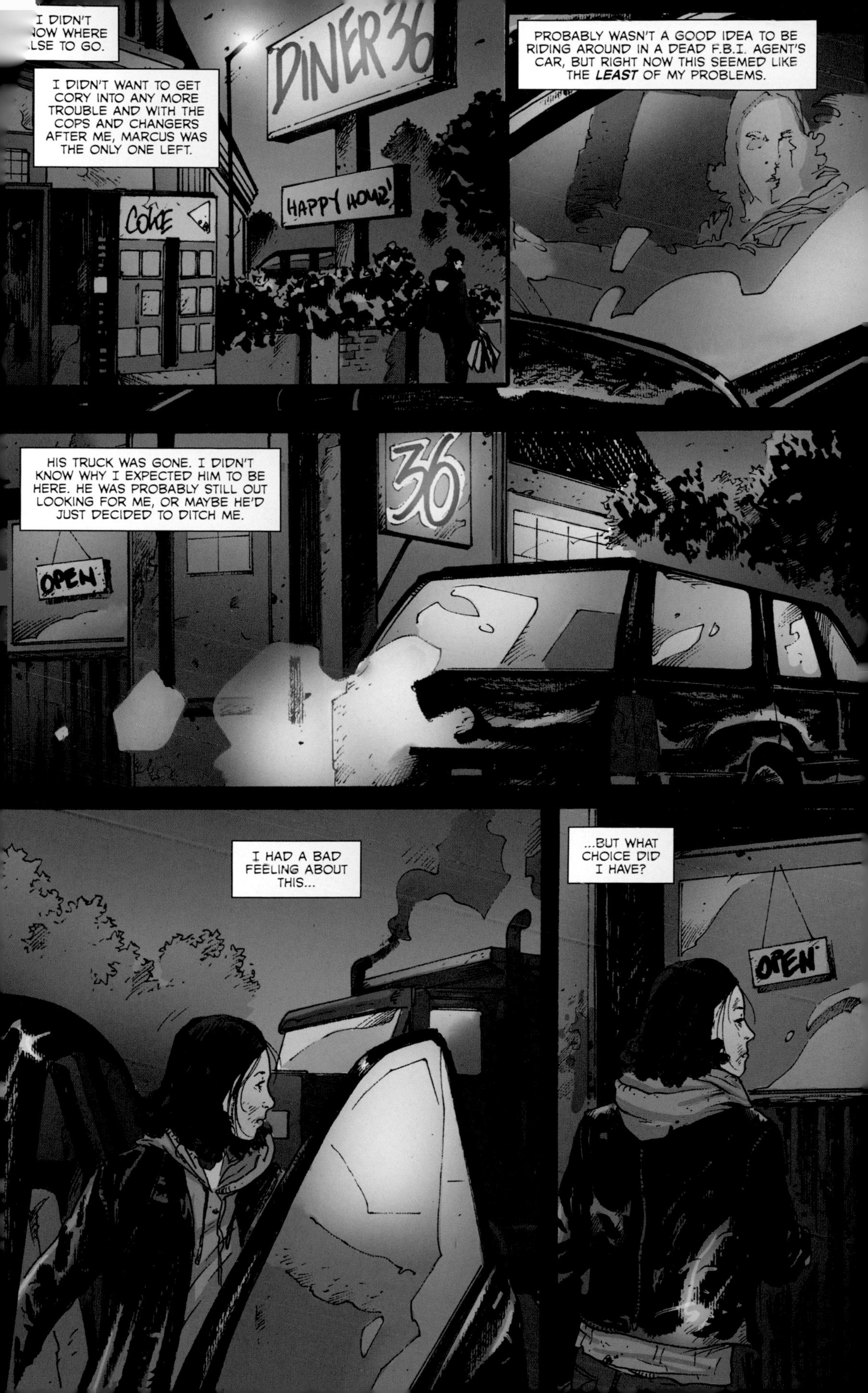
I DIDN'T
NOW WHERE
LSE TO GO.
I DIDN'T WANT TO GET CORY INTO ANY MORE TROUBLE AND WITH THE COPS AND CHANGERS AFTER ME, MARCUS WAS THE ONLY ONE LEFT.
DINER 36
HAPPY HOUR!
COKE
PROBABLY WASN'T A GOOD IDEA TO BE RIDING AROUND IN A DEAD F.B.I. AGENT'S CAR, BUT RIGHT NOW THIS SEEMED LIKE THE *LEAST* OF MY PROBLEMS.
HIS TRUCK WAS GONE. I DIDN'T KNOW WHY I EXPECTED HIM TO BE HERE. HE WAS PROBABLY STILL OUT LOOKING FOR ME, OR MAYBE HE'D JUST DECIDED TO DITCH ME.
36
OPEN
I HAD A BAD FEELING ABOUT THIS...
...BUT WHAT CHOICE DID I HAVE?
OPEN

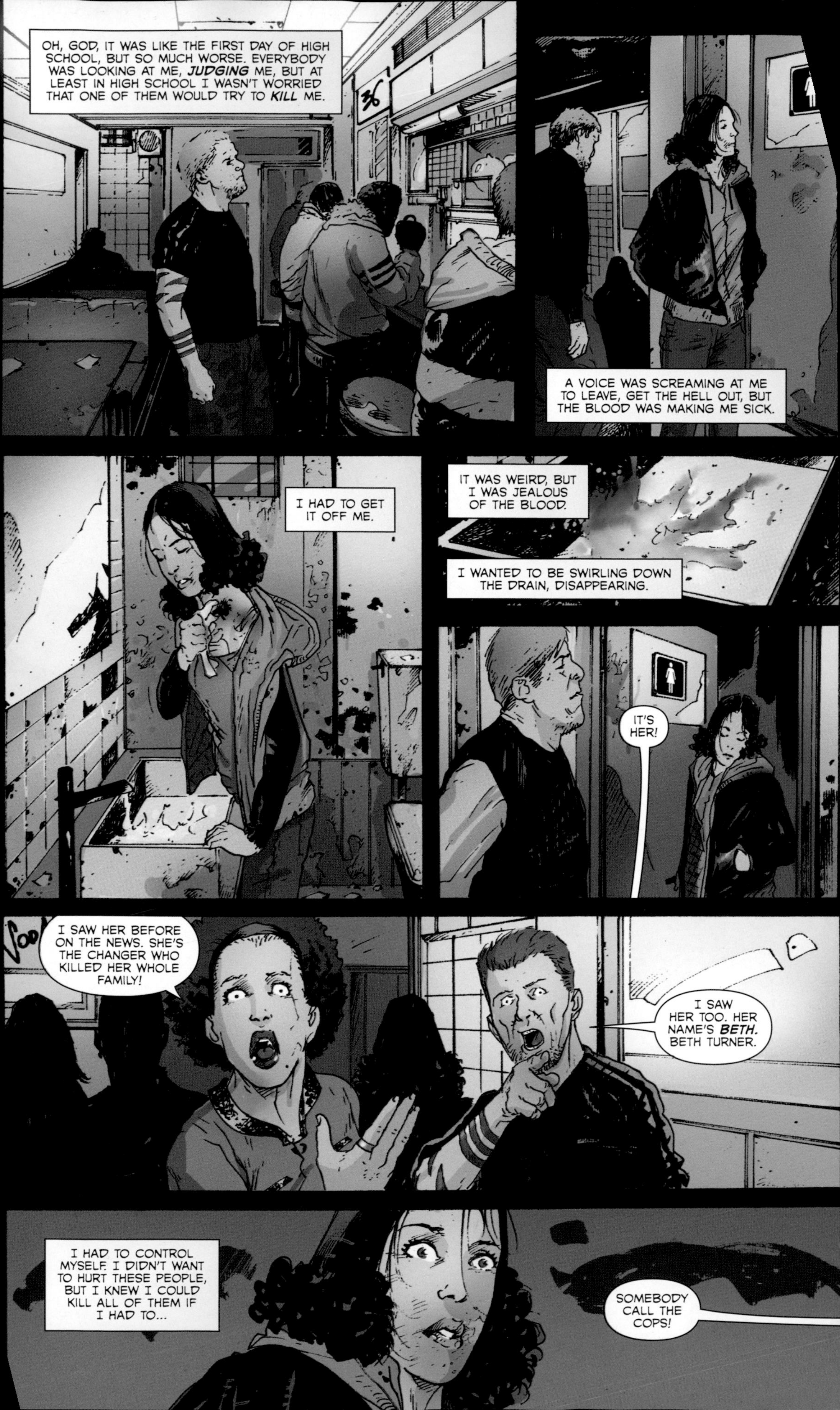
OH, GOD, IT WAS LIKE THE FIRST DAY OF HIGH SCHOOL, BUT SO MUCH WORSE. EVERYBODY WAS LOOKING AT ME, *JUDGING* ME, BUT AT LEAST IN HIGH SCHOOL I WASN'T WORRIED THAT ONE OF THEM WOULD TRY TO *KILL* ME.
A VOICE WAS SCREAMING AT ME TO LEAVE, GET THE HELL OUT, BUT THE BLOOD WAS MAKING ME SICK.
I HAD TO GET IT OFF ME.
IT WAS WEIRD, BUT I WAS JEALOUS OF THE BLOOD.
I WANTED TO BE SWIRLING DOWN THE DRAIN, DISAPPEARING.
IT'S HER!
I SAW HER BEFORE ON THE NEWS. SHE'S THE CHANGER WHO KILLED HER WHOLE FAMILY!
I SAW HER TOO. HER NAME'S *BETH.* BETH TURNER.
I HAD TO CONTROL MYSELF. I DIDN'T WANT TO HURT THESE PEOPLE, BUT I KNEW I COULD KILL ALL OF THEM IF I HAD TO...
SOMEBODY CALL THE COPS!

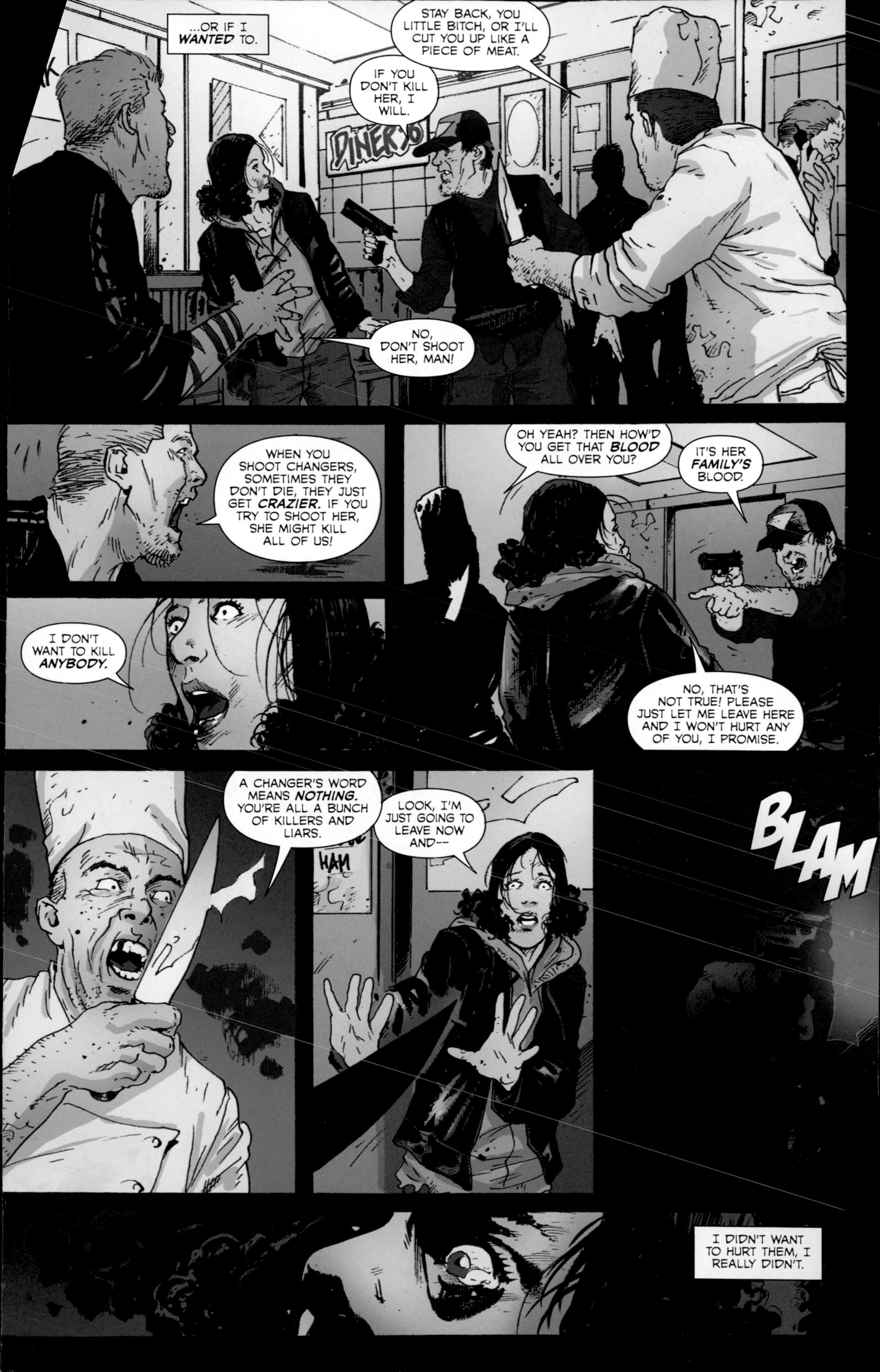
...OR IF I WANTED TO.
STAY BACK, YOU LITTLE BITCH, OR I'LL CUT YOU UP LIKE A PIECE OF MEAT.
IF YOU DON'T KILL HER, I WILL.
DINER
NO, DON'T SHOOT HER, MAN!
WHEN YOU SHOOT CHANGERS, SOMETIMES THEY DON'T DIE, THEY JUST GET CRAZIER. IF YOU TRY TO SHOOT HER, SHE MIGHT KILL ALL OF US!
OH YEAH? THEN HOW'D YOU GET THAT BLOOD ALL OVER YOU?
IT'S HER FAMILY'S BLOOD.
I DON'T WANT TO KILL ANYBODY.
NO, THAT'S NOT TRUE! PLEASE JUST LET ME LEAVE HERE AND I WON'T HURT ANY OF YOU, I PROMISE.
A CHANGER'S WORD MEANS NOTHING. YOU'RE ALL A BUNCH OF KILLERS AND LIARS.
LOOK, I'M JUST GOING TO LEAVE NOW AND--
HAM
BLAM
I DIDN'T WANT TO HURT THEM, I REALLY DIDN'T.

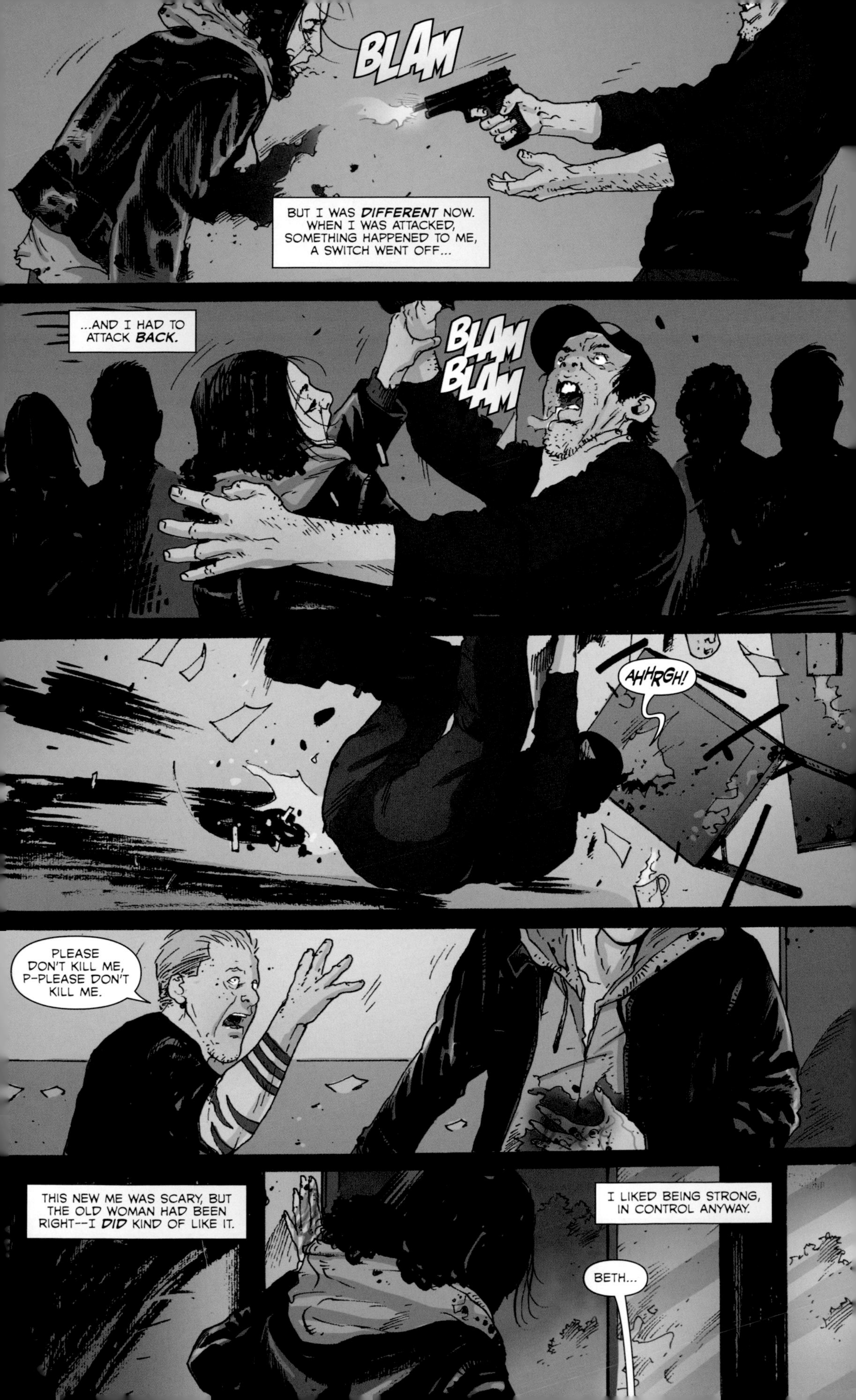
BLAM
BUT I WAS *DIFFERENT* NOW. WHEN I WAS ATTACKED, SOMETHING HAPPENED TO ME, A SWITCH WENT OFF...
...AND I HAD TO ATTACK *BACK.*
BLAM BLAM
AHHRGH!
PLEASE DON'T KILL ME, P-PLEASE DON'T KILL ME.
THIS NEW ME WAS SCARY, BUT THE OLD WOMAN HAD BEEN RIGHT--I *DID* KIND OF LIKE IT.
I LIKED BEING STRONG, IN CONTROL ANYWAY.
BETH...

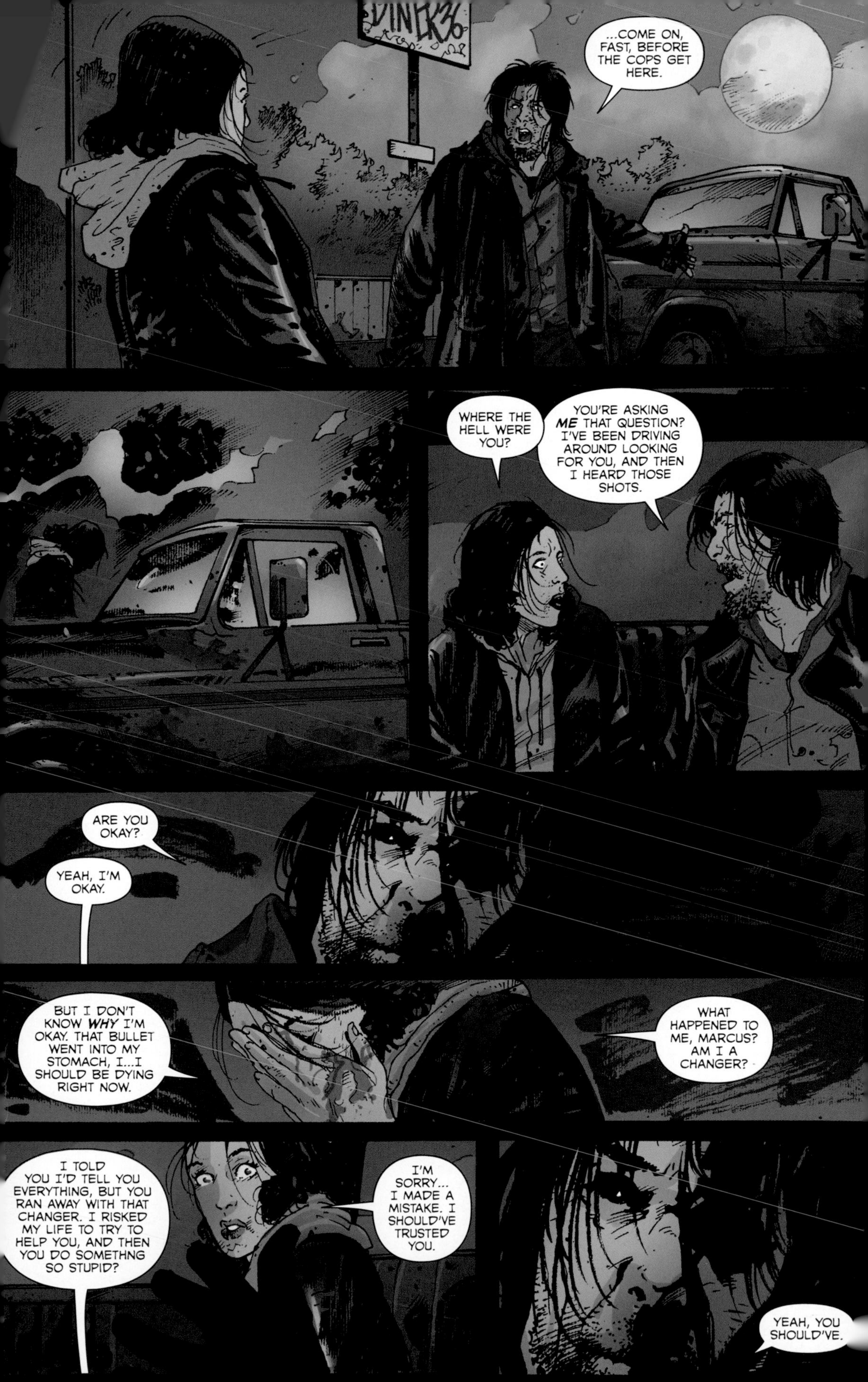

...COME ON, FAST, BEFORE THE COPS GET HERE.
WHERE THE HELL WERE YOU?
YOU'RE ASKING *ME* THAT QUESTION? I'VE BEEN DRIVING AROUND LOOKING FOR YOU, AND THEN I HEARD THOSE SHOTS.
ARE YOU OKAY?
YEAH, I'M OKAY.
BUT I DON'T KNOW *WHY* I'M OKAY. THAT BULLET WENT INTO MY STOMACH, I...I SHOULD BE DYING RIGHT NOW.
WHAT HAPPENED TO ME, MARCUS? AM I A CHANGER?
I TOLD YOU I'D TELL YOU EVERYTHING, BUT YOU RAN AWAY WITH THAT CHANGER. I RISKED MY LIFE TO TRY TO HELP YOU, AND THEN YOU DO SOMETHNG SO STUPID?
I'M SORRY... I MADE A MISTAKE. I SHOULD'VE TRUSTED YOU.
YEAH, YOU SHOULD'VE.

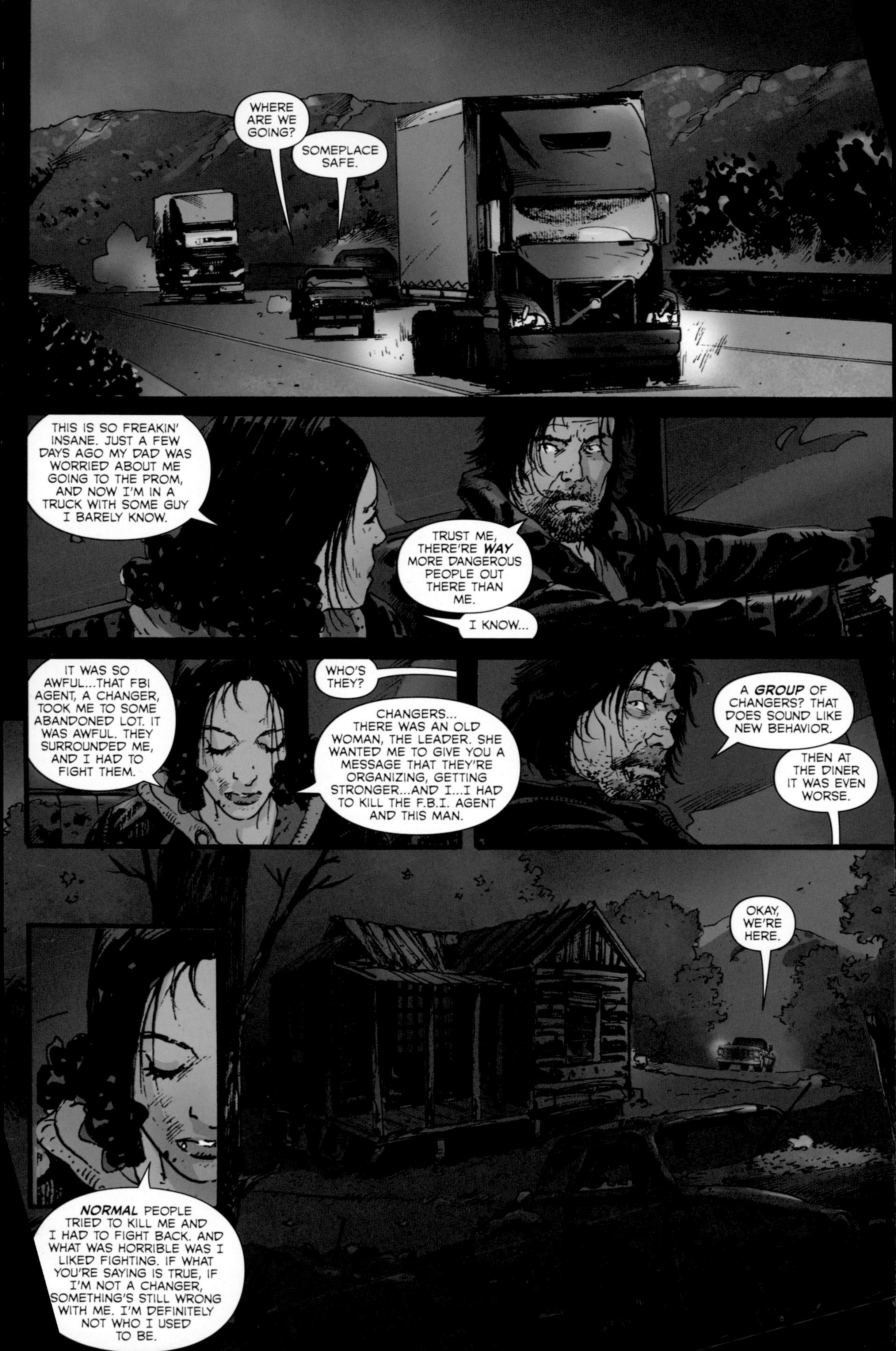

WHERE ARE WE GOING?
SOMEPLACE SAFE.
THIS IS SO FREAKIN' INSANE. JUST A FEW DAYS AGO MY DAD WAS WORRIED ABOUT ME GOING TO THE PROM, AND NOW I'M IN A TRUCK WITH SOME GUY I BARELY KNOW.
TRUST ME, THERE'RE *WAY* MORE DANGEROUS PEOPLE OUT THERE THAN ME.
I KNOW...
IT WAS SO AWFUL...THAT FBI AGENT, A CHANGER, TOOK ME TO SOME ABANDONED LOT. IT WAS AWFUL. THEY SURROUNDED ME, AND I HAD TO FIGHT THEM.
WHO'S THEY?
CHANGERS... THERE WAS AN OLD WOMAN, THE LEADER. SHE WANTED ME TO GIVE YOU A MESSAGE THAT THEY'RE ORGANIZING, GETTING STRONGER...AND I...I HAD TO KILL THE F.B.I. AGENT AND THIS MAN.
A *GROUP* OF CHANGERS? THAT DOES SOUND LIKE NEW BEHAVIOR.
THEN AT THE DINER IT WAS EVEN WORSE.
NORMAL PEOPLE TRIED TO KILL ME AND I HAD TO FIGHT BACK. AND WHAT WAS HORRIBLE WAS I LIKED FIGHTING. IF WHAT YOU'RE SAYING IS TRUE, IF I'M NOT A CHANGER, SOMETHING'S STILL WRONG WITH ME. I'M DEFINITELY NOT WHO I USED TO BE.
OKAY, WE'RE HERE.

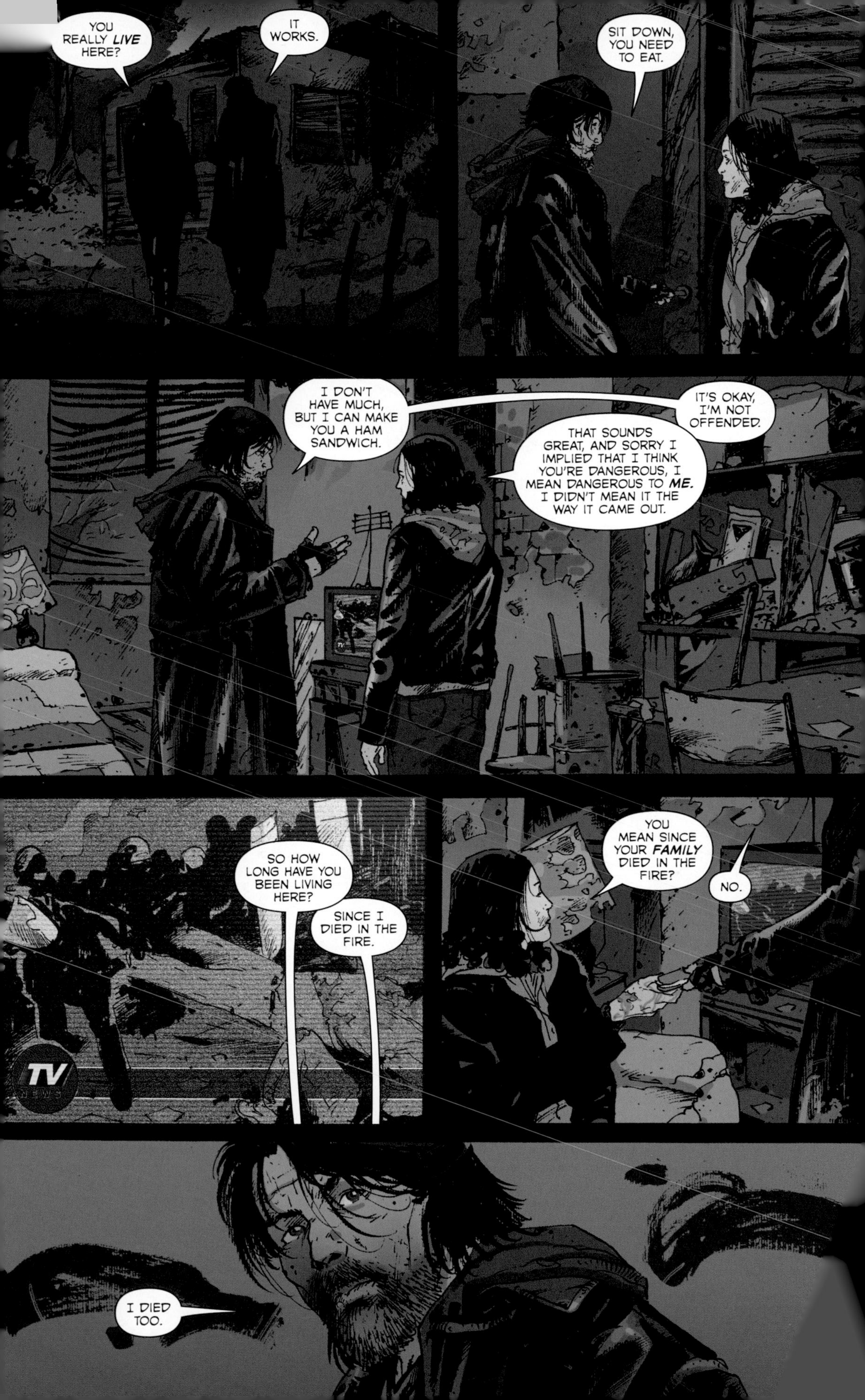
YOU REALLY LIVE HERE?
IT WORKS.
SIT DOWN, YOU NEED TO EAT.
I DON'T HAVE MUCH, BUT I CAN MAKE YOU A HAM SANDWICH.
THAT SOUNDS GREAT, AND SORRY I IMPLIED THAT I THINK YOU'RE DANGEROUS, I MEAN DANGEROUS TO ME. I DIDN'T MEAN IT THE WAY IT CAME OUT.
IT'S OKAY, I'M NOT OFFENDED.
TV
SO HOW LONG HAVE YOU BEEN LIVING HERE?
SINCE I DIED IN THE FIRE.
YOU MEAN SINCE YOUR FAMILY DIED IN THE FIRE?
NO.
I DIED TOO.

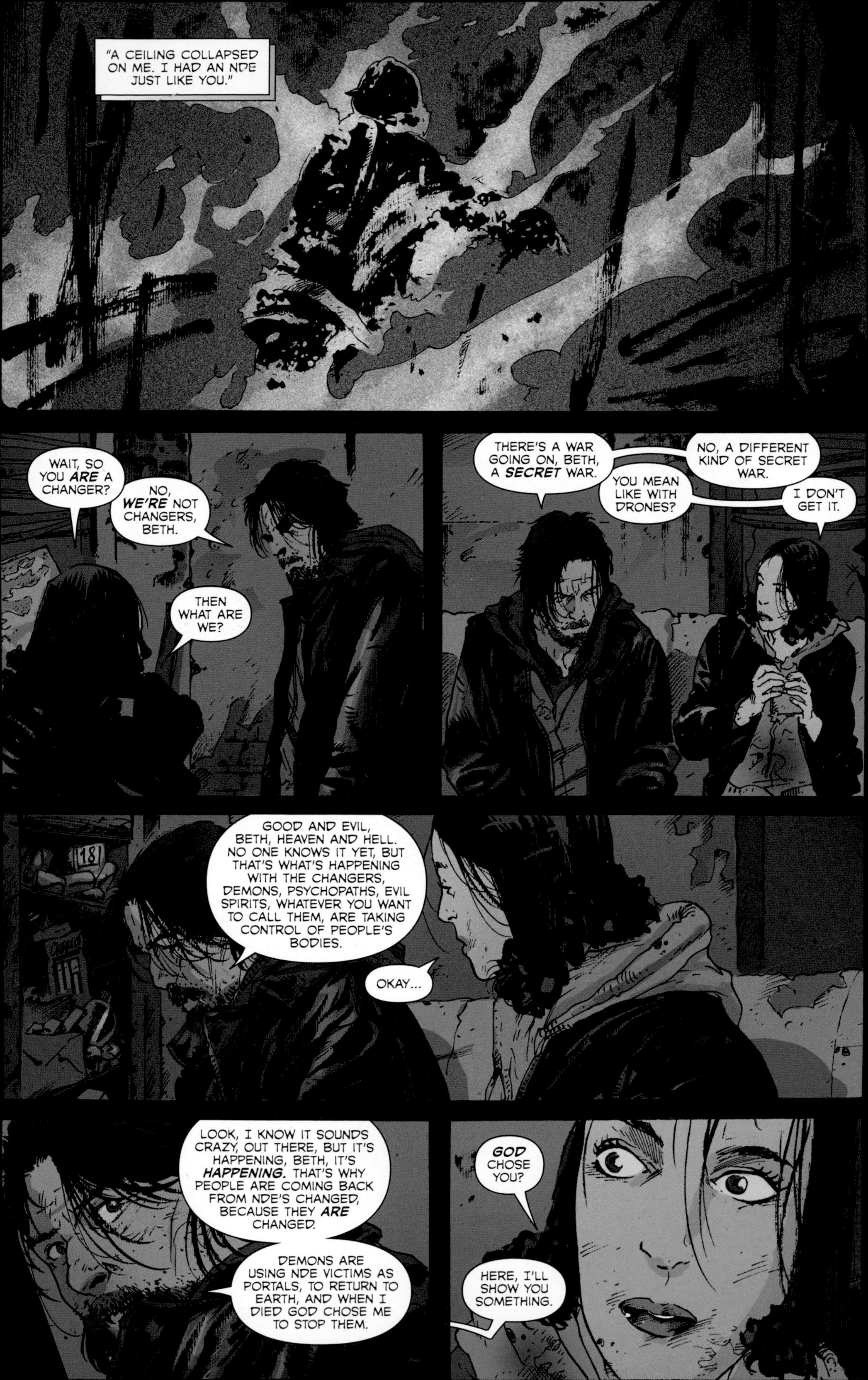
"A CEILING COLLAPSED ON ME. I HAD AN NDE JUST LIKE YOU."
WAIT, SO YOU ARE A CHANGER?
NO, WE'RE NOT CHANGERS, BETH.
THEN WHAT ARE WE?
THERE'S A WAR GOING ON, BETH, A SECRET WAR.
YOU MEAN LIKE WITH DRONES?
NO, A DIFFERENT KIND OF SECRET WAR.
I DON'T GET IT.
18
GOOD AND EVIL, BETH, HEAVEN AND HELL. NO ONE KNOWS IT YET, BUT THAT'S WHAT'S HAPPENING WITH THE CHANGERS, DEMONS, PSYCHOPATHS, EVIL SPIRITS, WHATEVER YOU WANT TO CALL THEM, ARE TAKING CONTROL OF PEOPLE'S BODIES.
OKAY...
LOOK, I KNOW IT SOUNDS CRAZY, OUT THERE, BUT IT'S HAPPENING, BETH, IT'S HAPPENING. THAT'S WHY PEOPLE ARE COMING BACK FROM NDE'S CHANGED, BECAUSE THEY ARE CHANGED.
DEMONS ARE USING NDE VICTIMS AS PORTALS, TO RETURN TO EARTH, AND WHEN I DIED GOD CHOSE ME TO STOP THEM.
GOD CHOSE YOU?
HERE, I'LL SHOW YOU SOMETHING.

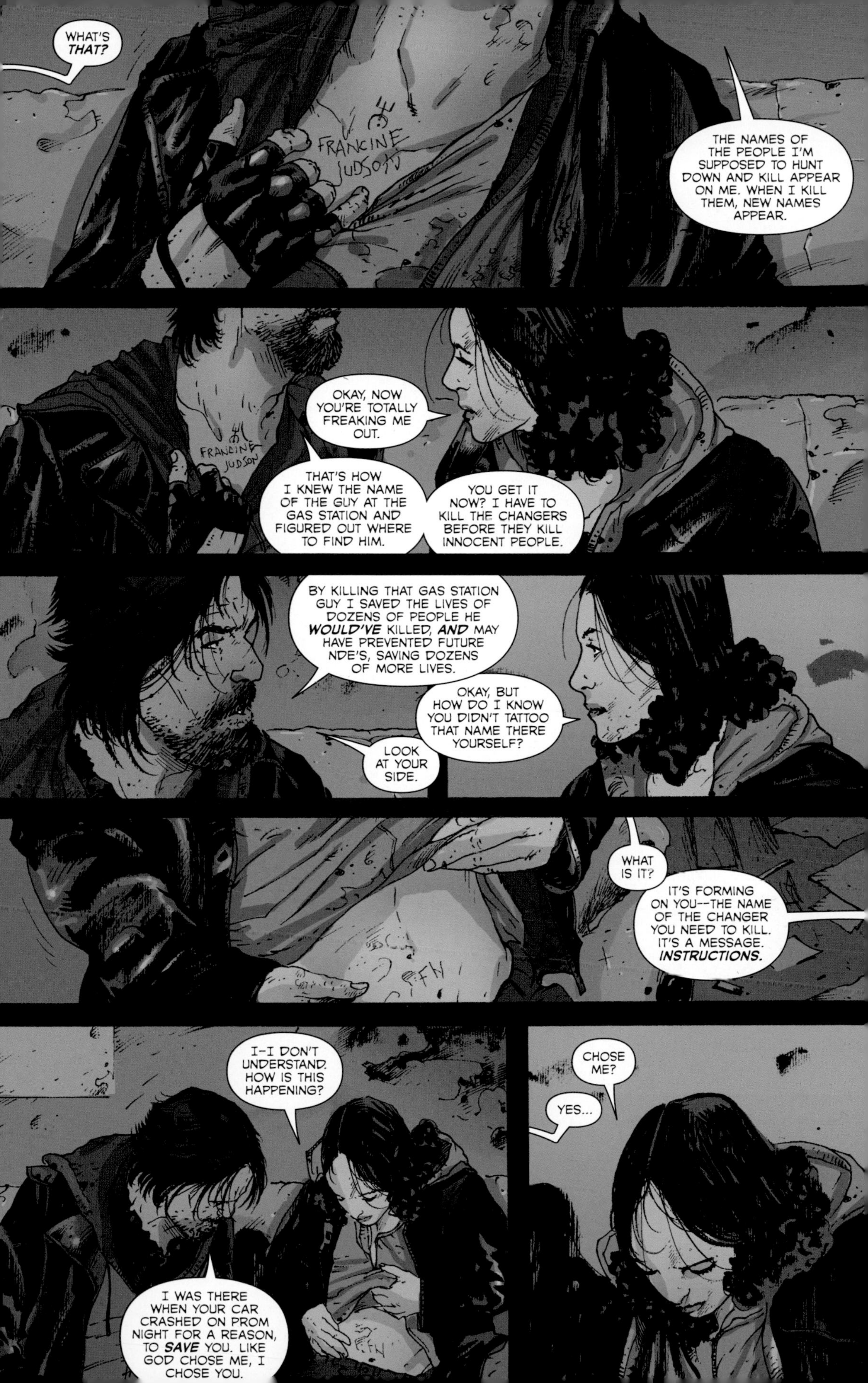
WHAT'S *THAT?*
FRANCINE JUDSON
THE NAMES OF THE PEOPLE I'M SUPPOSED TO HUNT DOWN AND KILL APPEAR ON ME. WHEN I KILL THEM, NEW NAMES APPEAR.
OKAY, NOW YOU'RE TOTALLY FREAKING ME OUT.
FRANCINE JUDSON
THAT'S HOW I KNEW THE NAME OF THE GUY AT THE GAS STATION AND FIGURED OUT WHERE TO FIND HIM.
YOU GET IT NOW? I HAVE TO KILL THE CHANGERS BEFORE THEY KILL INNOCENT PEOPLE.
BY KILLING THAT GAS STATION GUY I SAVED THE LIVES OF DOZENS OF PEOPLE HE ***WOULD'VE*** KILLED, ***AND*** MAY HAVE PREVENTED FUTURE NDE'S, SAVING DOZENS OF MORE LIVES.
OKAY, BUT HOW DO I KNOW YOU DIDN'T TATTOO THAT NAME THERE YOURSELF?
LOOK AT YOUR SIDE.
WHAT IS IT?
IT'S FORMING ON YOU--THE NAME OF THE CHANGER YOU NEED TO KILL. IT'S A MESSAGE. ***INSTRUCTIONS.***
I-I DON'T UNDERSTAND. HOW IS THIS HAPPENING?
I WAS THERE WHEN YOUR CAR CRASHED ON PROM NIGHT FOR A REASON, TO ***SAVE*** YOU. LIKE GOD CHOSE ME, I CHOSE YOU.
CHOSE ME?
YES...

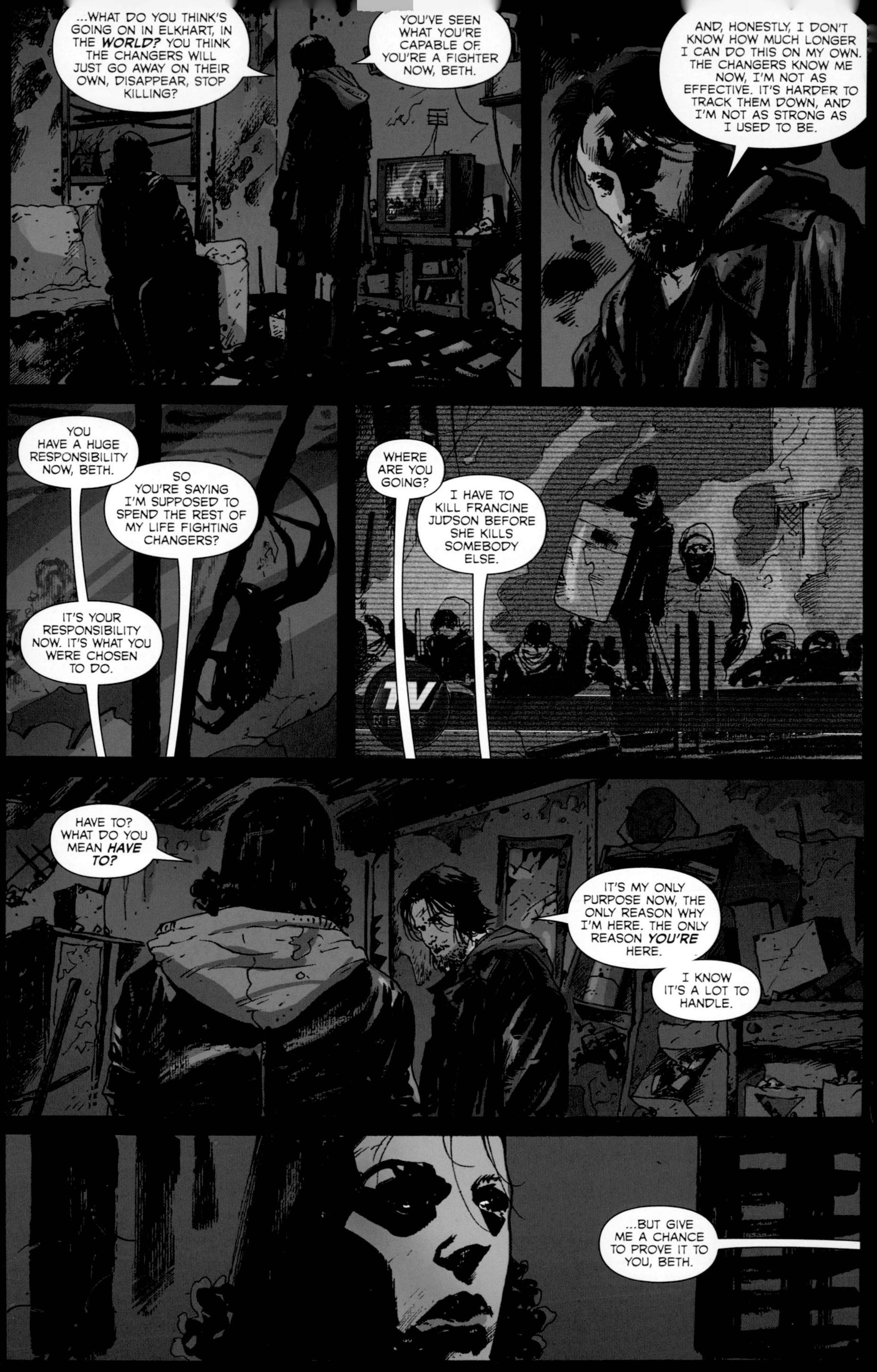
...WHAT DO YOU THINK'S GOING ON IN ELKHART, IN THE ***WORLD?*** YOU THINK THE CHANGERS WILL JUST GO AWAY ON THEIR OWN, DISAPPEAR, STOP KILLING?
YOU'VE SEEN WHAT YOU'RE CAPABLE OF. YOU'RE A FIGHTER NOW, BETH.
AND, HONESTLY, I DON'T KNOW HOW MUCH LONGER I CAN DO THIS ON MY OWN. THE CHANGERS KNOW ME NOW, I'M NOT AS EFFECTIVE. IT'S HARDER TO TRACK THEM DOWN, AND I'M NOT AS STRONG AS I USED TO BE.
YOU HAVE A HUGE RESPONSIBILITY NOW, BETH.
SO YOU'RE SAYING I'M SUPPOSED TO SPEND THE REST OF MY LIFE FIGHTING CHANGERS?
IT'S YOUR RESPONSIBILITY NOW. IT'S WHAT YOU WERE CHOSEN TO DO.
WHERE ARE YOU GOING?
I HAVE TO KILL FRANCINE JUDSON BEFORE SHE KILLS SOMEBODY ELSE.
TV
HAVE TO? WHAT DO YOU MEAN ***HAVE TO?***
IT'S MY ONLY PURPOSE NOW, THE ONLY REASON WHY I'M HERE. THE ONLY REASON ***YOU'RE*** HERE.
I KNOW IT'S A LOT TO HANDLE.
...BUT GIVE ME A CHANCE TO PROVE IT TO YOU, BETH.

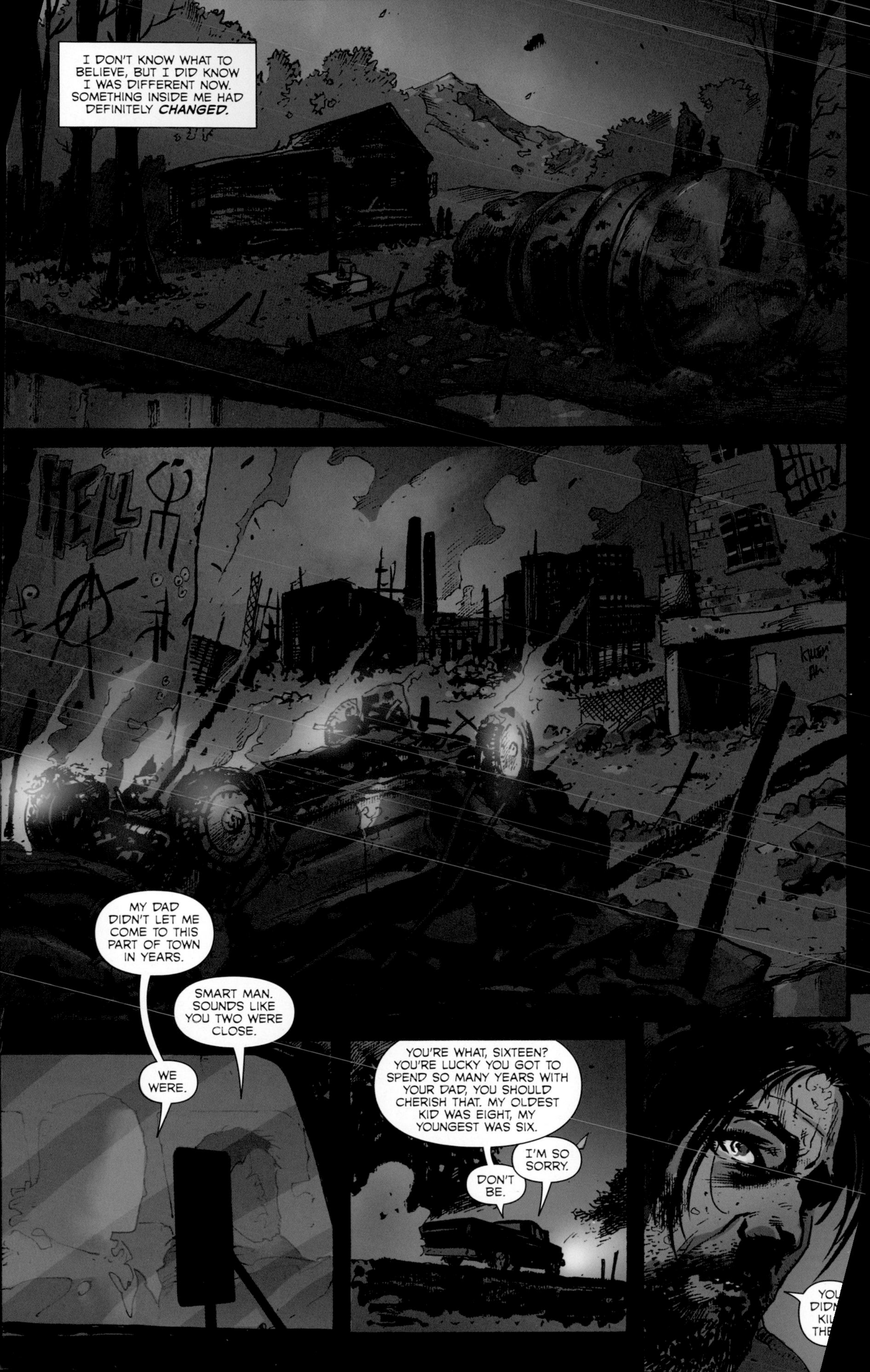

I DON'T KNOW WHAT TO BELIEVE, BUT I DID KNOW I WAS DIFFERENT NOW. SOMETHING INSIDE ME HAD DEFINITELY *CHANGED.*
HELL
MY DAD DIDN'T LET ME COME TO THIS PART OF TOWN IN YEARS.
SMART MAN. SOUNDS LIKE YOU TWO WERE CLOSE.
WE WERE.
YOU'RE WHAT, SIXTEEN? YOU'RE LUCKY YOU GOT TO SPEND SO MANY YEARS WITH YOUR DAD, YOU SHOULD CHERISH THAT. MY OLDEST KID WAS EIGHT, MY YOUNGEST WAS SIX.
I'M SO SORRY.
DON'T BE.

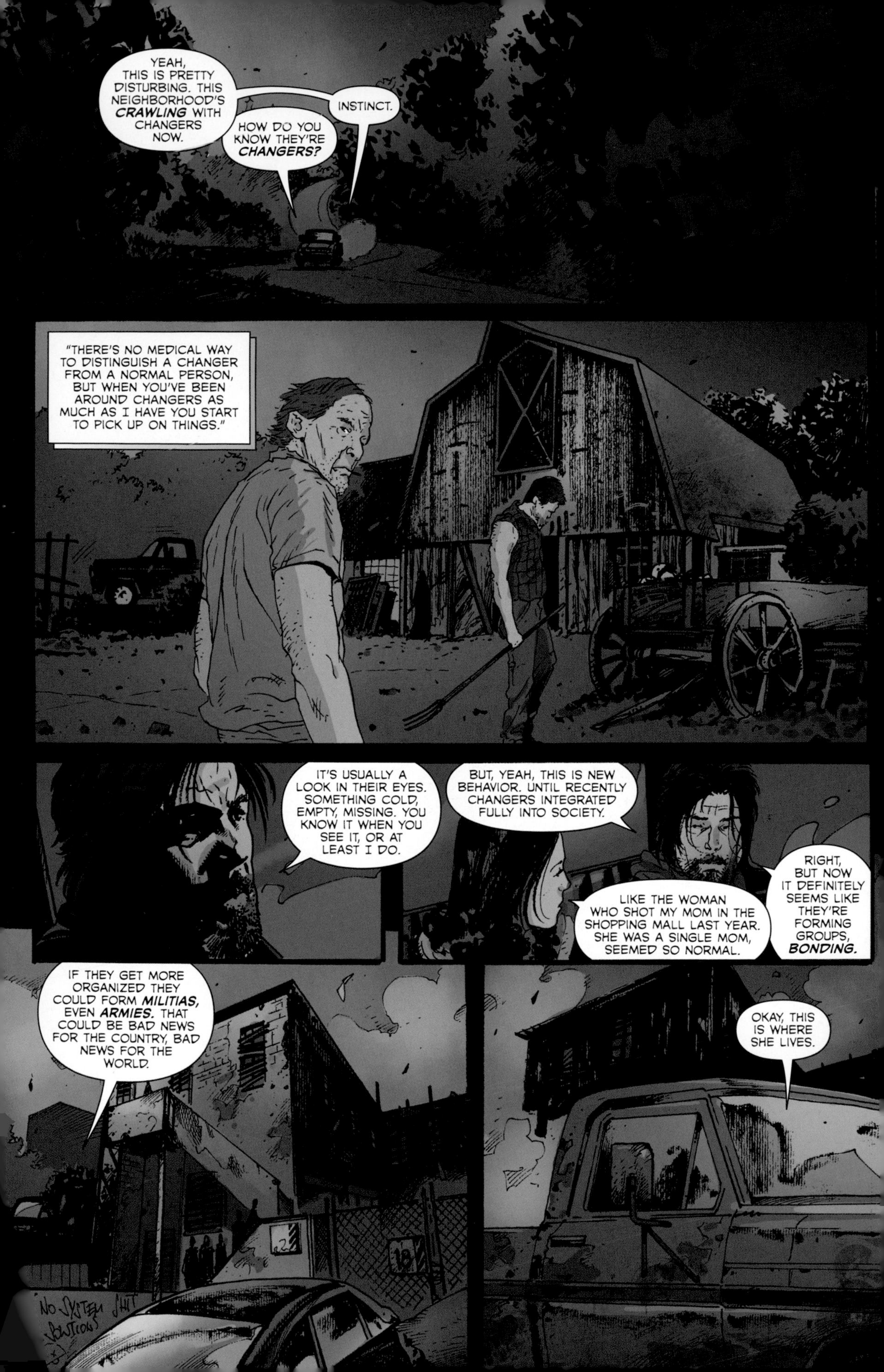
YEAH, THIS IS PRETTY DISTURBING. THIS NEIGHBORHOOD'S CRAWLING WITH CHANGERS NOW.
HOW DO YOU KNOW THEY'RE CHANGERS?
INSTINCT.
"THERE'S NO MEDICAL WAY TO DISTINGUISH A CHANGER FROM A NORMAL PERSON, BUT WHEN YOU'VE BEEN AROUND CHANGERS AS MUCH AS I HAVE YOU START TO PICK UP ON THINGS."
IT'S USUALLY A LOOK IN THEIR EYES. SOMETHING COLD, EMPTY, MISSING. YOU KNOW IT WHEN YOU SEE IT, OR AT LEAST I DO.
BUT, YEAH, THIS IS NEW BEHAVIOR. UNTIL RECENTLY CHANGERS INTEGRATED FULLY INTO SOCIETY.
LIKE THE WOMAN WHO SHOT MY MOM IN THE SHOPPING MALL LAST YEAR. SHE WAS A SINGLE MOM, SEEMED SO NORMAL.
RIGHT, BUT NOW IT DEFINITELY SEEMS LIKE THEY'RE FORMING GROUPS, BONDING.
IF THEY GET MORE ORGANIZED THEY COULD FORM MILITIAS, EVEN ARMIES. THAT COULD BE BAD NEWS FOR THE COUNTRY, BAD NEWS FOR THE WORLD.
OKAY, THIS IS WHERE SHE LIVES.

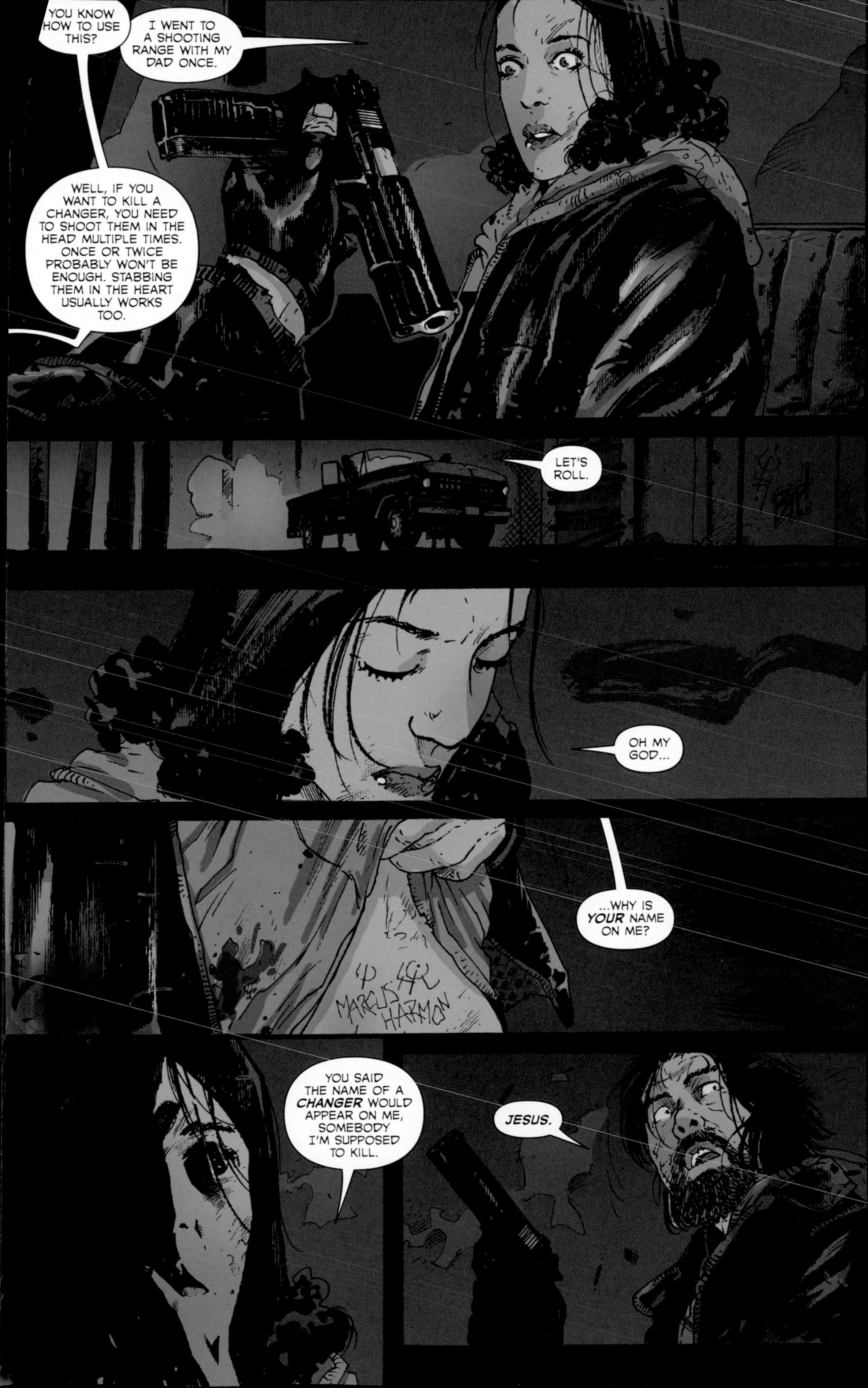
YOU KNOW HOW TO USE THIS?
I WENT TO A SHOOTING RANGE WITH MY DAD ONCE.
WELL, IF YOU WANT TO KILL A CHANGER, YOU NEED TO SHOOT THEM IN THE HEAD MULTIPLE TIMES. ONCE OR TWICE PROBABLY WON'T BE ENOUGH. STABBING THEM IN THE HEART USUALLY WORKS TOO.
LET'S ROLL.
OH MY GOD...
...WHY IS *YOUR* NAME ON ME?
MARCUS HARMON
YOU SAID THE NAME OF A *CHANGER* WOULD APPEAR ON ME, SOMEBODY I'M SUPPOSED TO KILL.
JESUS.

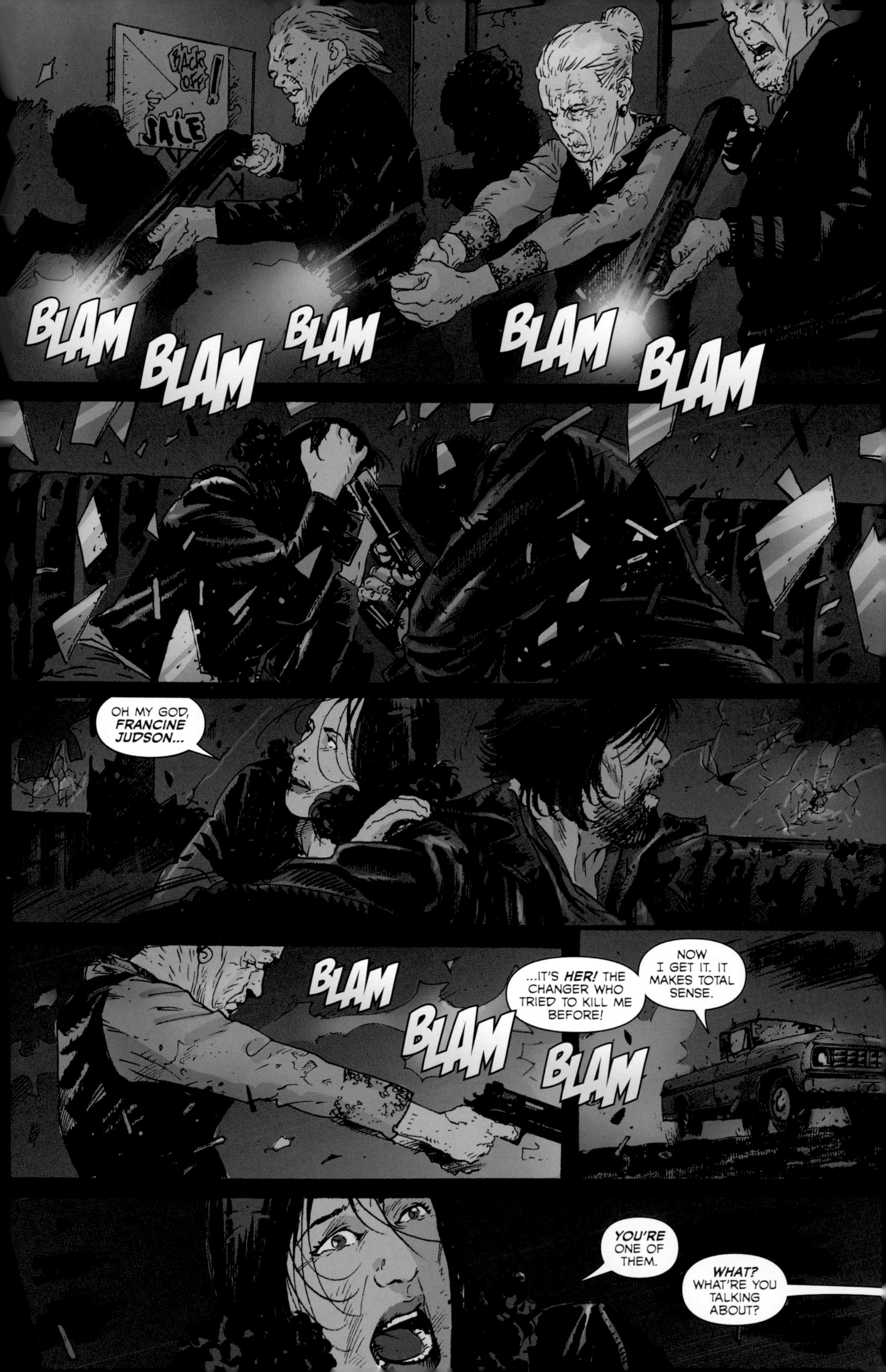
BACK OFF!
SALE
BLAM
BLAM
BLAM
BLAM
BLAM
OH MY GOD, FRANCINE JUDSON...
BLAM
BLAM
BLAM
...IT'S HER! THE CHANGER WHO TRIED TO KILL ME BEFORE!
NOW I GET IT. IT MAKES TOTAL SENSE.
YOU'RE ONE OF THEM.
WHAT? WHAT'RE YOU TALKING ABOUT?

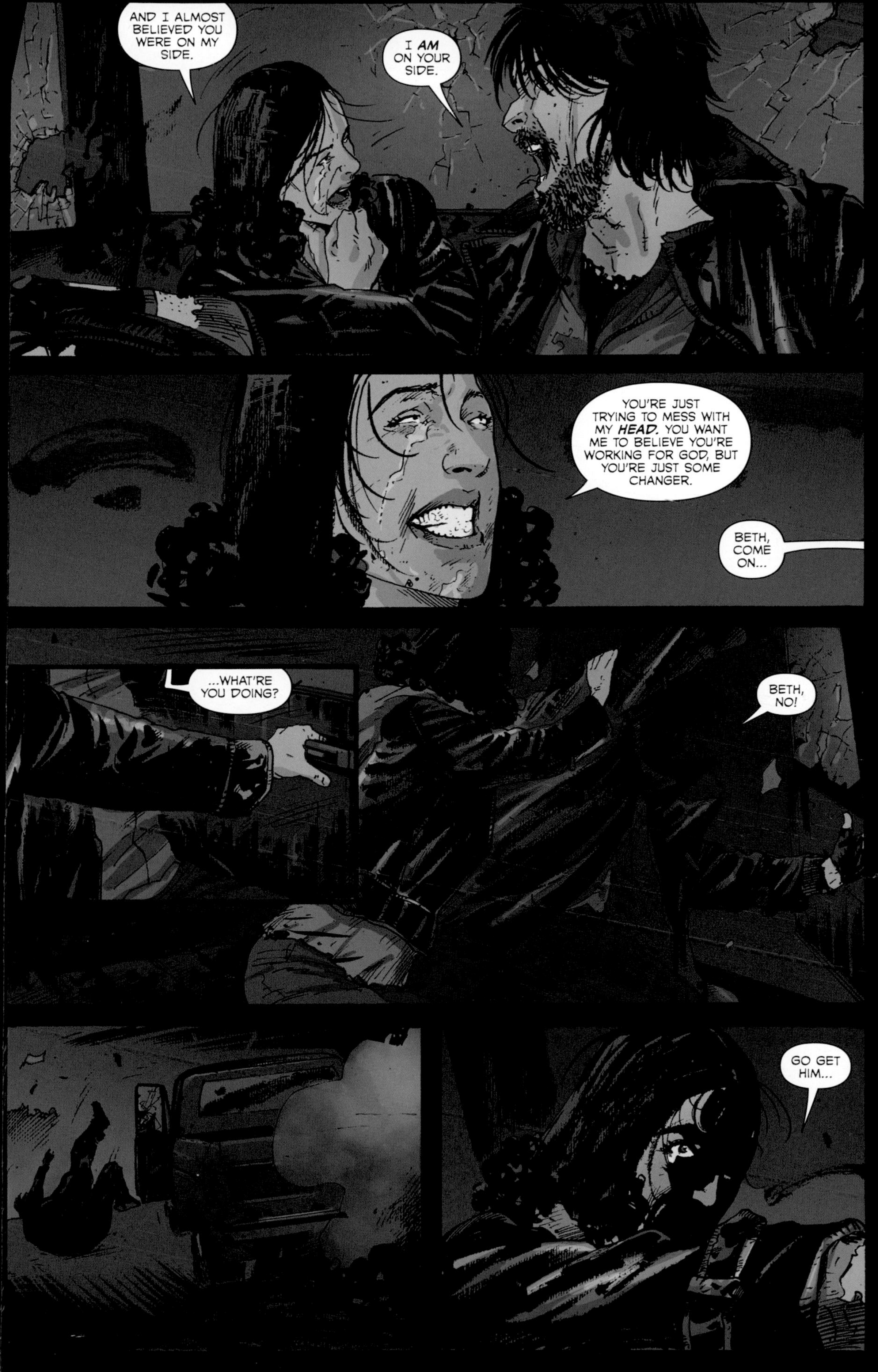
AND I ALMOST BELIEVED YOU WERE ON MY SIDE.
I AM ON YOUR SIDE.
YOU'RE JUST TRYING TO MESS WITH MY HEAD. YOU WANT ME TO BELIEVE YOU'RE WORKING FOR GOD, BUT YOU'RE JUST SOME CHANGER.
BETH, COME ON...
...WHAT'RE YOU DOING?
BETH, NO!
GO GET HIM...

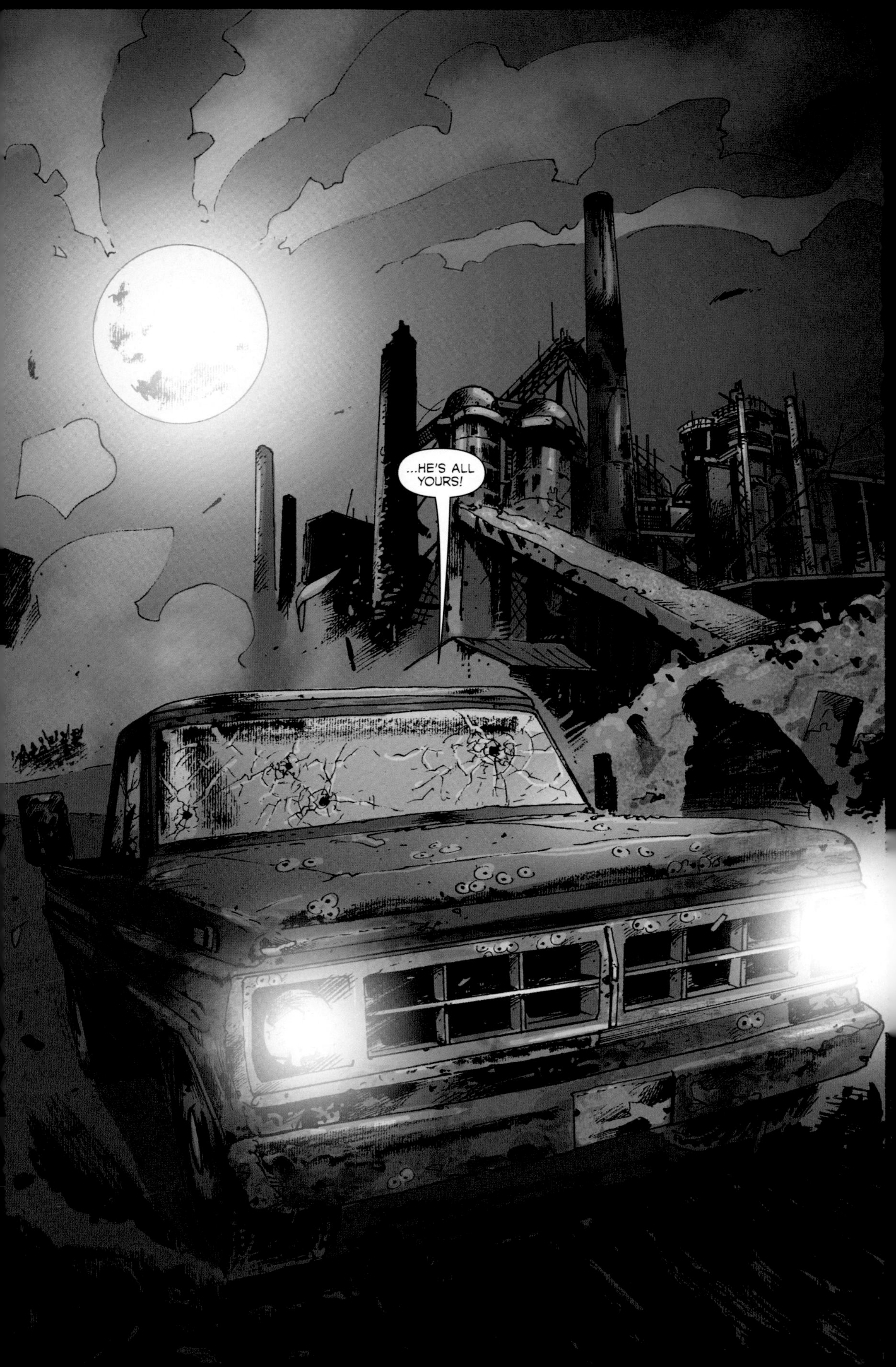
...HE'S ALL YOURS!

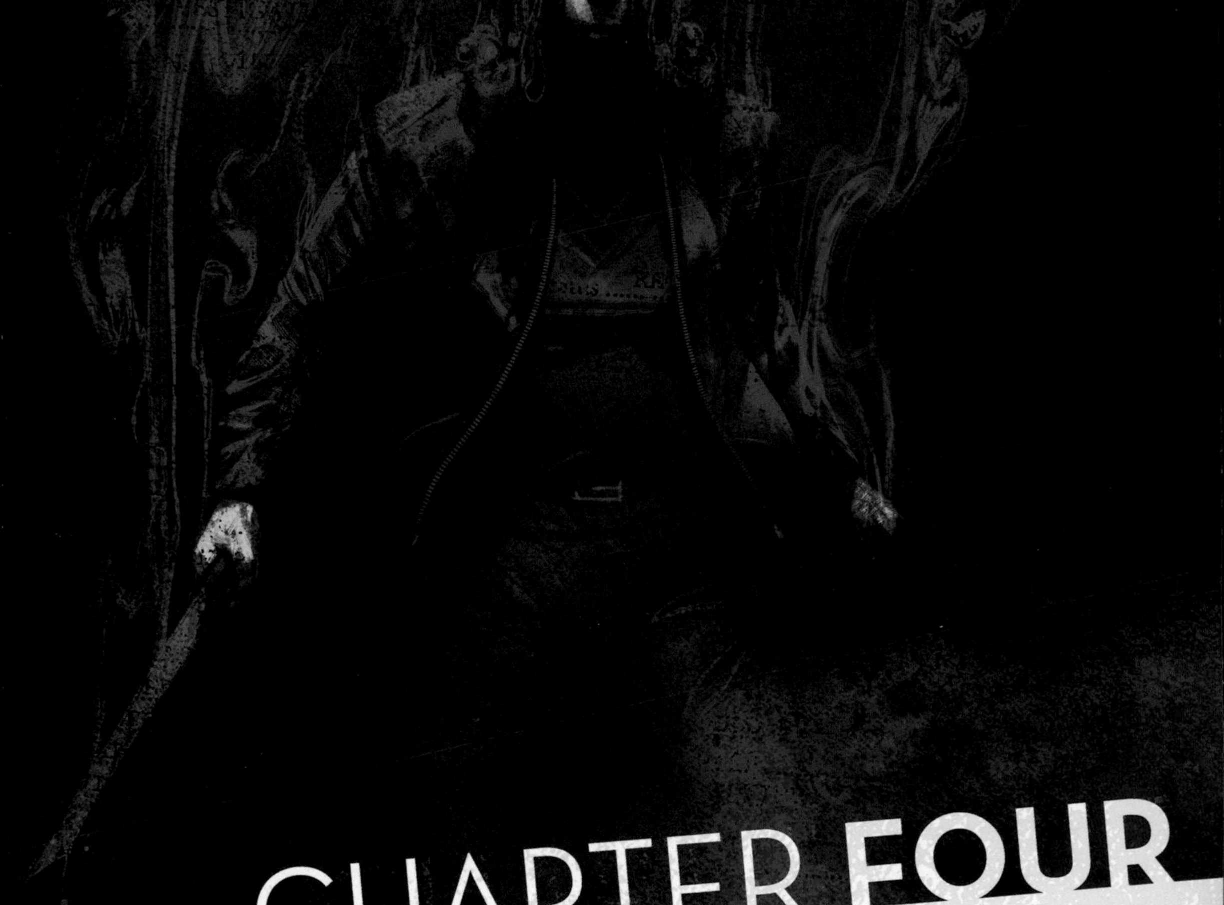

CHAPTER FOUR

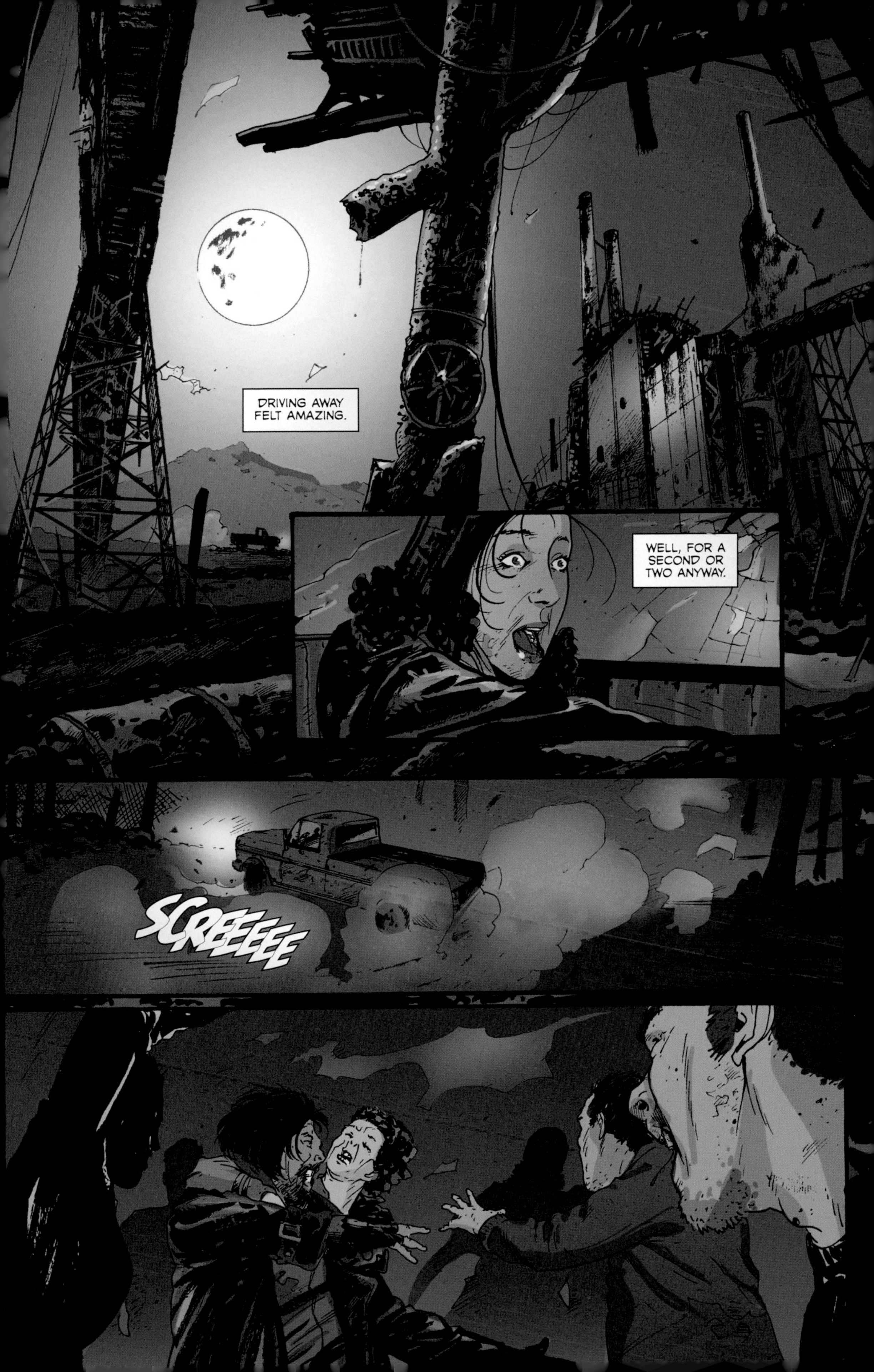
DRIVING AWAY FELT AMAZING.
WELL, FOR A SECOND OR TWO ANYWAY.
SCREEEEEE

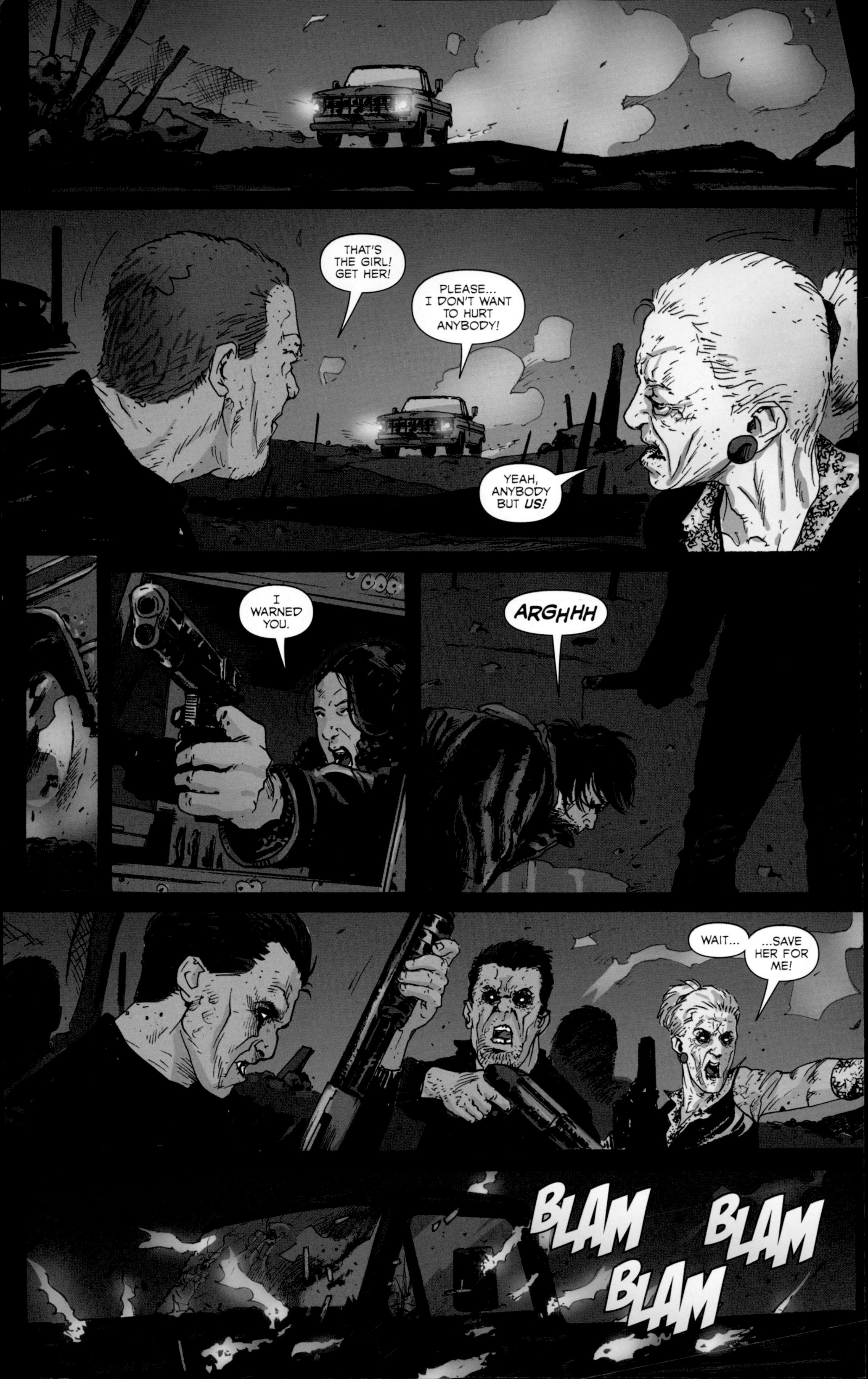

THAT'S THE GIRL! GET HER!
PLEASE... I DON'T WANT TO HURT ANYBODY!
YEAH, ANYBODY BUT US!
I WARNED YOU.
ARGHHH
WAIT...
...SAVE HER FOR ME!
BLAM BLAM BLAM

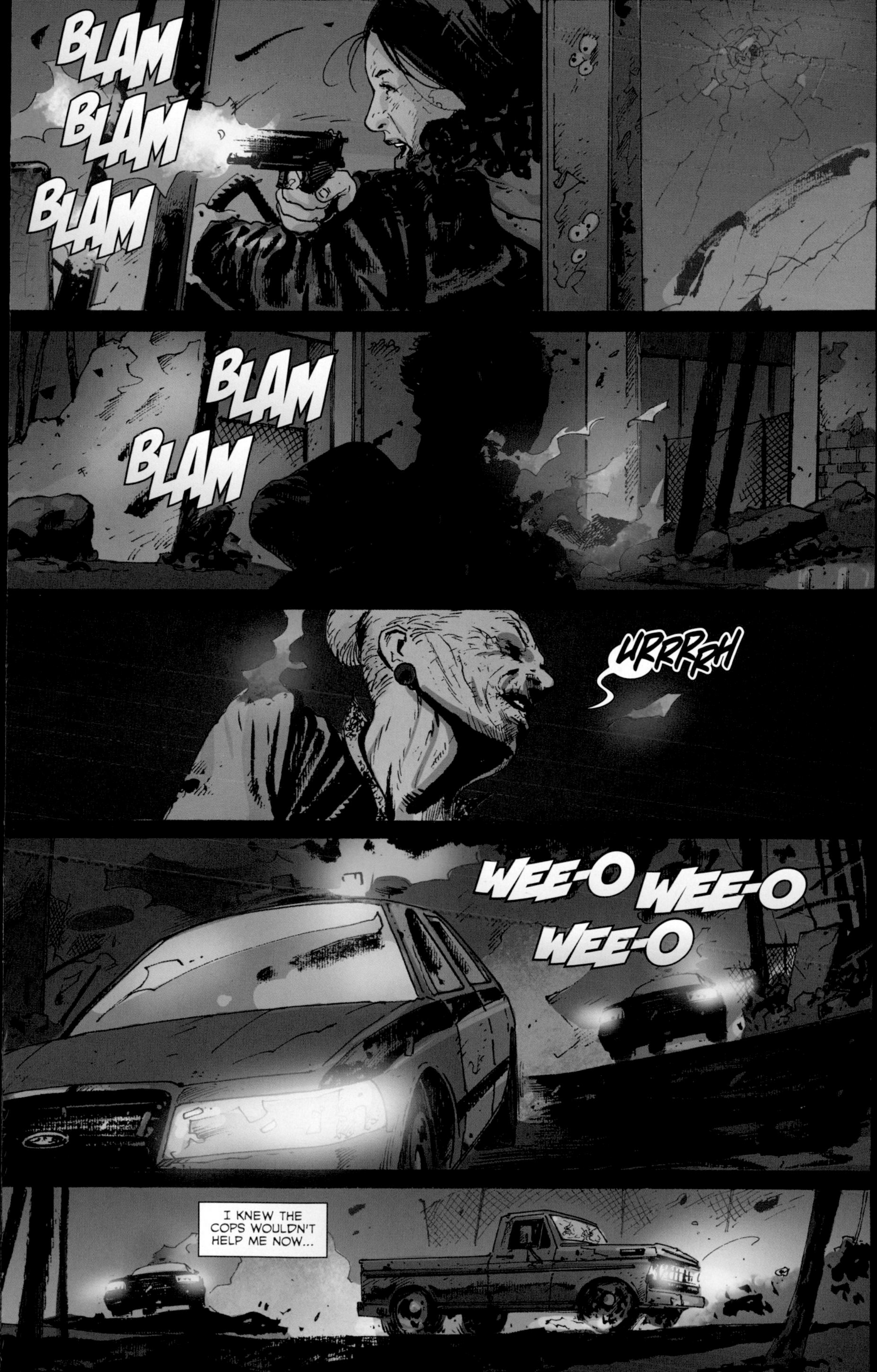
BLAM
BLAM
BLAM
BLAM
BLAM
URRRRH
WEE-O WEE-O
WEE-O
I KNEW THE COPS WOULDN'T HELP ME NOW...

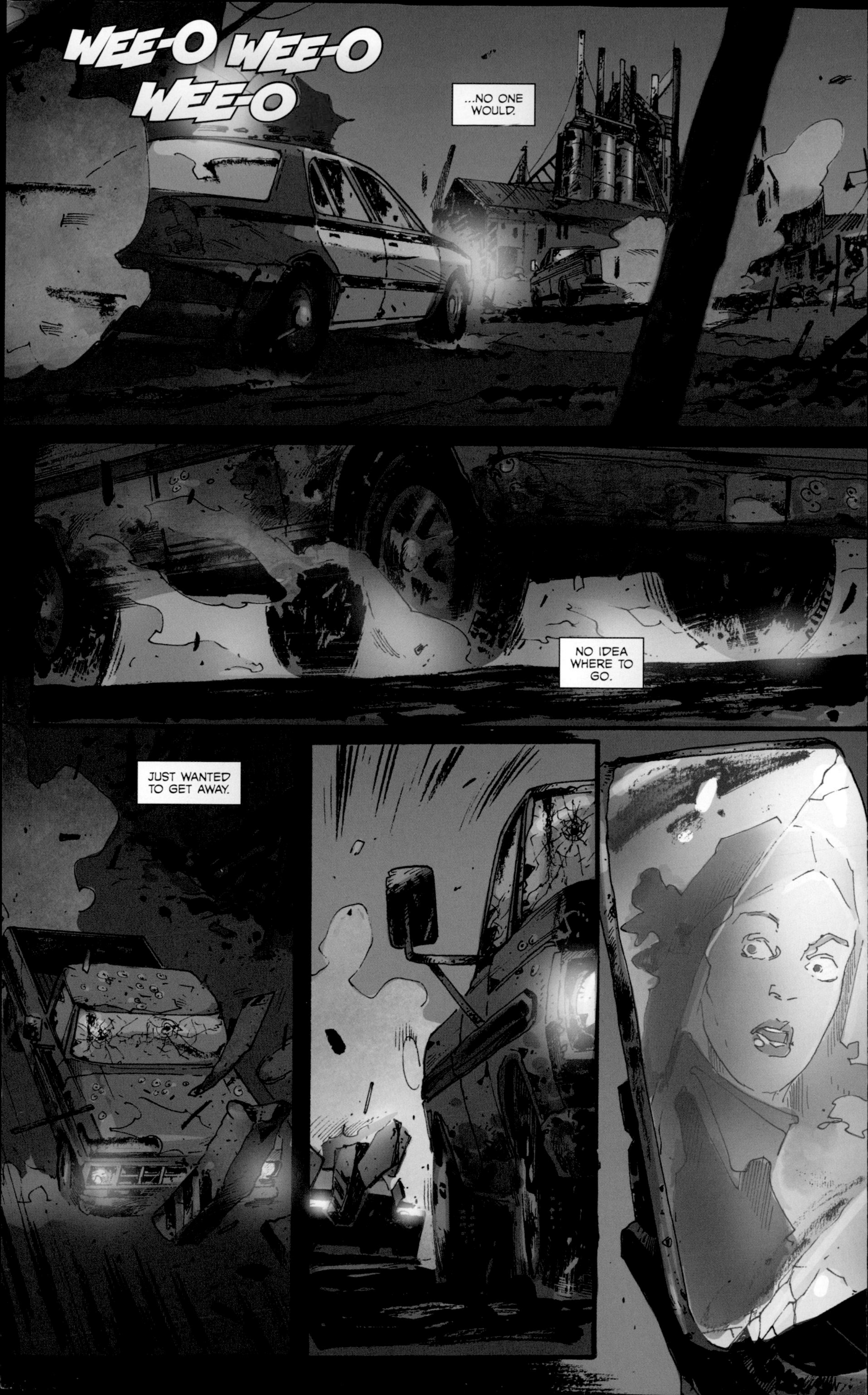
WEE-O WEE-O WEE-O
...NO ONE WOULD.
NO IDEA WHERE TO GO.
JUST WANTED TO GET AWAY.

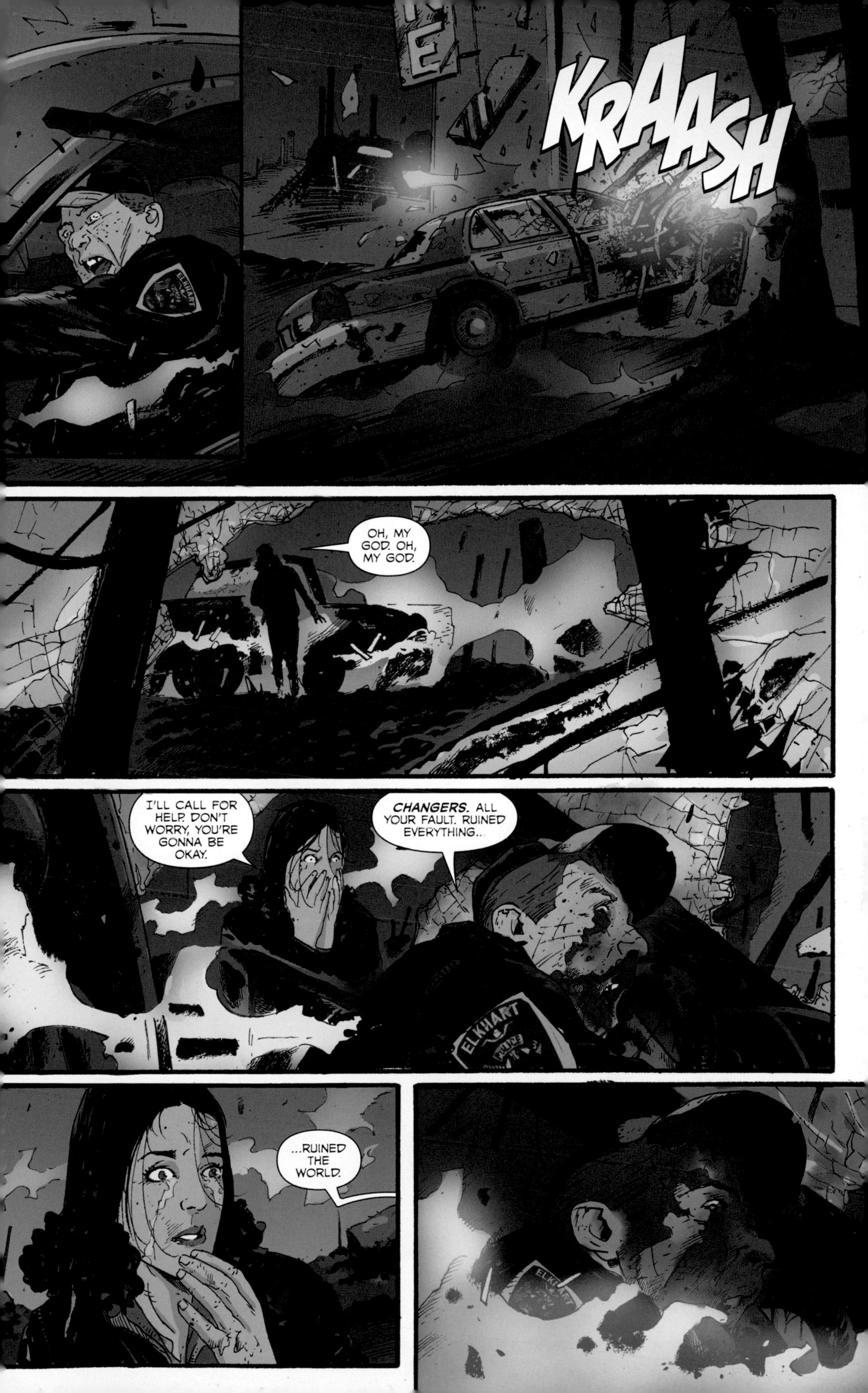
KRAAASH
OH, MY GOD. OH, MY GOD.
I'LL CALL FOR HELP. DON'T WORRY, YOU'RE GONNA BE OKAY.
CHANGERS. ALL YOUR FAULT. RUINED EVERYTHING...
...RUINED THE WORLD.

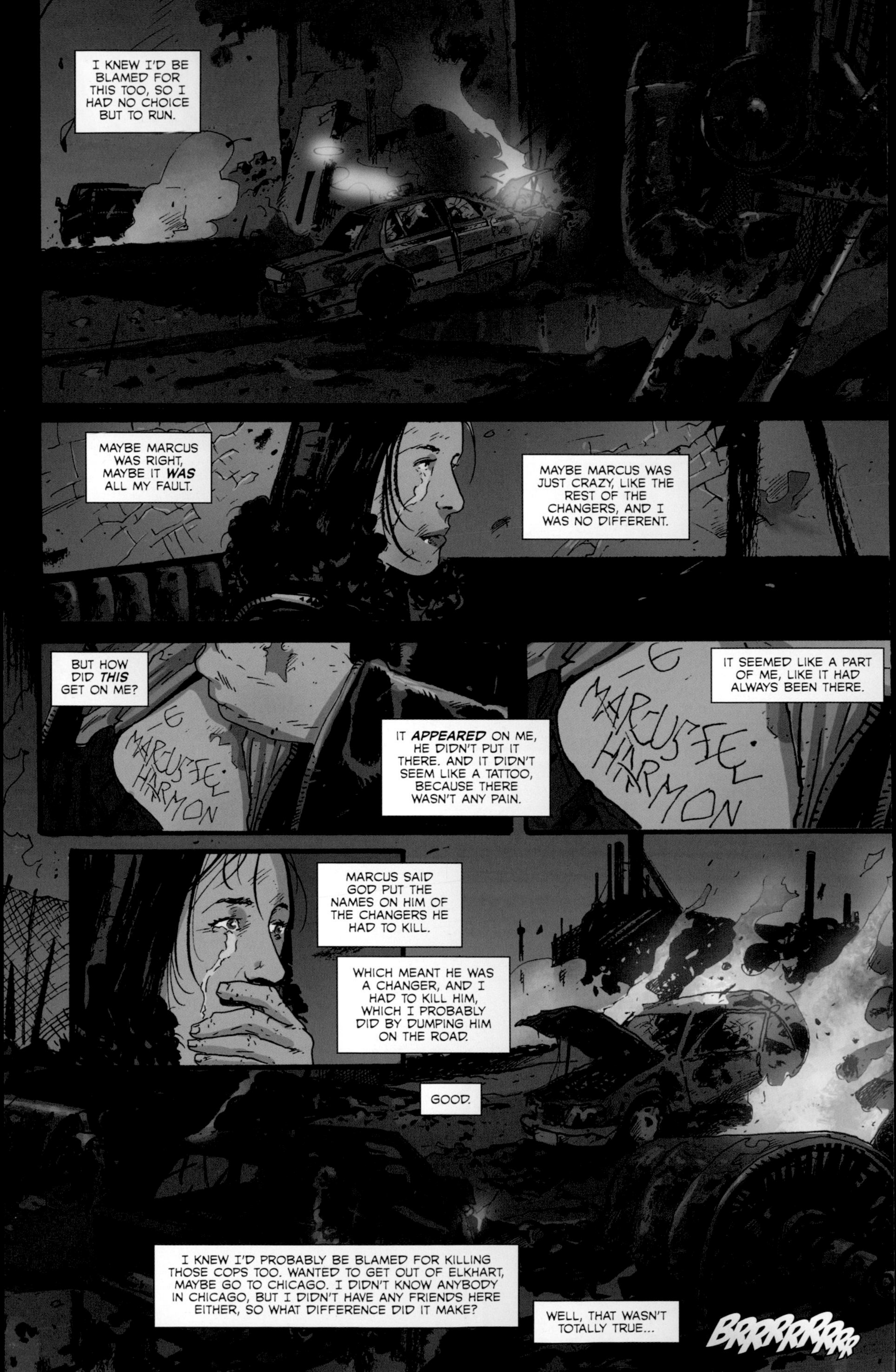
I KNEW I'D BE BLAMED FOR THIS TOO, SO I HAD NO CHOICE BUT TO RUN.
MAYBE MARCUS WAS RIGHT, MAYBE IT **WAS** ALL MY FAULT.
MAYBE MARCUS WAS JUST CRAZY, LIKE THE REST OF THE CHANGERS, AND I WAS NO DIFFERENT.
BUT HOW DID **THIS** GET ON ME?
MARCUS HARMON
IT **APPEARED** ON ME, HE DIDN'T PUT IT THERE. AND IT DIDN'T SEEM LIKE A TATTOO, BECAUSE THERE WASN'T ANY PAIN.
IT SEEMED LIKE A PART OF ME, LIKE IT HAD ALWAYS BEEN THERE.
MARCUS HARMON
MARCUS SAID GOD PUT THE NAMES ON HIM OF THE CHANGERS HE HAD TO KILL.
WHICH MEANT HE WAS A CHANGER, AND I HAD TO KILL HIM, WHICH I PROBABLY DID BY DUMPING HIM ON THE ROAD.
GOOD.
I KNEW I'D PROBABLY BE BLAMED FOR KILLING THOSE COPS TOO. WANTED TO GET OUT OF ELKHART, MAYBE GO TO CHICAGO. I DIDN'T KNOW ANYBODY IN CHICAGO, BUT I DIDN'T HAVE ANY FRIENDS HERE EITHER, SO WHAT DIFFERENCE DID IT MAKE?
WELL, THAT WASN'T TOTALLY TRUE...
BRRRRRRRR

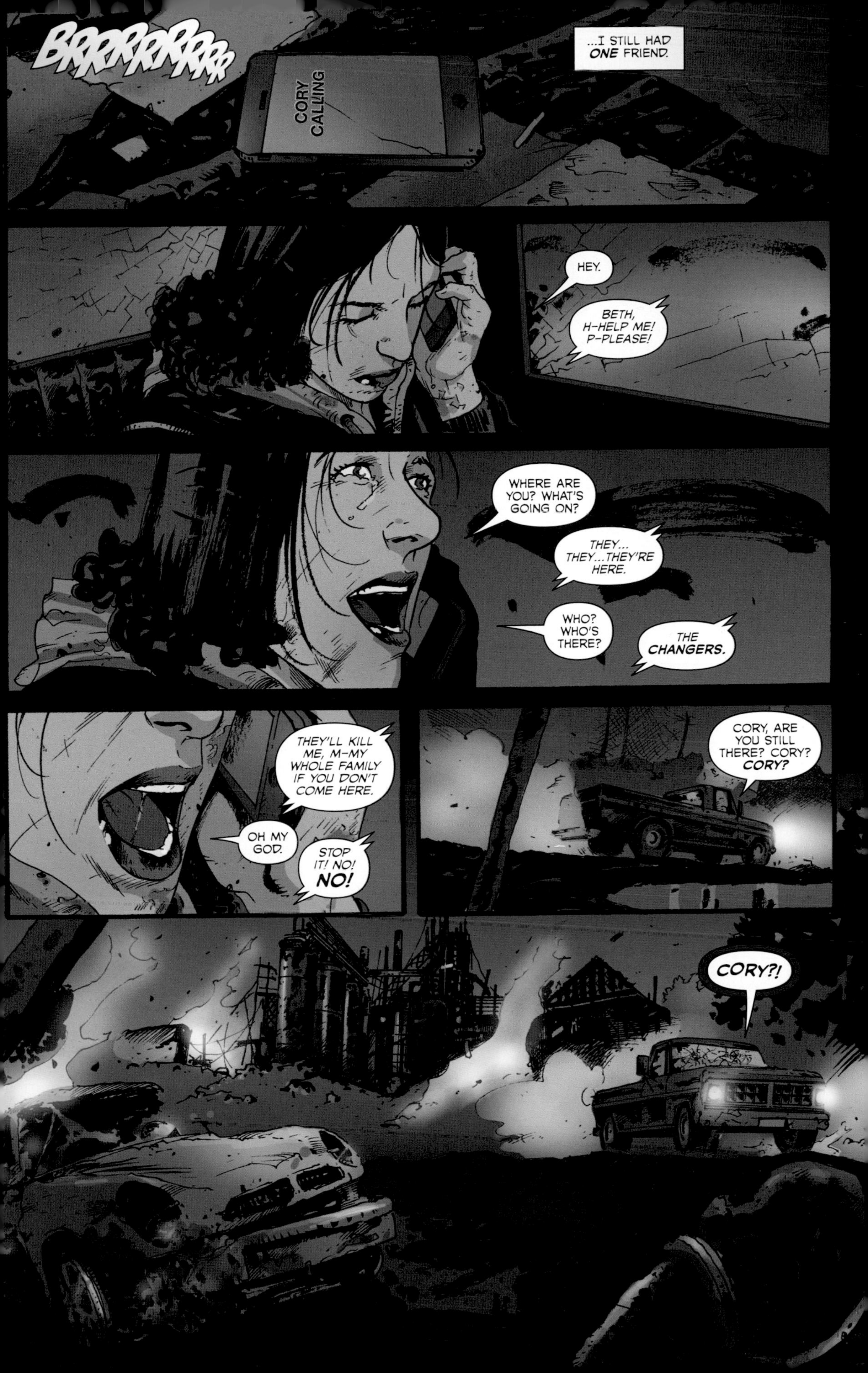
BRRRRRRRRR
CORY CALLING
...I STILL HAD ONE FRIEND.
HEY.
BETH, H-HELP ME! P-PLEASE!
WHERE ARE YOU? WHAT'S GOING ON?
THEY... THEY...THEY'RE HERE.
WHO? WHO'S THERE?
THE CHANGERS.
THEY'LL KILL ME, M-MY WHOLE FAMILY IF YOU DON'T COME HERE.
OH MY GOD.
STOP IT! NO! NO!
CORY, ARE YOU STILL THERE? CORY? CORY?
CORY?!

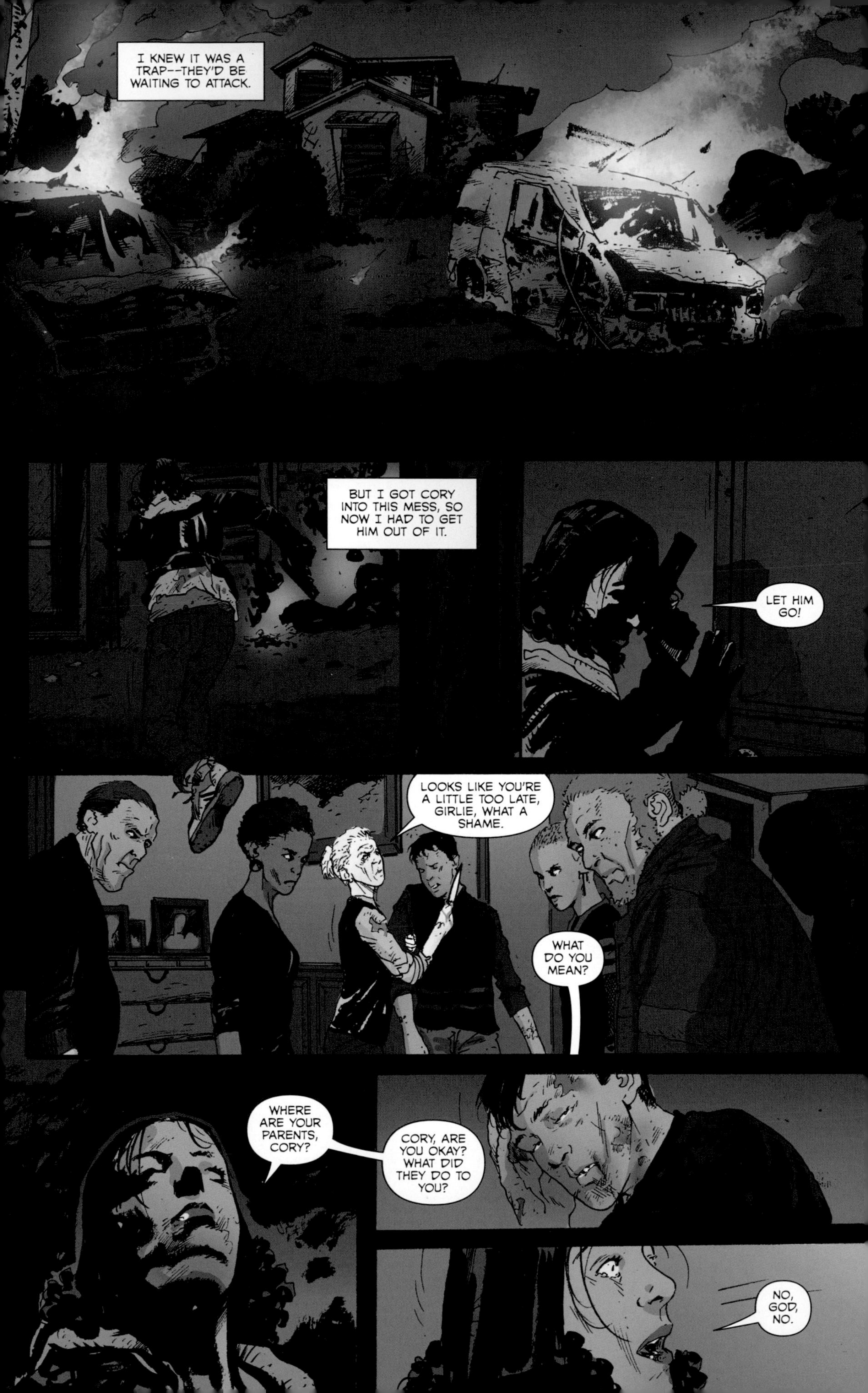
I KNEW IT WAS A TRAP--THEY'D BE WAITING TO ATTACK.
BUT I GOT CORY INTO THIS MESS, SO NOW I HAD TO GET HIM OUT OF IT.
LET HIM GO!
LOOKS LIKE YOU'RE A LITTLE TOO LATE, GIRLIE, WHAT A SHAME.
WHAT DO YOU MEAN?
CORY, ARE YOU OKAY? WHAT DID THEY DO TO YOU?
WHERE ARE YOUR PARENTS, CORY?
NO, GOD, NO.

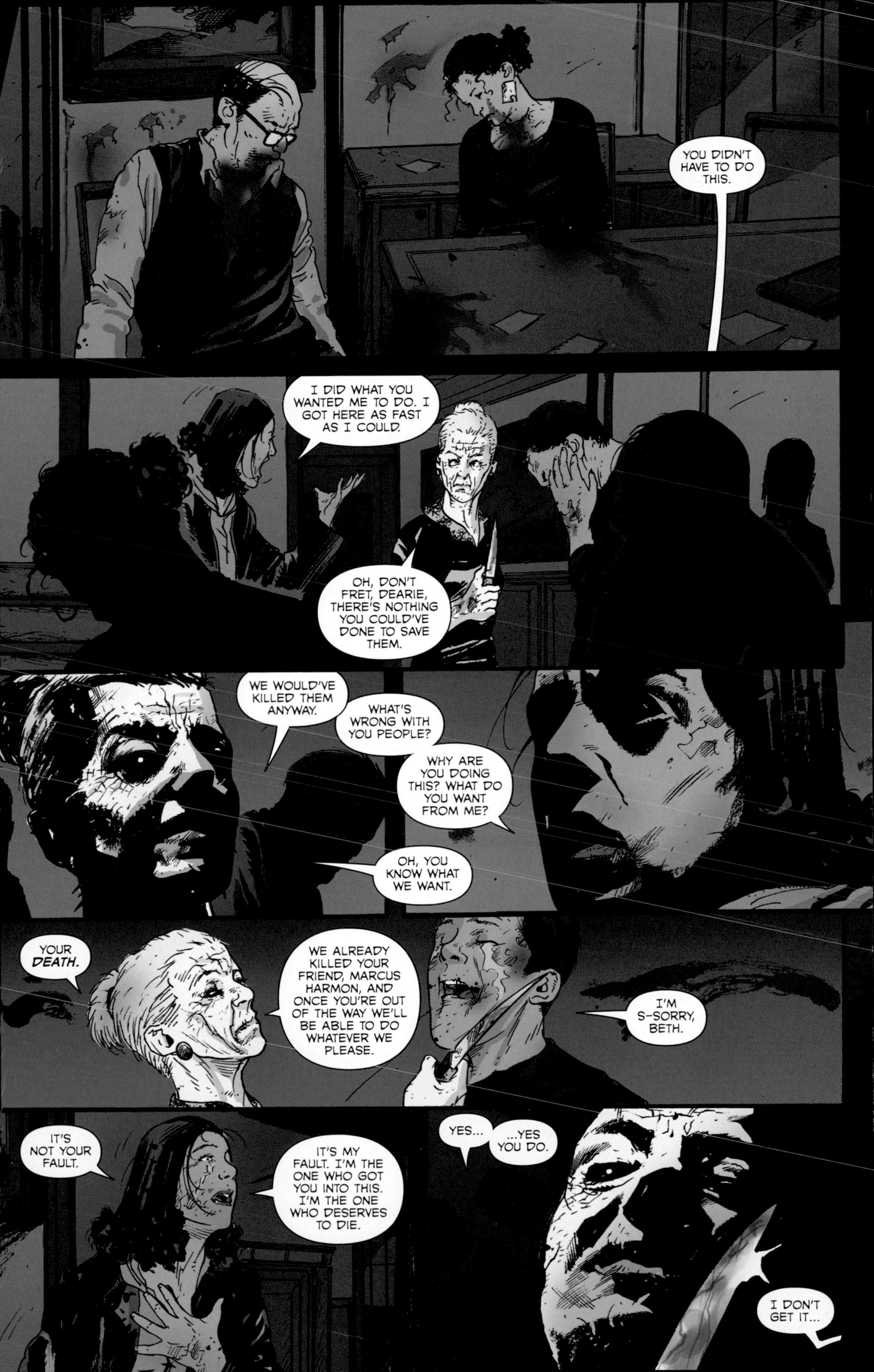
YOU DIDN'T HAVE TO DO THIS.
I DID WHAT YOU WANTED ME TO DO. I GOT HERE AS FAST AS I COULD.
OH, DON'T FRET, DEARIE, THERE'S NOTHING YOU COULD'VE DONE TO SAVE THEM.
WE WOULD'VE KILLED THEM ANYWAY.
WHAT'S WRONG WITH YOU PEOPLE?
WHY ARE YOU DOING THIS? WHAT DO YOU WANT FROM ME?
OH, YOU KNOW WHAT WE WANT.
YOUR *DEATH.*
WE ALREADY KILLED YOUR FRIEND, MARCUS HARMON, AND ONCE YOU'RE OUT OF THE WAY WE'LL BE ABLE TO DO WHATEVER WE PLEASE.
I'M S-SORRY, BETH.
IT'S NOT YOUR FAULT.
IT'S MY FAULT. I'M THE ONE WHO GOT YOU INTO THIS. I'M THE ONE WHO DESERVES TO DIE.
YES...
...YES YOU DO.
I DON'T GET IT...

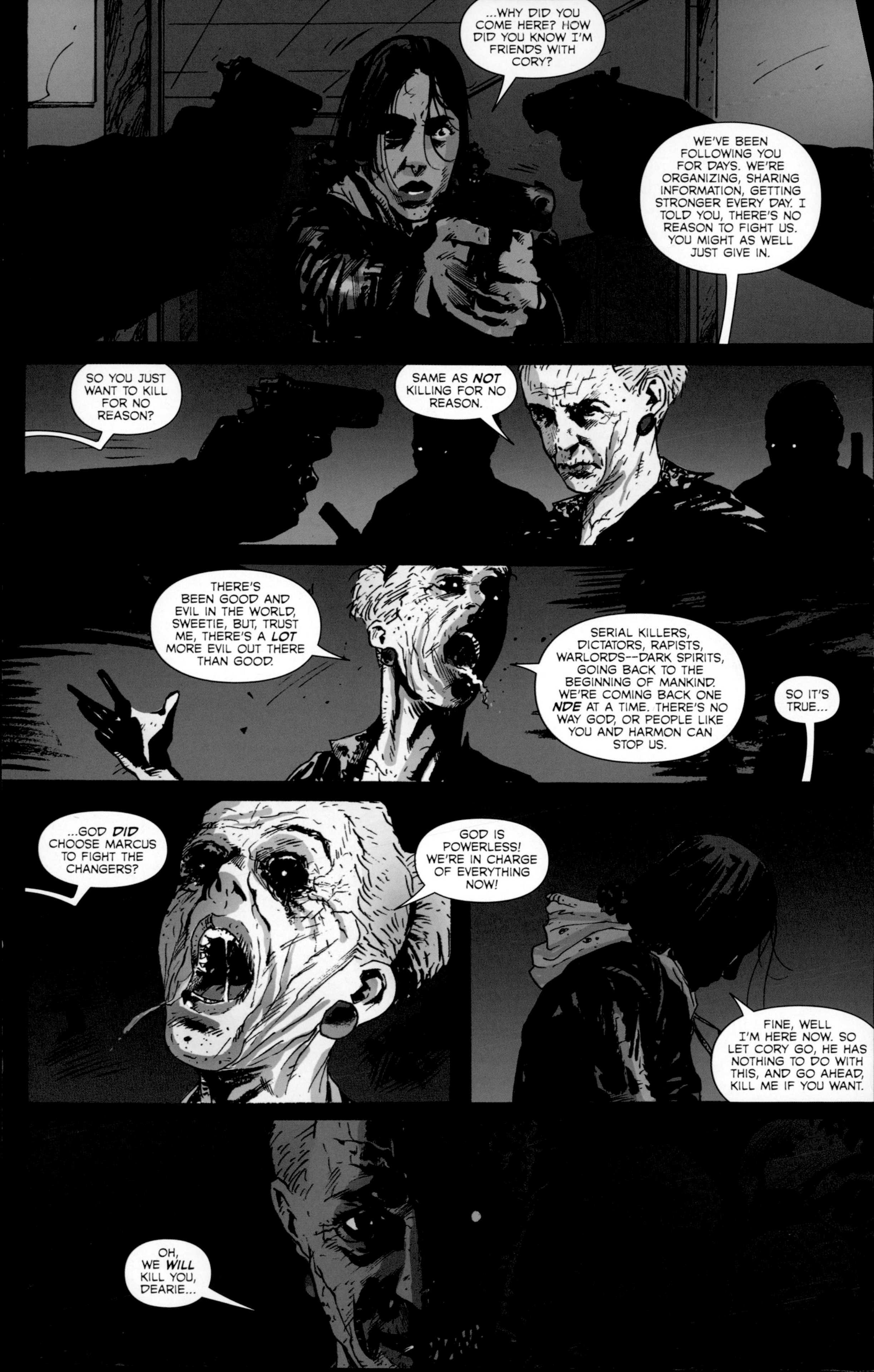
...WHY DID YOU COME HERE? HOW DID YOU KNOW I'M FRIENDS WITH CORY?
WE'VE BEEN FOLLOWING YOU FOR DAYS. WE'RE ORGANIZING, SHARING INFORMATION, GETTING STRONGER EVERY DAY. I TOLD YOU, THERE'S NO REASON TO FIGHT US. YOU MIGHT AS WELL JUST GIVE IN.
SO YOU JUST WANT TO KILL FOR NO REASON?
SAME AS *NOT* KILLING FOR NO REASON.
THERE'S BEEN GOOD AND EVIL IN THE WORLD, SWEETIE, BUT, TRUST ME, THERE'S A *LOT* MORE EVIL OUT THERE THAN GOOD.
SERIAL KILLERS, DICTATORS, RAPISTS, WARLORDS--DARK SPIRITS, GOING BACK TO THE BEGINNING OF MANKIND. WE'RE COMING BACK ONE *NDE* AT A TIME. THERE'S NO WAY GOD, OR PEOPLE LIKE YOU AND HARMON CAN STOP US.
SO IT'S TRUE...
...GOD *DID* CHOOSE MARCUS TO FIGHT THE CHANGERS?
GOD IS POWERLESS! WE'RE IN CHARGE OF EVERYTHING NOW!
FINE, WELL I'M HERE NOW. SO LET CORY GO, HE HAS NOTHING TO DO WITH THIS, AND GO AHEAD, KILL ME IF YOU WANT.
OH, WE *WILL* KILL YOU, DEARIE...

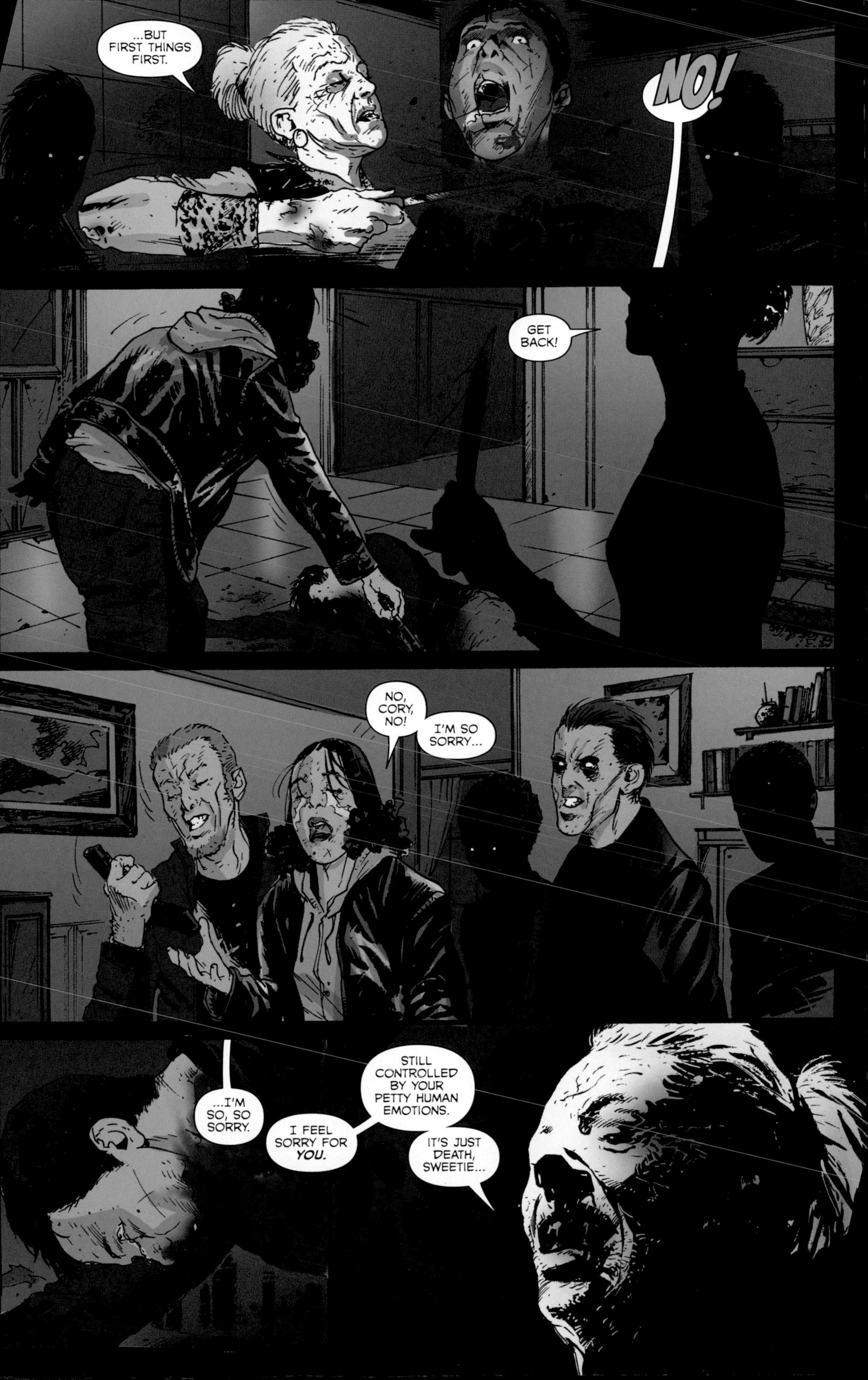

...BUT FIRST THINGS FIRST.
NO!
GET BACK!
NO, CORY, NO!
I'M SO SORRY...
...I'M SO, SO SORRY.
I FEEL SORRY FOR *YOU.*
STILL CONTROLLED BY YOUR PETTY HUMAN EMOTIONS.
IT'S JUST DEATH, SWEETIE...

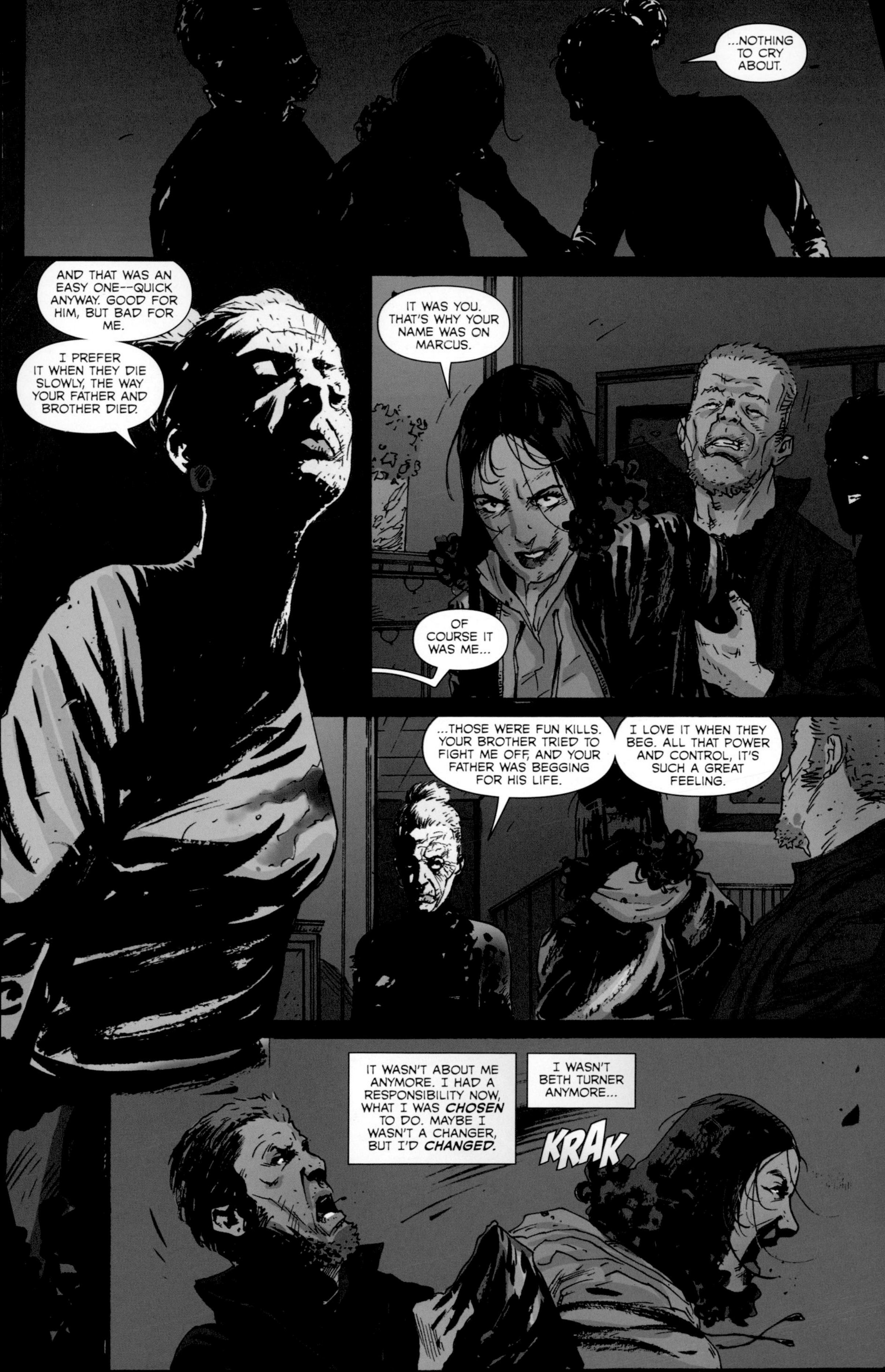
...NOTHING TO CRY ABOUT.
AND THAT WAS AN EASY ONE--QUICK ANYWAY. GOOD FOR HIM, BUT BAD FOR ME.
I PREFER IT WHEN THEY DIE SLOWLY, THE WAY YOUR FATHER AND BROTHER DIED.
IT WAS YOU. THAT'S WHY YOUR NAME WAS ON MARCUS.
OF COURSE IT WAS ME...
...THOSE WERE FUN KILLS. YOUR BROTHER TRIED TO FIGHT ME OFF, AND YOUR FATHER WAS BEGGING FOR HIS LIFE.
I LOVE IT WHEN THEY BEG. ALL THAT POWER AND CONTROL, IT'S SUCH A GREAT FEELING.
IT WASN'T ABOUT ME ANYMORE. I HAD A RESPONSIBILITY NOW, WHAT I WAS ***CHOSEN*** TO DO. MAYBE I WASN'T A CHANGER, BUT I'D ***CHANGED.***
I WASN'T BETH TURNER ANYMORE...
KRAK

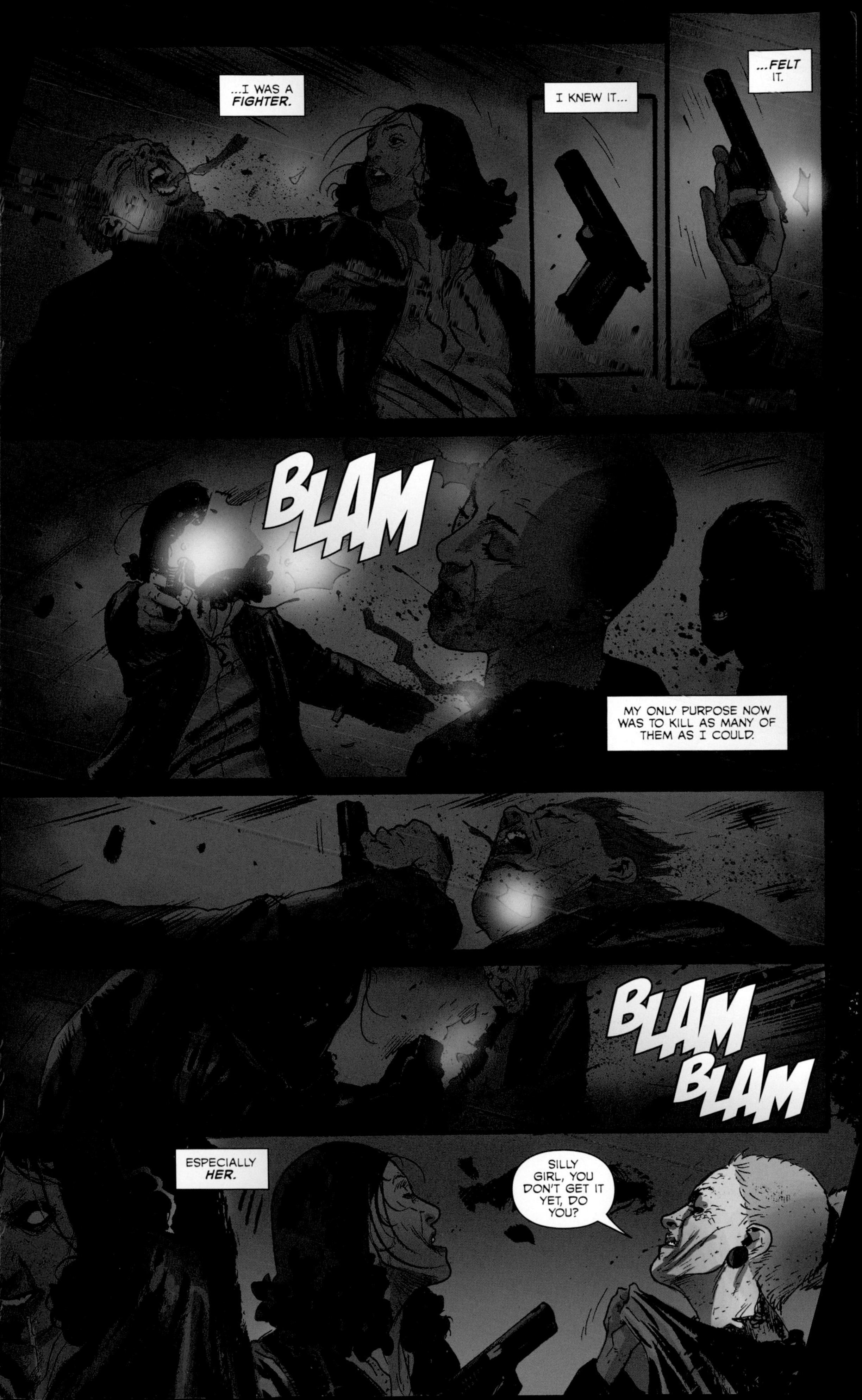
...I WAS A *FIGHTER.*
I KNEW IT...
...*FELT* IT.
BLAM
MY ONLY PURPOSE NOW WAS TO KILL AS MANY OF THEM AS I COULD.
BLAM BLAM
ESPECIALLY *HER.*
SILLY GIRL, YOU DON'T GET IT YET, DO YOU?

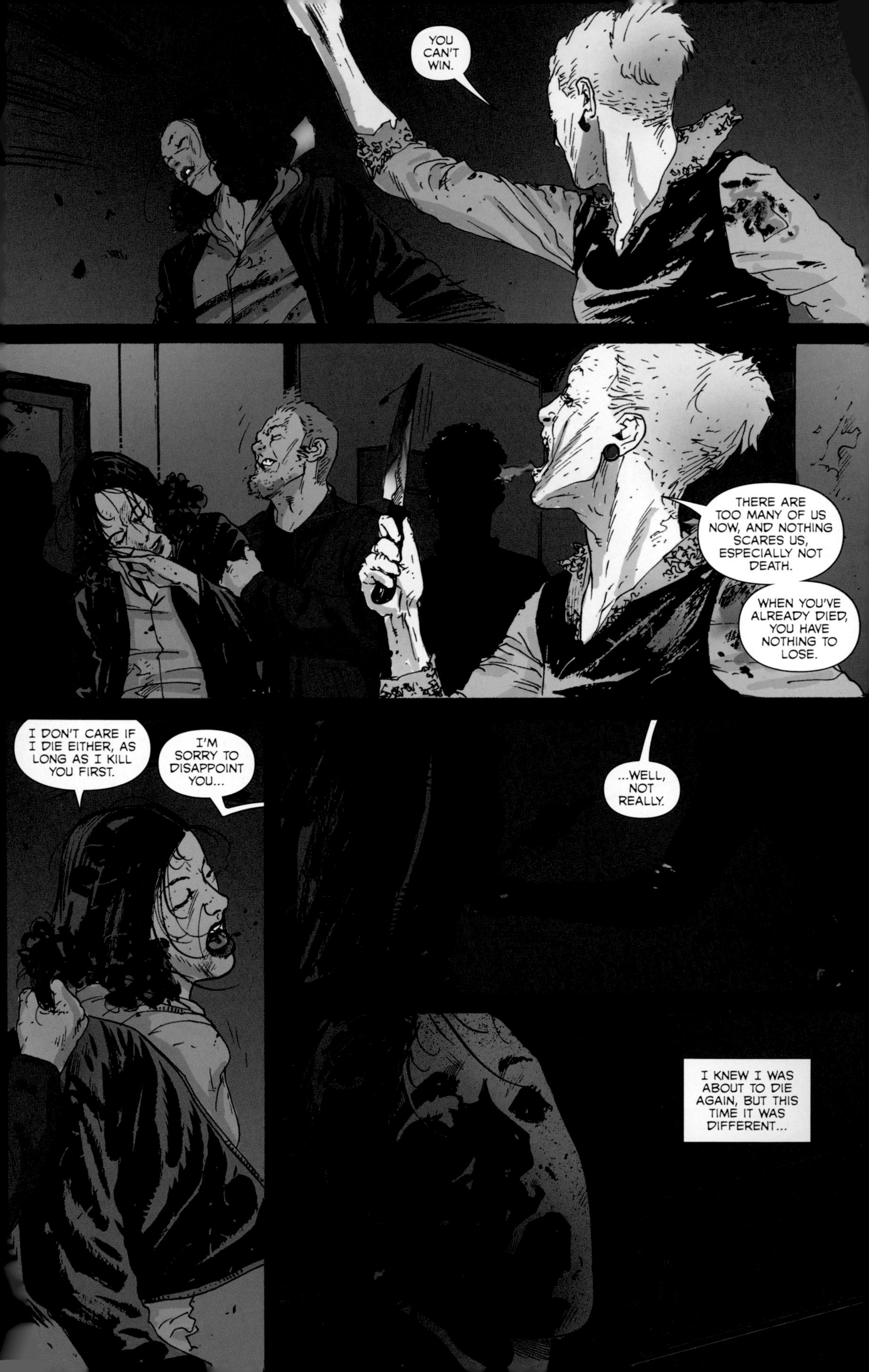
YOU CAN'T WIN.
THERE ARE TOO MANY OF US NOW, AND NOTHING SCARES US, ESPECIALLY NOT DEATH.
WHEN YOU'VE ALREADY DIED, YOU HAVE NOTHING TO LOSE.
I DON'T CARE IF I DIE EITHER, AS LONG AS I KILL YOU FIRST.
I'M SORRY TO DISAPPOINT YOU...
...WELL, NOT REALLY.
I KNEW I WAS ABOUT TO DIE AGAIN, BUT THIS TIME IT WAS DIFFERENT...

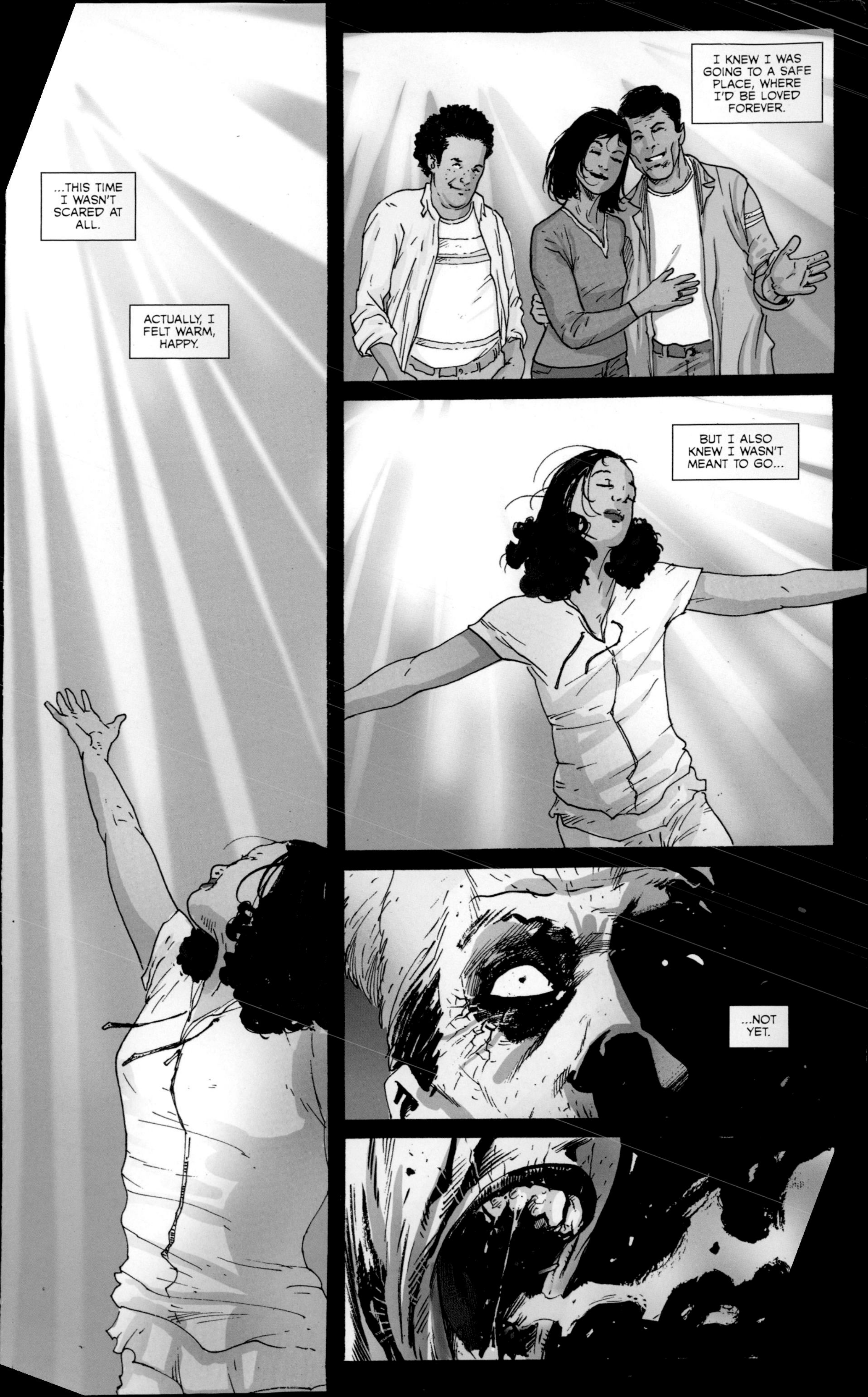
...THIS TIME I WASN'T SCARED AT ALL.
ACTUALLY, I FELT WARM, HAPPY.
I KNEW I WAS GOING TO A SAFE PLACE, WHERE I'D BE LOVED FOREVER.
BUT I ALSO KNEW I WASN'T MEANT TO GO...
...NOT YET.

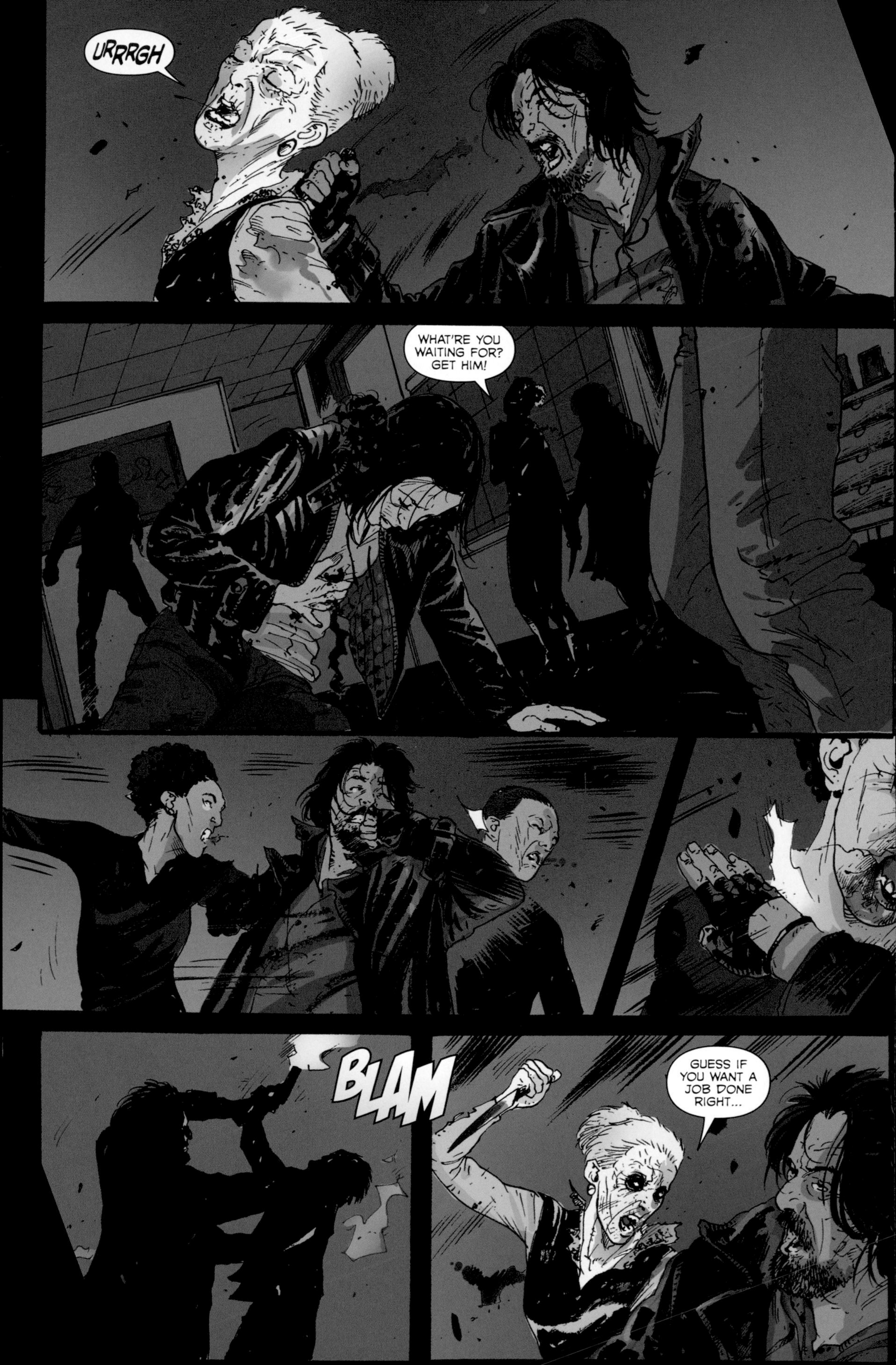

URRRGH
WHAT'RE YOU WAITING FOR? GET HIM!
BLAM
GUESS IF YOU WANT A JOB DONE RIGHT...

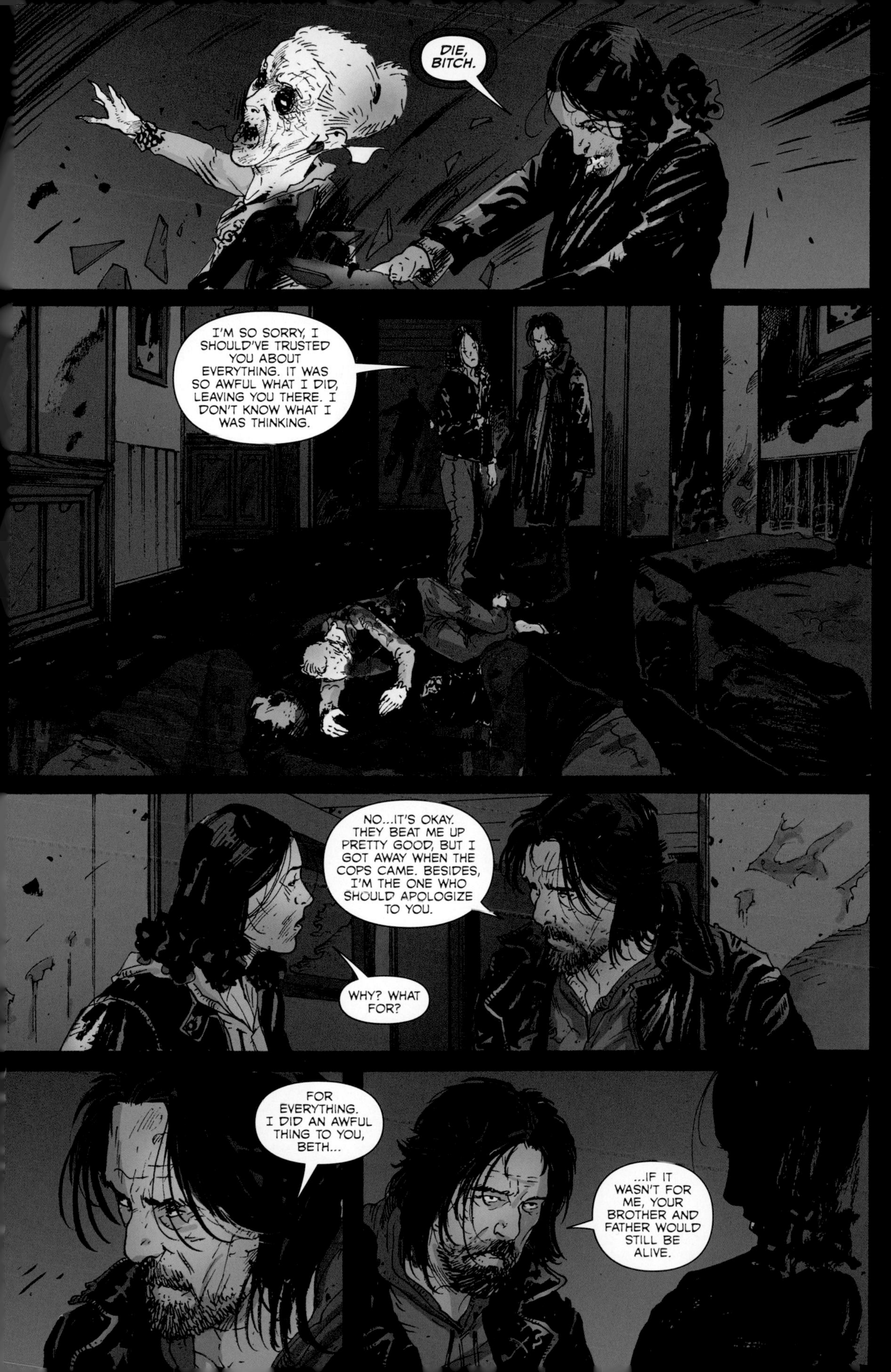
DIE, BITCH.
I'M SO SORRY, I SHOULD'VE TRUSTED YOU ABOUT EVERYTHING. IT WAS SO AWFUL WHAT I DID, LEAVING YOU THERE. I DON'T KNOW WHAT I WAS THINKING.
NO...IT'S OKAY. THEY BEAT ME UP PRETTY GOOD, BUT I GOT AWAY WHEN THE COPS CAME. BESIDES, I'M THE ONE WHO SHOULD APOLOGIZE TO YOU.
WHY? WHAT FOR?
FOR EVERYTHING. I DID AN AWFUL THING TO YOU, BETH...
...IF IT WASN'T FOR ME, YOUR BROTHER AND FATHER WOULD STILL BE ALIVE.

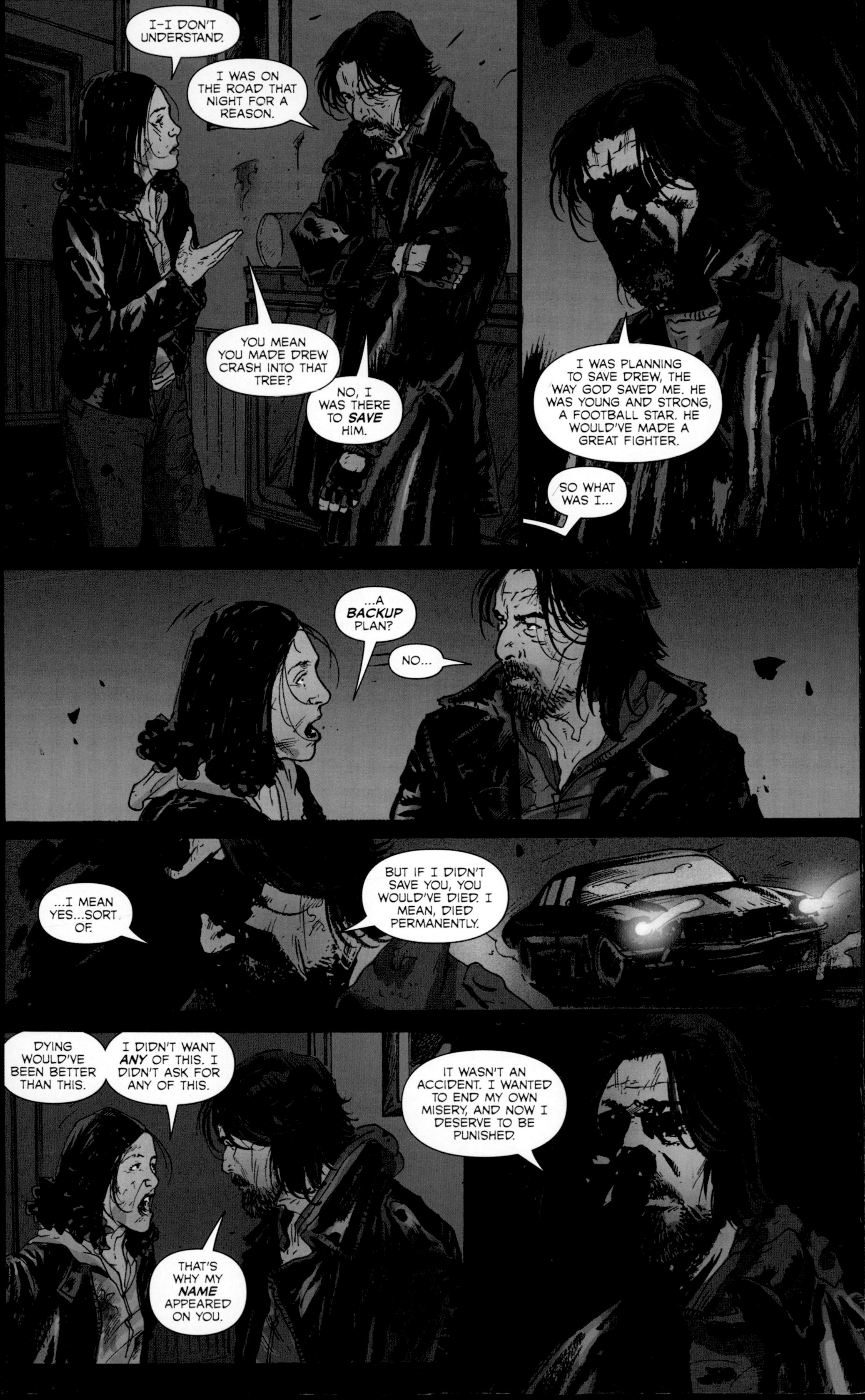
I-I DON'T UNDERSTAND.
I WAS ON THE ROAD THAT NIGHT FOR A REASON.
YOU MEAN YOU MADE DREW CRASH INTO THAT TREE?
NO, I WAS THERE TO *SAVE* HIM.
I WAS PLANNING TO SAVE DREW, THE WAY GOD SAVED ME. HE WAS YOUNG AND STRONG, A FOOTBALL STAR. HE WOULD'VE MADE A GREAT FIGHTER.
SO WHAT WAS I...
...A *BACKUP* PLAN?
NO...
...I MEAN YES...SORT OF.
BUT IF I DIDN'T SAVE YOU, YOU WOULD'VE DIED. I MEAN, DIED PERMANENTLY.
DYING WOULD'VE BEEN BETTER THAN THIS.
I DIDN'T WANT *ANY* OF THIS. I DIDN'T ASK FOR ANY OF THIS.
THAT'S WHY MY *NAME* APPEARED ON YOU.
IT WASN'T AN ACCIDENT. I WANTED TO END MY OWN MISERY, AND NOW I DESERVE TO BE PUNISHED.

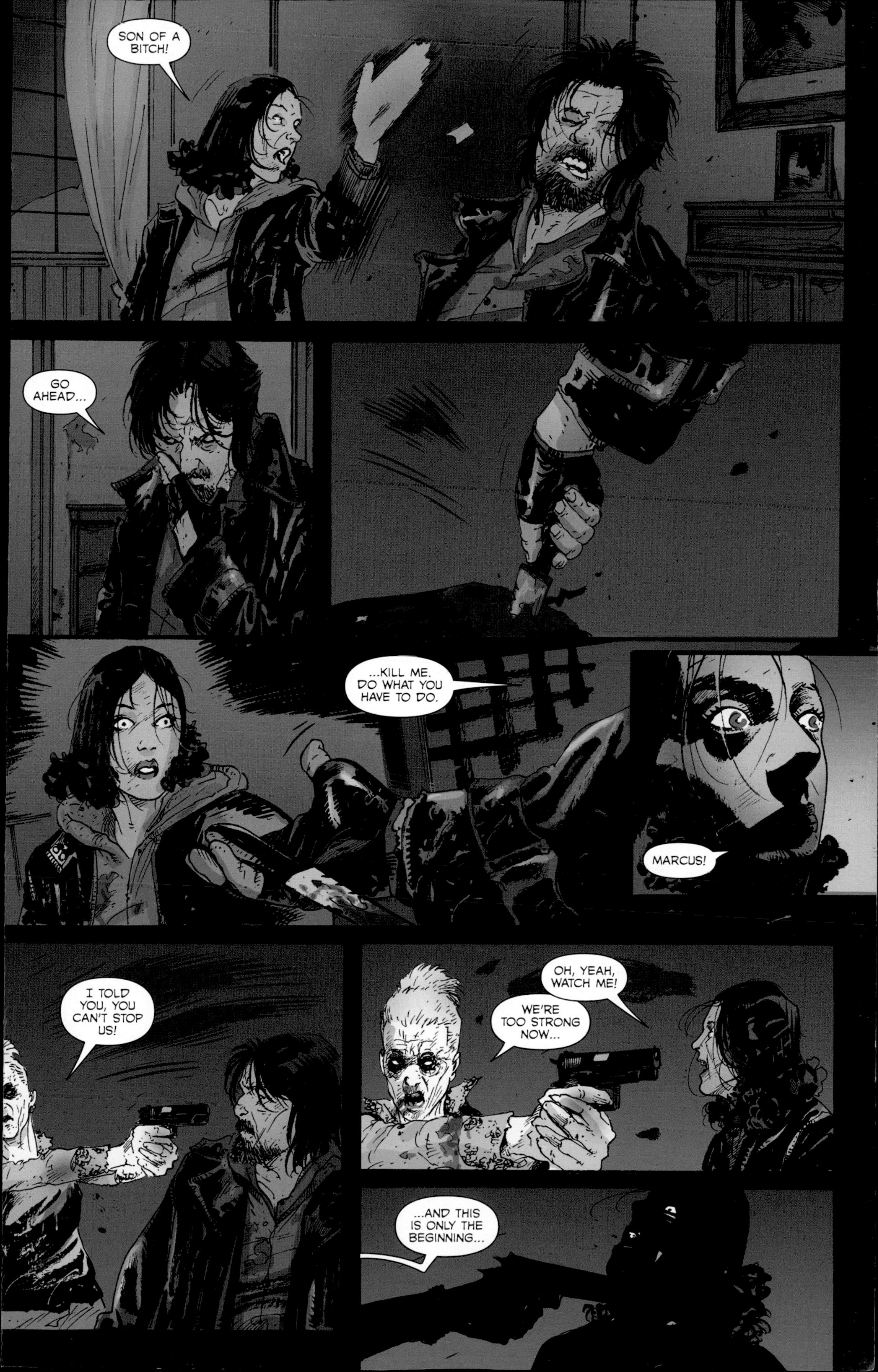
SON OF A BITCH!
GO AHEAD...
...KILL ME. DO WHAT YOU HAVE TO DO.
MARCUS!
I TOLD YOU, YOU CAN'T STOP US!
WE'RE TOO STRONG NOW...
OH, YEAH, WATCH ME!
...AND THIS IS ONLY THE BEGINNING...

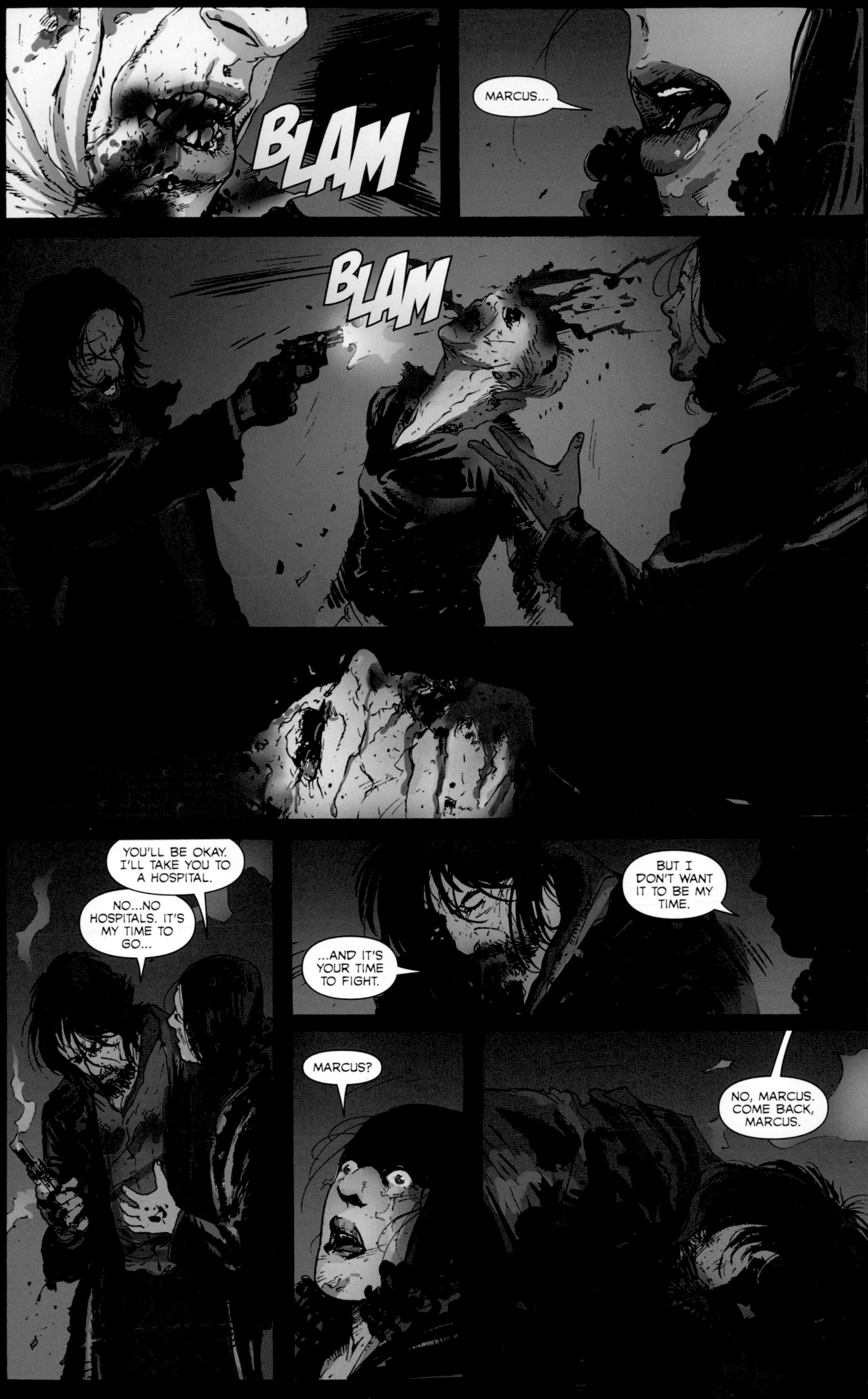
BLAM
MARCUS...
BLAM
YOU'LL BE OKAY. I'LL TAKE YOU TO A HOSPITAL.
NO...NO HOSPITALS. IT'S MY TIME TO GO...
...AND IT'S YOUR TIME TO FIGHT.
BUT I DON'T WANT IT TO BE MY TIME.
MARCUS?
NO, MARCUS. COME BACK, MARCUS.

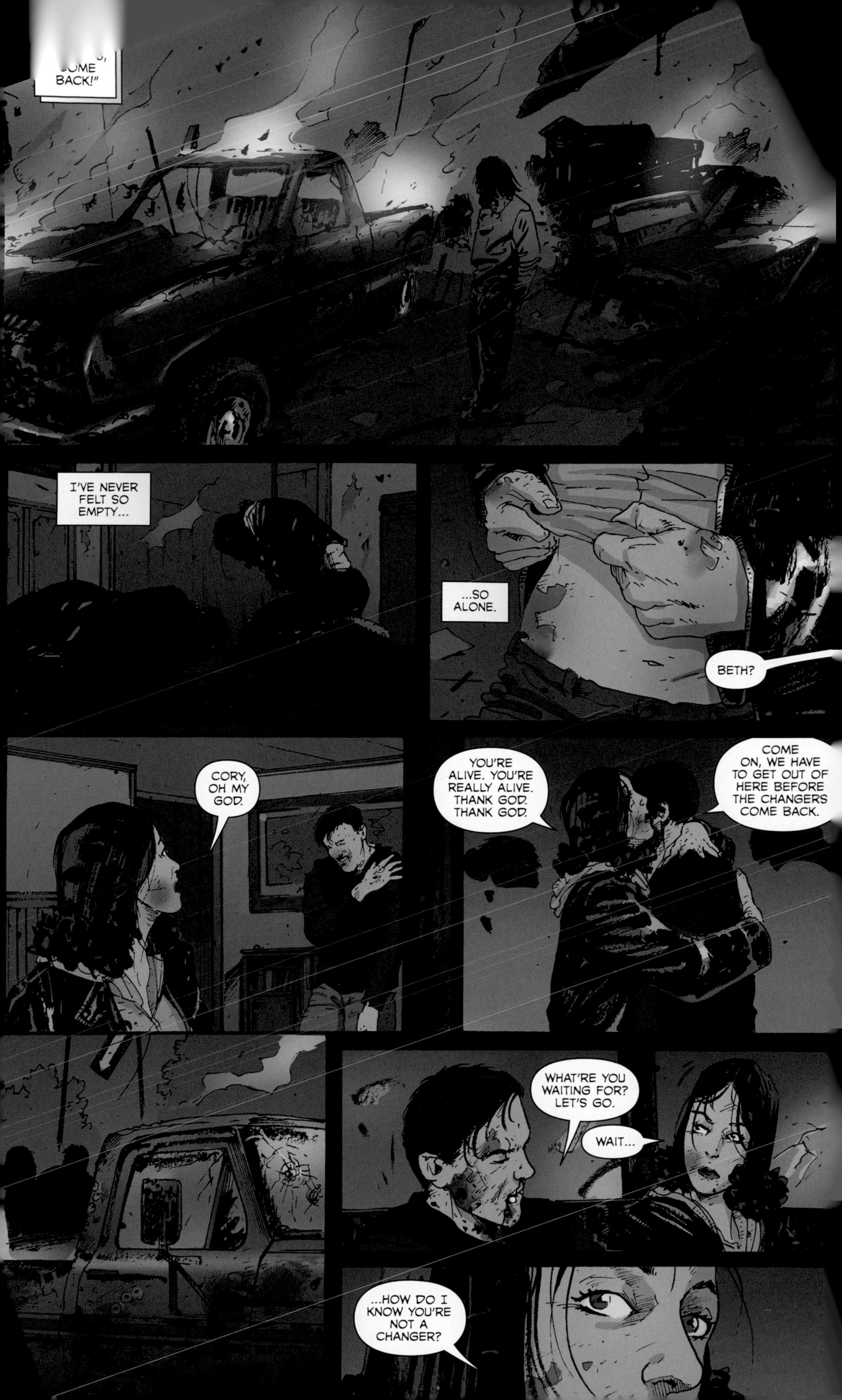

OME BACK!"
I'VE NEVER FELT SO EMPTY...
...SO ALONE.
BETH?
CORY, OH MY GOD.
YOU'RE ALIVE. YOU'RE REALLY ALIVE. THANK GOD. THANK GOD.
COME ON, WE HAVE TO GET OUT OF HERE BEFORE THE CHANGERS COME BACK.
WHAT'RE YOU WAITING FOR? LET'S GO.
WAIT...
...HOW DO I KNOW YOU'RE NOT A CHANGER?

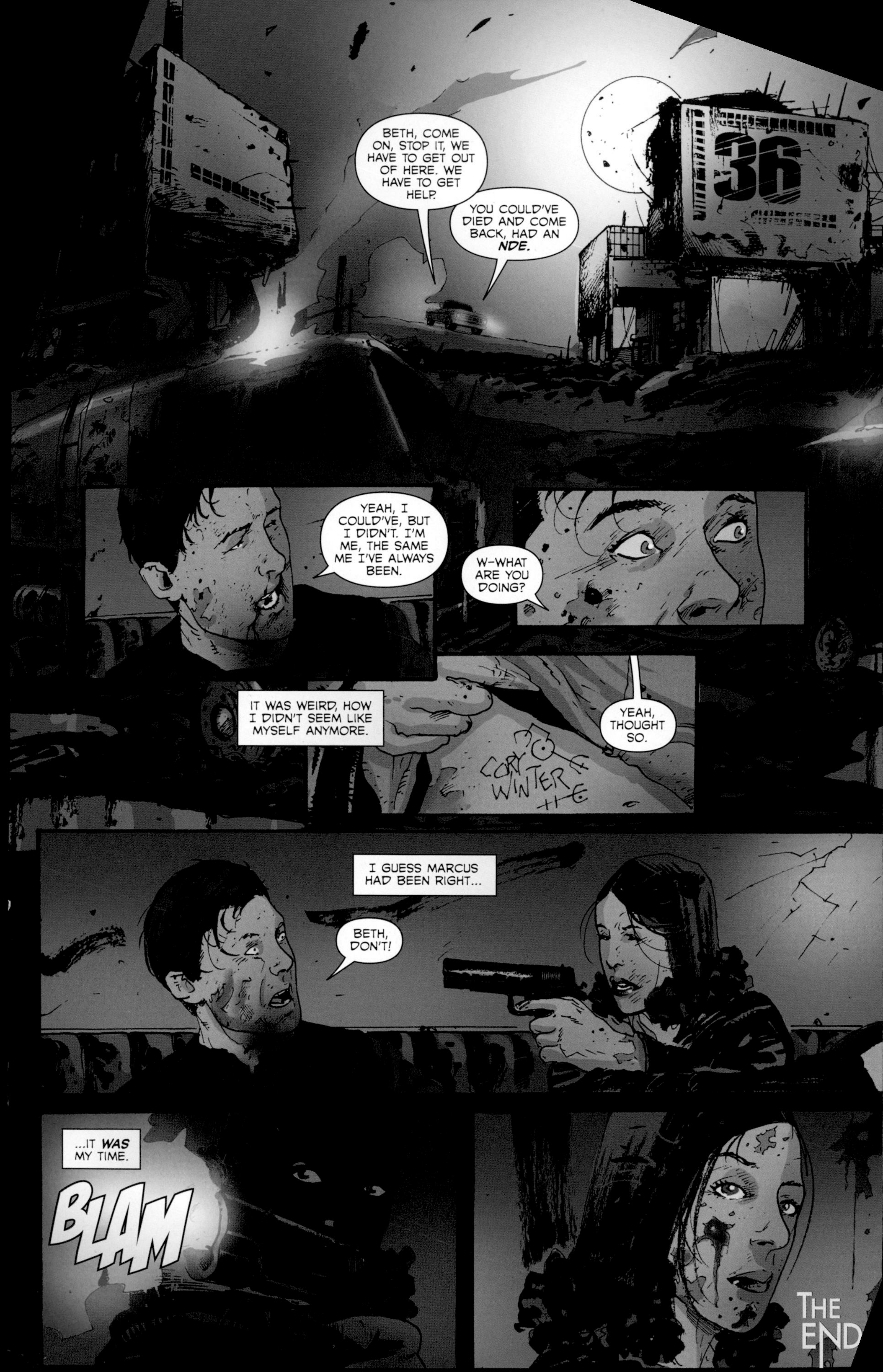
BETH, COME ON, STOP IT, WE HAVE TO GET OUT OF HERE. WE HAVE TO GET HELP.
YOU COULD'VE DIED AND COME BACK, HAD AN NDE.
YEAH, I COULD'VE, BUT I DIDN'T. I'M ME, THE SAME ME I'VE ALWAYS BEEN.
W-WHAT ARE YOU DOING?
IT WAS WEIRD, HOW I DIDN'T SEEM LIKE MYSELF ANYMORE.
YEAH, THOUGHT SO.
CORY WINTER
I GUESS MARCUS HAD BEEN RIGHT...
BETH, DON'T!
...IT WAS MY TIME.
BLAM
THE END

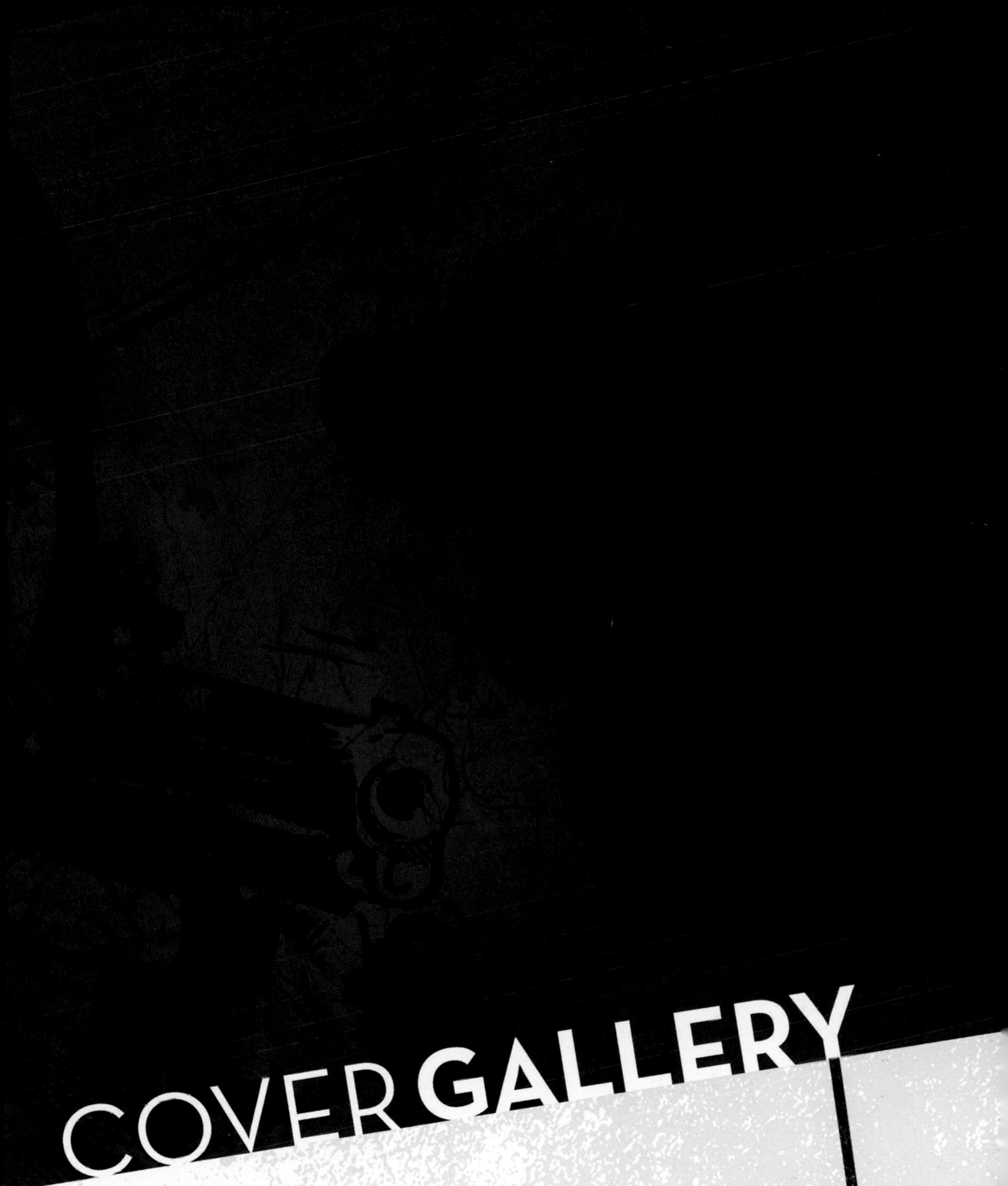

COVER GALLERY

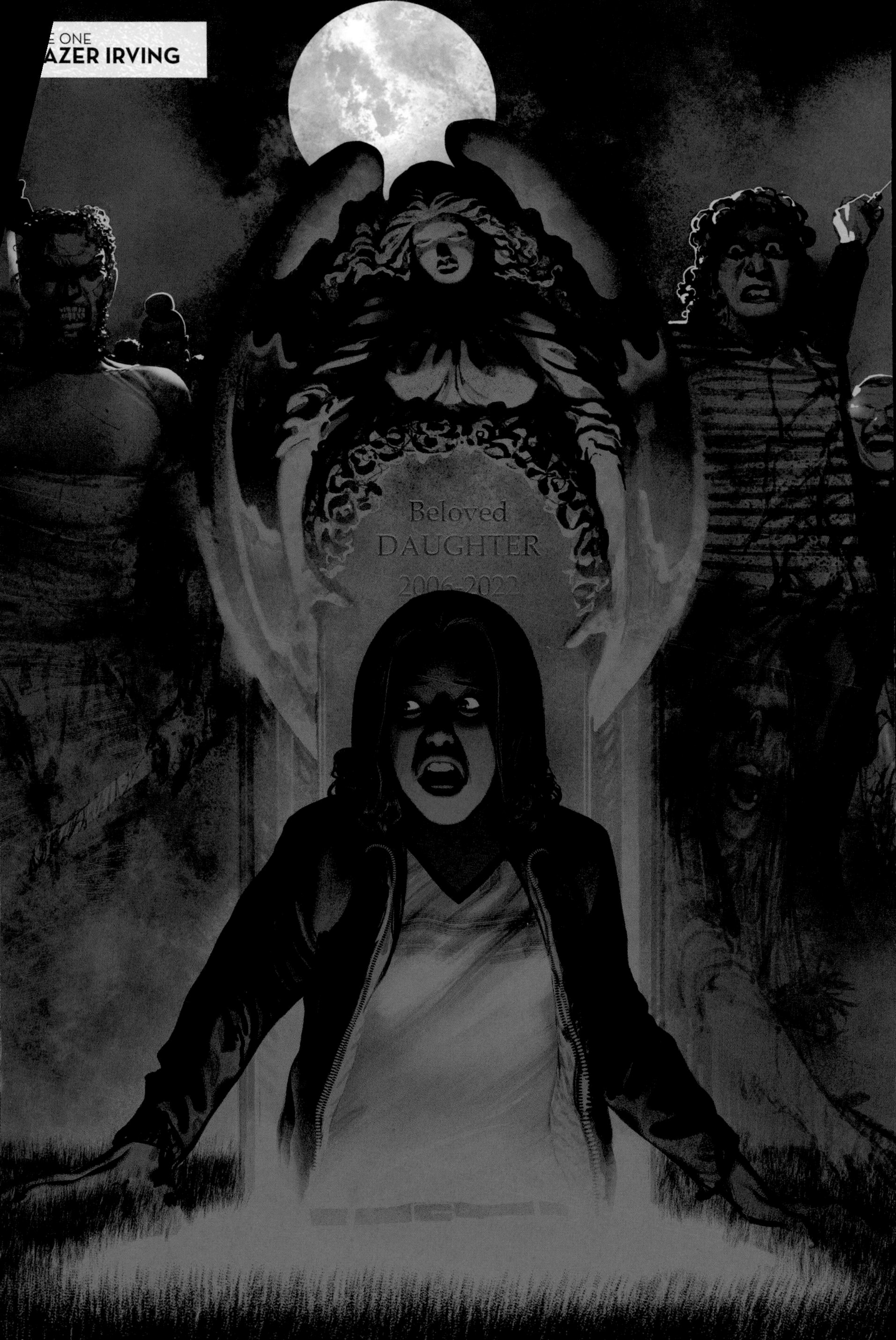
E ONE
AZER IRVING
Beloved
DAUGHTER
2006-2022

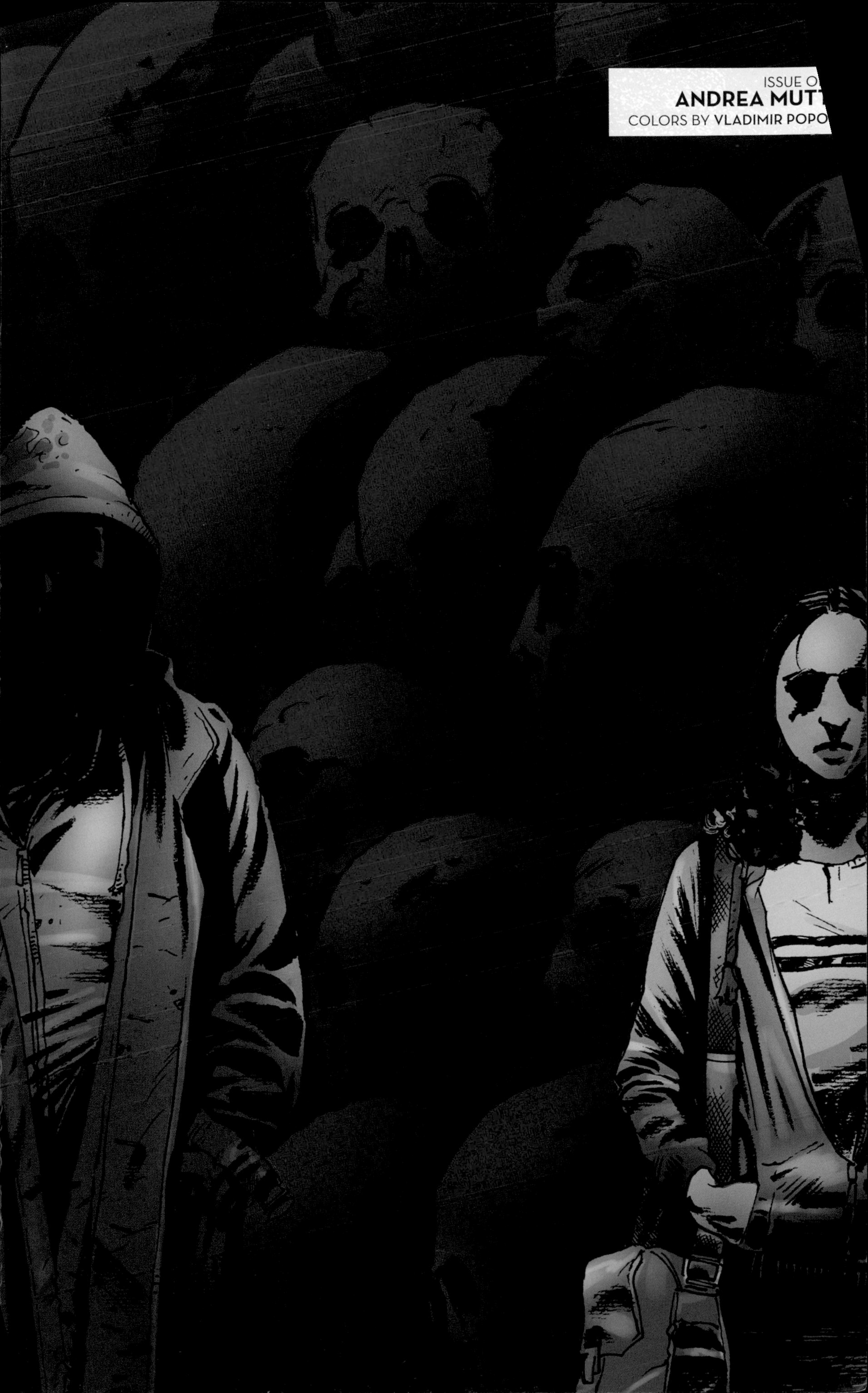
ISSUE O
ANDREA MUTT
COLORS BY VLADIMIR POPO

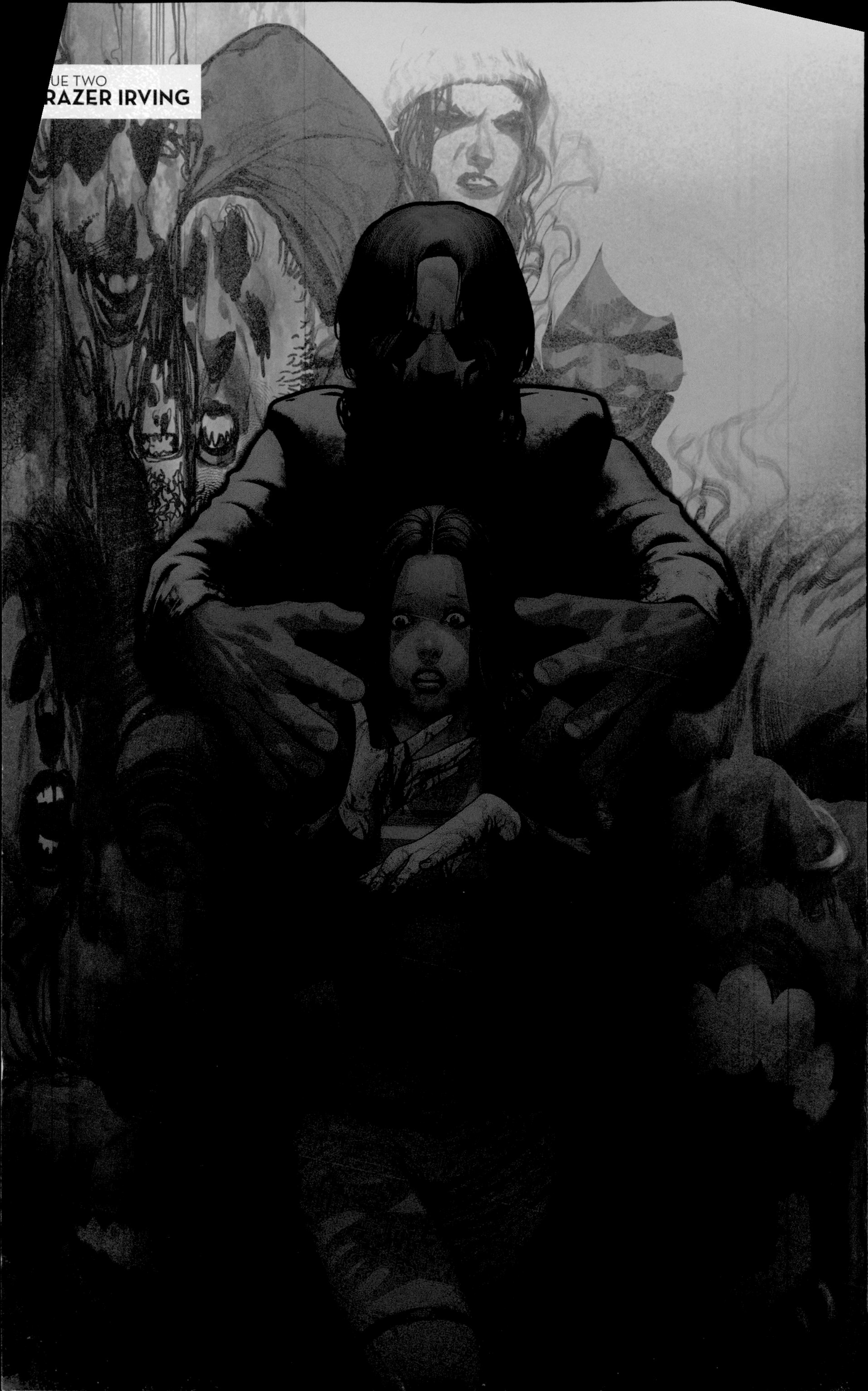
UE TWO
RAZER IRVING

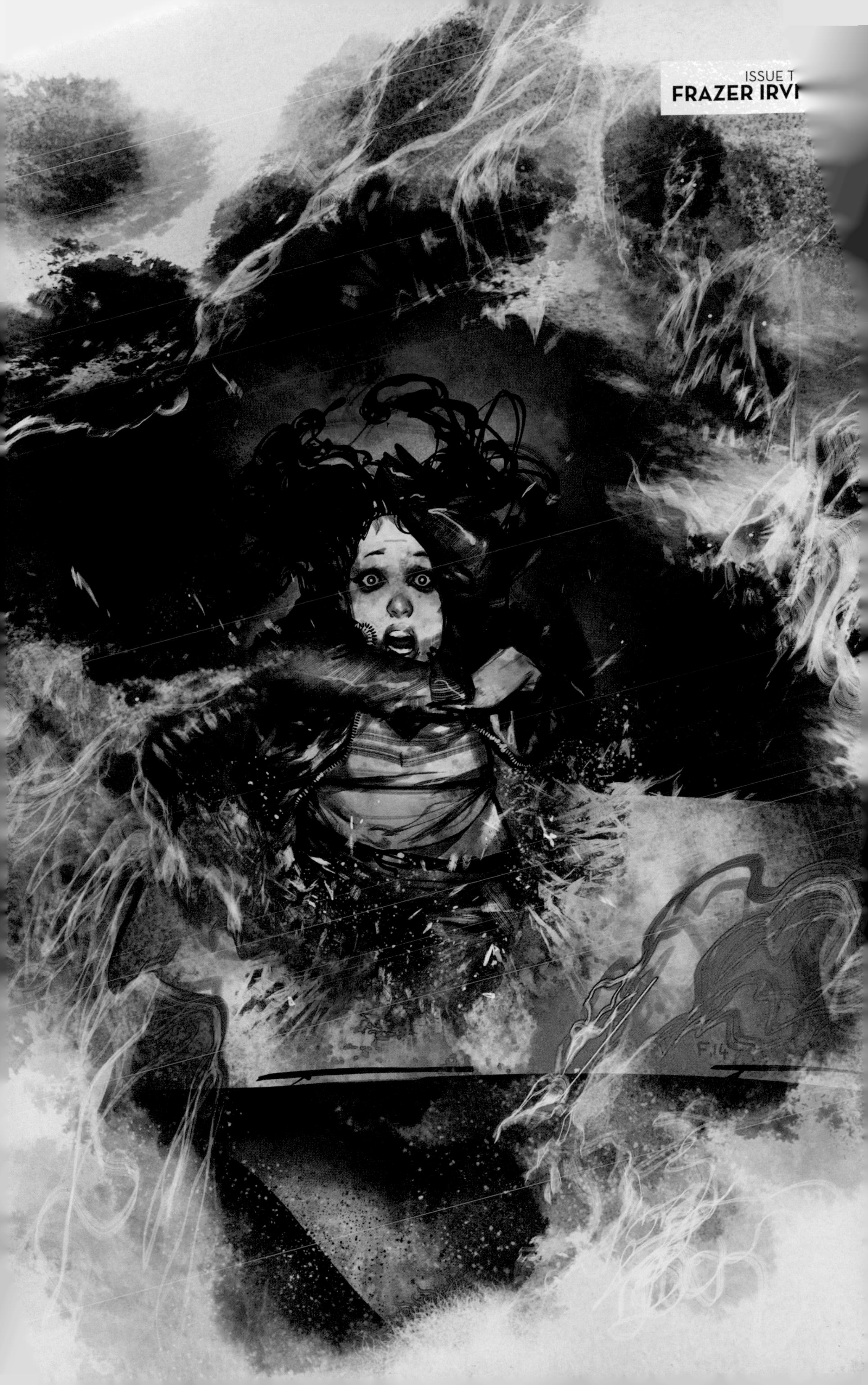
ISSUE T
FRAZER IRV
F.14

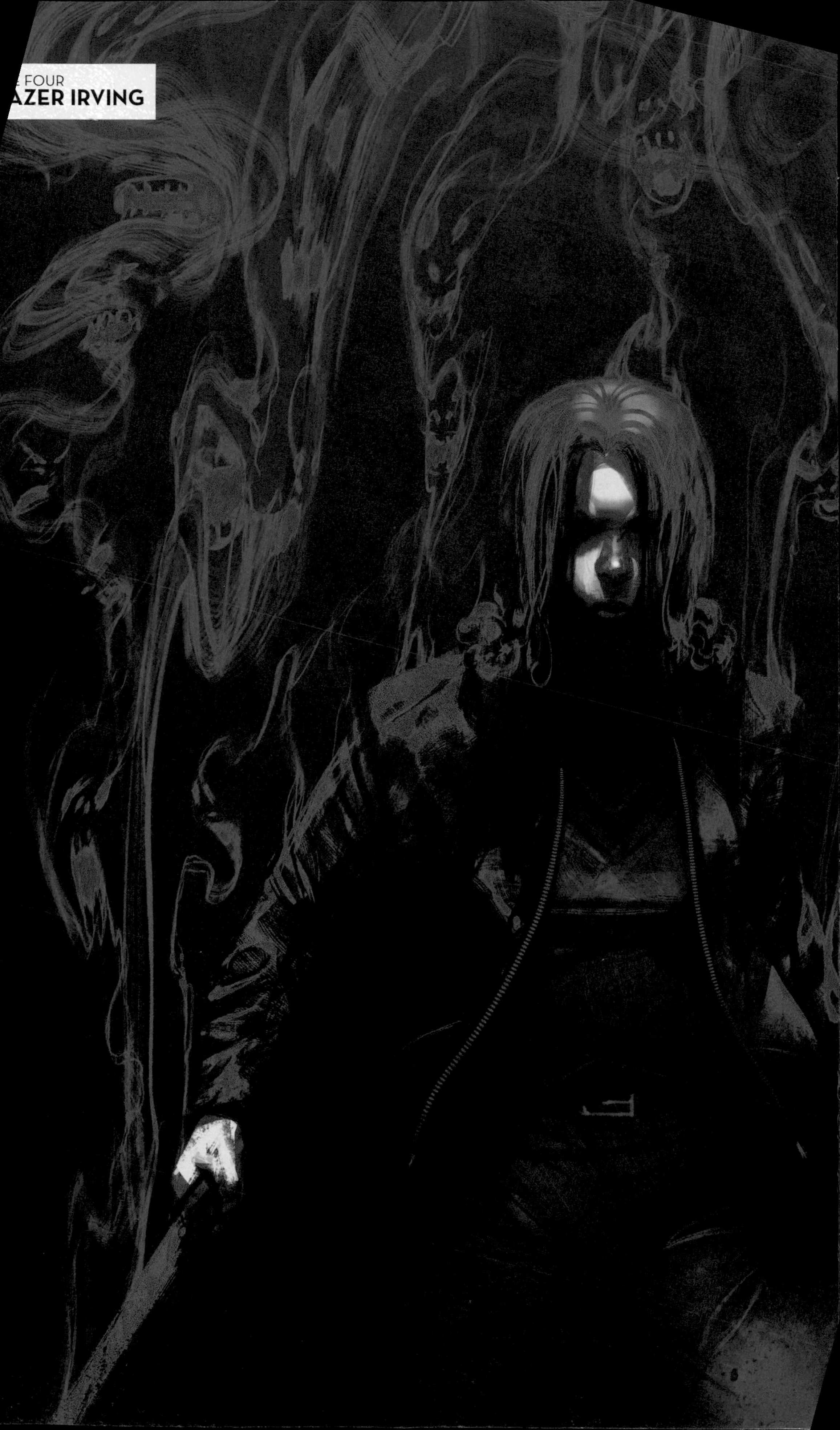
FOUR
AZER IRVING